By A Woman's Hand

By a Woman's Hand

A GUIDE TO MYSTERY FICTION BY WOMEN

Jean Swanson and Dean James

BERKLEY BOOKS, NEW YORK

BY A WOMAN'S HAND

A Berkley Book / published by arrangement with
the authors

PRINTING HISTORY
Berkley trade paperback edition / May 1994

ISBN: 0-425-14143-8

BERKLEY®
Berkley Books are published by The Berkley Publishing Group,
200 Madison Avenue, New York, New York 10016.
BERKLEY and the "B" design
are trademarks belonging to Berkley Publishing Corporation.

PRINTED IN THE UNITED STATES OF AMERICA

10 9 8 7 6 5 4 3 2 1

For James,
and in memory of Ellen Strid Swanson.

JS

For my mother,
and in memory of my father.

DJ

Contents

Acknowledgments

From both of us, special thanks to Martha Farrington, owner of Murder by the Book bookstore in Houston, for her friendship to us both, for introducing us in the first place, and for providing such a wonderful environment for mystery lovers; to the inter-library loan staff of the University of Redlands Library and the Houston Academy of Medicine–Texas Medical Center Library, for helping to find much-needed books quickly and efficiently; to our editor, Natalee Rosenstein, for answering questions patiently and cheerfully and for making this experience considerably less nerve-wracking than it might have been; to Carolyn G. Hart, for encouragement; and to Jim Thompson and Edith Brown, for assistance with information on certain authors.

From Dean, thanks to my friends and coworkers at Murder by the Book, Megan Bladen-Blinkoff, Edith Brown, Barbara Douglas, Jerry Miller, and David Thompson, who have graciously endured the painful birthing process and have offered friendship and encouragement when they were sorely needed.

From Jean, thanks to Art Plotnik, for help in developing the original idea; to Klaus Musmann, Sandi Richey, Kay Flowers, and Peanut Thompson for easing the way and listening; to Trisha

Aurelio and Jean Higginson for their daily support; to Ruth, Arthur, and Eric Swanson for their familial pep talks; most of all, to my father, Arthur Swanson, for teaching me how to write in the first place and for editing my work; and to my husband, Jim Thompson, for reading the manuscript and making valuable suggestions and for his unfailing encouragement and moral support.

Preface

I recall that when I'd read every book by Agatha Christie I could find, I despaired of ever discovering any other writer like her. I didn't want to try other mystery writers. What if they weren't as good? What if I wasted my money or time on their books? And how could I even begin to guess which ones among all of those other mystery novels at the libraries and bookstores might offer me a reading experience that was even close to the joy I obtained from a good Christie? If only I'd had this book!

There is, of course, no writer just like any other, but with a volume like this one in hand, I could have turned to an entry for Christie, Agatha—who was still alive at that time and so would have been included as a contemporary author—and I might have read: "Readers who enjoy English settings might also try the work of Dorothy L. Sayers, Josephine Tey, and Ngaio Marsh."

I'd have been a happy reader! I think you will be, too, with this masterful compendium to assist you. Jean Swanson and Dean James have created a tour de force of a reference source on contemporary women mystery writers, an armchair detective's dream, a veritable Fodor's—that is, a guidebook—of mystery, which may gently and tactfully but firmly and knowledgeably point you down the roads you most want to travel in your mystery reading.

I envy you this book! As you travel happily from Christie to Hart to Churchill, or from Muller to MacGregor to Dunlap, or from Melville to O'Donnell to Maron and beyond, think of those earlier adventurers, like me, who traversed this terrain without a map.

This is your map to the grand world of mysteries written by contemporary women, and you may safely follow its expert recommendations to five-star reading pleasure.

NANCY PICKARD

Introduction

Women writers have always held an important place in the development of mystery fiction in the English-speaking world. Agatha Christie is probably the best-known mystery writer in much of the world; even those who are not devoted mystery readers know the name of Christie and the type of literature with which it is associated. Christie, moreover, has exerted a powerful influence over the development of the mystery novel, either because writers have attempted to follow her patterns of plot and timing, or because they consciously have worked to escape many of the conventions that seemed to control Christie's writing.

As eminent as Christie's place has been in mystery fiction, she is certainly not the only woman writer of historical importance to the genre. Mary Roberts Rinehart, Mignon G. Eberhart, and Phoebe Atwood Taylor in America, and Margery Allingham, Ngaio Marsh, Dorothy L. Sayers, and Josephine Tey in England all lent their distinctive voices to give an impressive imprimatur to the mystery novel as written by women. The mysteries written by these women are, in many ways, reflective of the societies in which the authors themselves were raised. These societies were convention-bound, and the roles of women in them were restricted. Perhaps in consequence, these women from earlier in the century wrote novels of mystery that steered clear of the "mean streets" so beloved of the hard-boiled, wisecracking private eye school and centered rather upon the drawing room, the family in both its nuclear and extended definitions, or some other form of the small, enclosed community in which murder is bred from the relationships of the people involved.

As the decades have passed and the social rules have changed, the number of women mystery writers has increased greatly. These authors come from widely varying backgrounds, and their personal attitudes and styles lend many different perspectives to the fiction they write and the characters they create. In consequence, mystery fiction is richer in diversity than ever before, for the range of women authors and women characters is wider and is expanding all the time. Writers like Pat Burden, Betty Rowlands, and Carolyn G. Hart may write mysteries in the vein of Agatha Christie, but they add a decidedly modern twist. Sue Grafton, Marcia Muller, Sara Paretsky, and many other authors write about strong women characters who have little relation to an earlier version of the female detective, Miss Jane Marple. Ruth Rendell, Margaret Millar, and Frances Hegarty/ Fyfield write novels of psychological complexity and realism very unlike the mainstream of mystery fiction from the Golden Age.

There is much to celebrate in the current boom in mystery fiction, which is in many ways dominated by women writers. Unfortunately, the supportive and reference literature has not yet caught up with this trend; women writers often have been ignored or undervalued by critics in the field. This led to formation of the group, Sisters in Crime, which has, with some success, lobbied for more book reviews of women authors and greater critical consideration. We hope that our book will help to fill this gap in the critical literature.

The overwhelming bounty of mystery fiction can cause problems for readers with definite likes and dislikes among mystery styles and types of characters. Readers who love psychological suspense novels might not care for the cozy, traditional mysteries in the Christie vein, for example. Once readers identify a particular type of mystery, a typical kind of series character, or mysteries with a regional setting, they often try to find similar writers. Thus, one common question in libraries and bookstores alike is, "I've just read my last novel by P. D. James [or Sue Grafton or Elizabeth Peters or whomever]. If I like her, whom should I read next?"

By a Woman's Hand is an attempt to help readers answer this question. This guide is arranged alphabetically by author, and each author entry offers a description of the salient features of the author's style, series characters, and other important characteristics. We include the title and the original American publication information of initial books in series, along with other books of importance among the more prolific writers' works. (This is not intended to be a bibliography; there are a number of reference works that fill that need.) These entries are intended as an analysis of each particular author, not to render our own opinions of the writer's standing in the genre as a whole, but rather to assess what there is about this writer's work that appeals to readers. We are well aware, however, of the critical reputation of the writers included in this guide, and we have attempted to indicate those writers who consistently are judged among the best in the field by critics. We have also mentioned award-winning works whenever possible. The Edgars are given by the Mystery Writers of America in various categories, and the Gold and Silver Daggers are awarded by the British Crime Writers' Association. Other than these peer awards, we have also mentioned awards given by fans: the Agatha, bestowed by the Malice Domestic Mystery Convention (which is devoted to the traditional mystery), the Anthony, awarded by the Bouchercon (the World Mystery Convention), and the Macavity, given by the readership of the *Mystery Readers Journal* of Mystery Readers International. Finally, each entry ends with recommendations of other writers who might share some characteristic with the writer under discussion. These recommendations are based on our own extensive reading in the field. Most often, the recommendations given are to other women writers covered in this guide, if those are the most appropriate references.

One important question in the reader's mind is, no doubt, how we chose the writers included in this guide. We concentrate upon contemporary women mystery writers. We took as our rough starting date the year 1977, when Marcia Muller's first Sharon McCone novel, *Edwin of the Iron Shoes* (McKay Washburn), was published. Muller's book is often considered to have ushered in the era of the modern female private eye. From the late 1970s to the present day, we see the result of this trend in the many types of women characters no longer bound by the conventions of the Golden Age mystery novel. In drawing up our list of writers for this guide, we chose authors whose first work has been published since 1977, such as Elizabeth George or Frances Hegarty, who also uses the pen name Frances Fyfield, or writers published before that time who are still consistently producing, such as P. D. James and Ellis Peters. We tend to concentrate mostly on writers of mystery and detective fiction, though we also include writers of suspense novels, such as Mary Higgins Clark, Mary Stewart, and Margaret Millar, because of their importance to the field. We do not include writers like Evelyn Anthony or Helen MacInnes, whose chief output is in the field of espionage thrillers. We cover English-language writers, with an emphasis on American, Canadian, and British authors. We have not analyzed short stories, but we provide a bibliography of important short story anthologies that contain stories by women authors. Finally, we have also included women who have written a minimum of three books. As space and time have permitted, we have included authors who have written two books and whose third books seem imminent. No doubt, readers will come up with writers whom we failed to include for some reason, but we have included as many writers as we could without going blind and broke in the process.

In the appendices of the book, readers will find various index lists—lists by type of detective (such as private eye, amateur, police), regional setting, and series character and author. Finally, a word on definitions. The terms *cozy* and *traditional mystery* are used interchangeably throughout the book to refer to mysteries written largely in the tradition of Agatha Christie and other Golden Age authors. In other words, traditional mysteries are those with an enclosed setting, a series detective, little explicit violence, and a good puzzle to be solved. Cozies have come a long way since *The Body in the Library*, with gifted writers like Nancy Pickard, Carolyn G. Hart, and Frances Fyfield, among many others, stretching the boundaries. *Hard-boiled* refers to mysteries in which there might be violence and lots of action, but chiefly the term indicates a mood, a connection to what Raymond Chandler called the "mean streets." A great deal of upheaval has occurred in the hard-boiled mystery tradition in recent years, with the addition of female private eyes created by fine authors like Sara Paretsky, Liza Cody, and Sue Grafton. *Psychological* suspense refers to those books in which the emphasis is more on whydunit than whodunit, though writers like Ruth Rendell and Margaret Millar can fascinate the reader easily with both questions. A *thriller* or *suspense* novel might be defined as a story that keeps the reader turning the pages to find out what's going to happen next, with the emphasis on how it's going to turn out, rather than simply whodunit. Readers may look for classic practitioners of this art like Mary Higgins Clark and Dorothy Dunnett. The *police procedural* can be a detective story or a thriller, but generally, this type of novel relies on the routines of police activity in order to answer the vital questions, whodunit, whydunit, or howdunit. The emergence of policewomen as protagonists in novels by Susan Dunlap, Lillian O'Donnell, Katherine V. Forrest, and other women writers has created a welcome change in this area.

The mystery reader's motto might easily be, "So many books, so little time." We certainly discovered that fact as we immersed ourselves in the wealth of diversity of mystery fiction written by women. We hope that *By a Woman's Hand* can serve to help readers find those books and authors who most fit their tastes. This book was a voyage of discovery for its authors; may it be no less for its readers.

JEAN SWANSON

DEAN JAMES

Authors Included in the Book

Deborah Adams
M. J. Adamson
Catherine Aird
Margot Arnold
Marian Babson
Mignon F. Ballard
Linda Barnes
M. C. Beaton
K. K. Beck
Sophie Belfort
Carole Berry
Malacai Black
Veronica Black
Anne Blaisdell
J. S. Borthwick
Eleanor Boylan
Lilian Jackson Braun
D. C. Brod
Rita Mae Brown
Pat Burden
Gwendoline Butler
Dorothy Cannell
P. M. Carlson

Sarah Caudwell
Elizabeth Chaplin
Kate Charles
Joyce Christmas
Jill Churchill
Mary Higgins Clark
Anna Clarke
Melissa Cleary
Ann Cleeves
Liza Cody
Janet Cohen
Susan Conant
Natasha Cooper
Susan Rogers Cooper
Patricia D. Cornwell
Alisa Craig
Caroline Crane
Hamilton Crane
Trella Crespi
Deborah Crombie
Amanda Cross
Clare Curzon
Mary Daheim

Catherine Dain
Barbara D'Amato
Gloria Dank
Diane Mott Davidson
Dorothy Salisbury Davis
Lindsey Davis
Janet Dawson
Jane Dentinger
R. B. Dominic
Carole Nelson Douglas
Lauren Wright Douglas
Alison Drake
Sarah Dreher
Sarah Dunant
Susan Dunlap
Dorothy Dunnett
Jack Early
Marjorie Eccles
Ruth Dudley Edwards
Lesley Egan
Elizabeth Eyre
Ann C. Fallon
Jean Femling
E. X. Ferrars
Katherine V. Forrest
Anthea Fraser
Antonia Fraser
Margaret Frazer
Celia Fremlin
Mickey Friedman
Frances Fyfield
Judith Garwood
Elizabeth George
B. M. Gill
Dorothy Gilman
Jaqueline Girdner
E. X. Giroux
Alison Gordon
Paula Gosling
Sue Grafton

Caroline Graham
Ann Granger
Linda Grant
Lesley Grant-Adamson
Gallagher Gray
Kate Green
D. M. Greenwood
L. B. Greenwood
Martha Grimes
Sally Gunning
Jane Haddam
Joan Hadley
Jean Hager
Mary Bowen Hall
Mollie Hardwick
Charlaine Harris
Cynthia Harrod-Eagles
Carolyn G. Hart
Ellen Hart
S. T. Haymon
Frances Hegarty
Joan Hess
Patricia Highsmith
Isabelle Holland
Hazel Holt
Kay Hooper
Wendy Hornsby
Marian J. A. Jackson
Nancy Baker Jacobs
P. D. James
J. A. Jance
Trish Janeshutz
Velda Johnston
Lucille Kallen
Faye Kellerman
Nora Kelly
Susan Kelly
Susan B. Kelly
Judith Kelman
Susan Kenney

Authors

Karen Kijewski
Mary Kittredge
Alanna Knight
Kathryn Lasky Knight
Gabrielle Kraft
Rochelle Majer Krich
Jane Langton
Janet LaPierre
Emma Lathen
Janet Laurence
Janice Law
Elizabeth Lemarchand
Donna Leon
Elizabeth Linington
Gillian Linscott
Nancy Livingston
Caroline Llewellyn
Margaret Logan
M. K. Lorens
T. J. MacGregor
Charlotte MacLeod
Jessica Mann
Margaret Maron
Lee Martin
Sarah J. Mason
Lia Matera
Stefanie Matteson
A. E. Maxwell
Taylor McCafferty
Vicki P. McConnell
Sharyn McCrumb
Val McDermid
Jill McGown
Claire McNab
M. R. D. Meek
Jennie Melville
D. R. Meredith
Barbara Mertz
Annette Meyers
Maan Meyers

Barbara Michaels
Margaret Millar
D. F. Mills
Kay Mitchell
Gwen Moffat
Miriam Grace Monfredo
Susan Moody
Kate Morgan
Anne Morice
B. J. Morison
Patricia Moyes
Marcia Muller
Amy Myers
Magdalen Nabb
Janet Neel
Meg O'Brien
Maxine O'Callaghan
Lillian O'Donnell
B. J. Oliphant
Sister Carol Anne O'Marie
A. J. Orde
Katherine Hall Page
Orania Papazoglou
Sara Paretsky
Barbara Paul
Anne Perry
Elizabeth Peters
Ellis Peters
Audrey Peterson
Nancy Pickard
Marissa Piesman
Deborah Powell
Mary Monica Pulver
Erica Quest
Sheila Radley
J. M. Redmann
Ruth Rendell
Virginia Rich
Gillian Roberts
Annette Roome

Jennifer Rowe
Betty Rowlands
Medora Sale
Eve K. Sandstrom
Corinne Holt Sawyer
Sandra Scoppettone
Kate Sedley
Diane K. Shah
Sarah Shankman
Dell Shannon
Stella Shepherd
Celestine Sibley
Dorothy Simpson
L. V. Sims
Shelley Singer
Gillian Slovo
Evelyn E. Smith
Janet L. Smith
Joan Smith
Julie Smith
Rosamond Smith
Patricia H. Sprinkle
Dana Stabenow
Susannah Stacey
Mary Stewart
Alice Storey
Dorothy Sucher
Elizabeth Atwood Taylor

June Thomson
Elizabeth Travis
Kathy Hogan Trocheck
Margaret Truman
Kerry Tucker
Dorothy Uhnak
Deborah Valentine
Judith Van Gieson
Barbara Vine
Marilyn Wallace
Minette Walters
Martha G. Webb
Carolyn Wheat
Teri White
Barbara Whitehead
Phyllis A. Whitney
Kate Wilhelm
Barbara Wilson
Chris Wiltz
Anne Wingate
Mary Wings
Valerie Wolzien
Sara Woods
Sherryl Woods
M. K. Wren
L. R. Wright
Chelsea Quinn Yarbro
Margaret Yorke

Adams, Deborah. This Tennessee author has taken the unusual tack of having a town serve as her series "character," rather than using a single person as the focal point of her books. The town is named Jesus Creek, and that should be a signal to the reader to expect Southern eccentricity as a chief ingredient of the mix. In the first of the series, *All the Great Pretenders* (Ballantine, 1992), a rich young woman disappears, and a psychic tries to find her, while Jesus Creek is in the midst of its sesquicentennial celebrations. The third, *All the Dark Disguises* (Ballantine, 1993), offers a serial killer working in the area, dispatching pretty blondes to eternal rest, while the town concentrates on its Saint Patrick's Day festivities. As the series progresses, some characters become regulars, like the police chief, the town's librarian, the town's beauty queen hopeful, and, of all things, an eccentric Yankee. Adams pitches her mélange of eccentricity and gently satiric humor in a low key, so there is never an extravagance of humor or character to veer off into caricature. Jesus Creek might be an unusual place, but it's a charmingly offbeat one to visit on a tour of the fictional South. *All the Great Pretenders* was nominated for an Agatha for Best First Novel.

Readers looking for other Southern mysteries with humor might try the Elizabeth MacPherson novels of Sharyn McCrumb, the work of Charlaine Harris, or the Samantha Adams novels of Sarah Shankman. Other Southern writers to note are Taylor McCafferty, Rita Mae Brown, Celestine Sibley, and Patricia H. Sprinkle.

Adamson, M. J. The island of Puerto Rico is the setting for Adamson's series of police procedurals. In the first novel, *Not Till a Hot January* (Bantam, 1987), New York homicide detective Balthazar Marten, recovering from a bombing incident in which his young wife was murdered, is sent to Puerto Rico on a "lend-lease" type of arrangement with the Puerto Rican police. Though of mixed Dutch and Irish ancestry, Marten speaks Spanish fluently and fits in easily with the locals. He is to be a consultant on a case involving gambling, an area in which he has considerable expertise, but in the beginning, he gets assigned to a homicide case in which someone is murdering young women in San Juan. Assigned to help Marten is young cop Sixto Cardenas, and the two work together through the rest of the series. The second novel, *A February Face* (Bantam, 1987), has Marten and Cardenas investigating mysterious Voodoo-related incidents in a small town not far from San Juan. The colorful setting of Puerto Rico makes a fascinating backdrop for the series, and Adamson weaves details of the history and culture into the fabric of her stories. Marten and Cardenas are intelligent, dedicated, and likable characters, an enjoyable duo in the great tradition of "buddy" detectives.

Readers who have read and enjoyed this out-of-print series might try other police procedural series, like the work of J. A. Jance, Elizabeth Linington, Dell Shannon, Lesley Egan, or Marilyn Wallace. Those looking for something of the Latin flavor might try the works of Paco Ignacio Taibo II, which are now being published in English.

Aird, Catherine. Aird created the English county of Calle-shire for her series of mysteries featuring Detective Inspector C. D. Sloan (''Seedy'' to his friends) and amusingly annoying Sergeant Crosby. Calleshire owes much to the England of the Golden Age; village life in this county is much like what readers encounter in the works of Christie or Marsh, with a more modern face, though Aird's territory is not quite the modern English village of Dorothy Simpson or Peter Robinson. In his debut, *The Religious Body* (Doubleday, 1966), Sloan solves a murder at a nunnery, and Aird describes the life of the community of nuns well. A later book, *The Stately Home Murder* (Doubleday, 1970; English title, *The Complete Steel*), allows Aird to display at full steam a deliciously wry sense of humor, as tourists invade a stately home full of armor and the remnants of feudalism. This novel's solution contains one of the great literary jokes of mystery fiction, and Aird pulls it off with great panache. Indeed, through much of her work, Aird's sense of humor is a strong undercurrent, lending a light touch that distinguishes Aird from some contemporaries for whom humor is sometimes a mystery in itself. Though she writes a little too infrequently for her fans, Aird provides solid entertainment in the field of the traditional English mystery.

Those who have enjoyed Aird might try in addition the work of Elizabeth Lemarchand, June Thomson, Patricia Moyes, Caroline Graham, or E. X. Ferrars. Other writers who use humor to good effect in their traditional English mysteries are Sarah J. Mason, who also writes as Hamilton Crane, M. C. Beaton, and Nancy Livingston.

Arnold, Margot. An anthropologist and educator in real life, the pseudonymous Arnold makes excellent use of her own background to endow her sprightly series of mysteries with authentic settings and archaeological detail. Her series characters, American anthropologist Penny Spring and Welsh archaeologist Toby (Sir Tobias) Glendower, are long-standing friends and fellows in different Oxford colleges. These two eminent professionals somehow manage to combine crime-solving with anthropology and archaeology, much to the delight of the reader. They also demonstrate that sixty-something sleuths can be just as capable at crime-solving as their younger counterparts. Both Penny and Toby bring a wealth of experience, academic and otherwise, to their investigations. Beginning with *Exit Actors, Dying* (Playboy, 1979), which is set in Greece, Penny and Toby have traveled widely to such places as Hawaii (*The Menehune Murders;* Foul Play, 1989); Israel (*Zadok's Treasure;* Playboy, 1979); Scotland (*Lament for a Lady Laird;* Playboy, 1982); and New Orleans (*Death of a Voodoo Doll;* Playboy, 1982). Whatever the venue, the result, in Arnold's hands, is sheer fun. Arnold has also written three novels in the thriller vein, deft mixtures of suspense, intrigue, and romance, including the recent *Sinister Purposes* (Fawcett, 1988).

Other writers who effectively use archaeology, anthropology, or art history as backgrounds for their work are Elizabeth Peters, Caroline Llewellyn, and Mary Stewart. Readers interested in other series about older sleuths should try the work of Eleanor Boylan, Gallagher Gray, and Dorothy Gilman.

Babson, Marian. Babson is an American author, long resident in England, who has written more than thirty mysteries in the traditional English style. Babson's skill with words, adroit depictions of quirky characters, and careful plot structures turn her novels into enjoyable reading experiences. *Pretty Lady* (Walker, 1990), for example, is a brief, suspenseful story of one violent incident and what happened in each character's life to lead up to it. Babson has used Douglas Perkins, a partner in the London public relations firm of Perkins & Tate, as a series character in some of her novels. The Perkins series begins with *Cover-up Story*. Babson also has written a series of humorous mysteries featuring Trixie Dolan and Evangeline Sinclair, who were movie stars in the Golden Age of Hollywood. The two elderly actors are attempting to revive their careers in London theater, but inevitably they become involved in murder. The series begins with *Reel Murder* (St. Martin, 1986). American readers be warned: some of Babson's books change titles when they are published in the U.S., and certain novels have appeared in America years after their initial British publication.

Babson's first mystery was *Cover-up Story* (St. Martin, 1988; London: Collins, 1971).

Readers who enjoy traditional cozy mysteries with idiosyncratic characters and humorous situations should look for the works of M. C. Beaton, K. K. Beck, Carolyn G. Hart, and Jill Churchill.

Ballard, Mignon F.   Ballard writes romantic suspense novels with a strong atmosphere of lurking menace. Touches of the supernatural and convoluted twists in the plot are characteristic Ballard plot devices. Her first novel was *Raven Rock* (Dodd, Mead, 1986). *Deadly Promise* (Carroll & Graf, 1989) is set in the small town of Harmony, Georgia. Molly Stonehouse, a young widow, has come back to her husband's ancestral home to investigate his death. Ballard effectively creates a rural Southern atmosphere for her story. In *The Widow's Woods* (Carroll & Graf, 1991), Jane Cannon returns to her hometown in South Carolina after being jilted. One day she finds that her neighbor has disappeared, leaving a pan of beans burning on the stove. This small domestic crisis leads Jane into a maelstrom of evil, Satanism, and murder. *Final Curtain* (Carroll & Graf, 1992) is the most ghostly and atmospheric of Ballard's novels. A young woman, Ginger Cameron, comes to Plumb-Nelly Tavern in Fiddler's Glen, North Carolina to look into the long-ago death of her great-aunt. The ghost of her aunt helps her in her search for the truth. Ballard's novels are as much Southern gothics as they are mysteries.

Readers of Ballard may want to look for romantic mysteries by Barbara Michaels, Sherryl Woods, Velda Johnston, and Carolyn G. Hart. Charlaine Harris writes atmospheric Southern crime novels.

Barnes, Linda.   The first series Linda Barnes wrote featured Michael Spraggue, an independently wealthy actor and detective. These stories are located in Boston, the Napa Valley, and New Orleans, and the first, *Blood Will Have Blood* (Avon, 1982), has a theatrical setting. Barnes's more recent series stars Carlotta Carlyle, Boston private eye and cab driver. Carlotta is six feet tall, half-Irish and half-Jewish, a former policewoman, and she is truly a memorable character. Barnes has endowed Carlotta with an active sense of humor and a wry outlook on life. Readers may enjoy Carlotta's personality as much as the lively and thought-provoking plots. The secondary characters are striking creations as well. Carlotta's tenant, Roz, is an eccentric artist. Sam Gianelli is a son (supposedly honest) of the local Mafia don; he and Carlotta have an occasional fling. Through the Little Sisters organization, Carlotta has found a young sister, Paolina, with whom she has a strong and fond connection. And, of course, a private eye may sometimes need a friend in the police department; Carlotta has Mooney, an old buddy from her days as a cop.

The first Carlotta Carlyle novel is *A Trouble of Fools* (St. Martin, 1987), and it was nominated for an Edgar Award for Best Novel.

Strongly characterized private eyes include Sue Grafton's Kinsey Millhone, Sarah Dunant's Hannah Wolfe, and Karen Kijewski's Kat Colorado. Other mysteries set in the Boston-Cambridge area are written by Susan Conant, Susan Kelly, Kathryn Lasky Knight, and Jane Langton. P. M. Carlson and Jane Dentinger also have mysteries with theatrical connections.

Beaton, M. C. Marion Chesney, a prolific writer of historical romances under her own name and the pseudonyms of Ann Fairfax, Jennie Tremaine, Helen Crampton, and Charlotte Ward, began writing mysteries in the 1980s under the name M. C. Beaton. Her first mysteries have been a series of unusual police procedurals that are witty, light, and full of eccentric characters. The novels are British cozies with an endearing Gaelic twist. The first mystery in the series is *Death of a Gossip* (St. Martin, 1985). The hero is Hamish Macbeth, constable of the small village of Lochdubh in northwestern Scotland. In his role as village bobby,

Hamish sometimes acts deliberately stupid, and he uses the stereotype of the lazy gormless Highlander to his advantage in dealing with suspects (especially snobbish English visitors). Hamish is also a crofter in the community, so he knows the characters and the idiosyncracies of the villagers only too well. This understanding allows him to solve murders in spite of the interference of his crass and bigoted superior in the police bureaucracy. Unfortunately, Hamish has to keep downplaying his successes; the last thing he wants is to be promoted out of his comfortable rural sinecure. Beaton has begun a new series with *Agatha Raisin and the Quiche of Death* (St. Martin, 1992). Agatha is a hard-hearted businesswoman who retires to a cottage in the Cotswolds and finds more than she bargained for when she encounters hostility from the locals and a mysterious death. Beaton's novels combine gentle comedy and memorable settings with the traditional British mystery format.

Readers of Beaton's mysteries may also enjoy Marian Babson's novels, with their unusual character studies, Gloria Dank's humorous mysteries, and Susannah Stacey's stories about Robert Bone, an English police superintendent. Alanna Knight sets her historical mysteries in Victorian Scotland.

Beck, K. K. A journalist and magazine editor in Seattle, Beck has shown herself to be a versatile mystery writer. Beck has a marvelous light touch, bringing sprightly humor and an engaging sense of fun to many of her books. Beck's first novel, *Death in a Deck Chair* (Walker, 1984), introduced one series character, 1920s college student Iris Cooper. Returning from a visit to England on an ocean liner, Iris and her aunt encounter murder on board the ship. With the aid of charmingly roguish reporter Jack Clancy, Iris solves the crime. In a similar light vein, Beck penned a novel of romantic intrigue, set in pre–World War I America and Europe, *Mrs. Cavendish and the Kaiser's Men* (Walker, 1987). Lately she has begun a new series with *A Hopeless Case* (Mysterious, 1992), featuring Jane da Silva as an investigator into seemingly hopeless cases. Jane inherited the business from a wealthy but eccentric uncle. All these works are entertaining evidence of Beck's skill with the light and breezy, but she has demonstrated that she can write a gripping suspense novel as well. In *Unwanted Attentions* (Walker, 1988), Beck offers a tense variation on the stalker novel, proving that she can handle the darker side just as well as she handles the light.

Readers looking for other Seattle-based mysteries might try the work of Mary Daheim and Janet L. Smith. Marian Babson also has an enjoyable light touch in many of her novels.

Belfort, Sophie. The academic mystery is a staple of contemporary mystery fiction, for the enclosed community of the academic world offers the mystery writer a ready-made setting for murder and mayhem. Belfort, a pseudonymous historian who lives in Massachusetts, writes novels that, to date, have combined the worlds of academia and politics in a readable and informative mixture. The main characters of the series are history professor Molly Rafferty, a specialist in the Renaissance and Reformation era, and Jesuit-educated policeman Nick Hannibal. The first novel in the series, *The Lace Curtain Murders* (Atheneum, 1986), is subtitled "A Romance" and is as much the story of Molly and Nick falling in love as it is the investigation of a politically motivated murder in Boston. In this first novel Belfort tackles the thorny issues, both political and moral, surrounding American support of the IRA. In a later work, *Eyewitness to Murder* (Donald I. Fine, 1992), Molly and Nick are involved in a case revolving around the prosecution of a Catholic priest accused of being a Nazi war criminal. Much of the novel takes place in Eastern Europe after the Soviet breakdown. Molly and Nick are appealing characters, and they make no bones about their opinions on issues both political and ethical. Subtle and complex, the plots of the novels offer much to the reader looking for an unusual twist on the academic mystery.

Fans of Amanda Cross and Nora Kelly will find much to enjoy

in Belfort's work. Also, those who admire writers who weave in the world of politics and contemporary ethics, like Sara Paretsky and Cross, should also enjoy Belfort. Other recommendations are the archaeological-anthropological mysteries of Margot Arnold, and the series by Gillian Roberts that features a thirty-something high school teacher involved with a homicide detective.

Berry, Carole. Berry's heroine in a continuing series is Bonnie Indermill, who has made a career of working as an office temporary. Berry uses the format of presenting a limited number of murder suspects in a colorful, insular setting. So far Bonnie has worked in a law office, a large corporation, a ballet company, and a resort hotel. Bonnie is personable, observant, casual, and funny. The first book in the series is *The Letter of the Law* (St. Martin, 1987). In *Goodnight, Sweet Prince* (St. Martin, 1990), Bonnie goes to work at a major ballet company, doing fund-raising. She inadvertently helps a famous Soviet dancer to defect; he is then murdered. In *Island Girl* (St. Martin, 1991), Bonnie is working at a rather seedy, down-at-the-heels resort in the Bahamas where she teaches fitness classes and finds herself in the midst of murder. The Bonnie Indermill books are light and entertaining reading. Berry also has written a novel of suspense, *Nightmare Point* (St. Martin, 1993), about a thirteen-year-old girl who is kidnapped while on vacation with her family on Cape Cod.

Other writers in a similar vein that readers might like include Annette Meyers, who writes about New York office workers from a more affluent viewpoint, and Trella Crespi, whose advertising agency employee and sleuth Simona Griffo is as perpetually broke as Bonnie Indermill.

Black, Malacai. See **D'Amato, Barbara.**

Black, Veronica. Black is a pseudonym for English author Maureen Peters, who also writes romance novels. *Last Seen Wear-*

ing (St. Martin, 1990) is a suspense novel about the kidnapping of a three-year-old girl. It explores the tension and anguish of waiting experienced by the child's mother and adds a touch of romance. With *A Vow of Silence* (St. Martin, 1990), Black began a series of clerical mysteries featuring Sister Joan. Sister Joan is a nun of the Order of the Daughters of Compassion; she lives in a convent in Cornwall and teaches at a small school on the moors. The strength of Black's clerical novels is in her detailed descriptions of the closely regulated lives of cloistered nuns. The outside world, with its evil and uncertainties, intrudes upon the nuns' peaceful routines, but never shakes Sister Joan's faith. The world inside the convent has its terrors as well; in *A Vow of Silence,* mysterious disappearances and deaths occur within the sister-hood. *A Vow of Chastity* (St. Martin, 1991) continues the series with a story about the disappearance of a gypsy child from Sister Joan's school. Black also has written a ghostly suspense novel, *My Name Is Polly Winter* (St. Martin, 1993). Jessica Cameron, a historical researcher, encounters murder and the specter of a long-dead child when she rents a room in a gloomy Victorian house in Liverpool.

Readers may also wish to look for clerical mysteries by Sister Carol Anne O'Marie and D. M. Greenwood.

Blaisdell, Anne.   See **Linington, Elizabeth.**

Borthwick, J. S.   Sarah Deane, graduate student in English literature and later a teaching fellow at a small college in Maine, is the central character in this series of traditional mysteries. In the first of the series, *The Case of the Hook-Billed Kites* (St. Martin, 1982), Sarah has joined her boyfriend in southern Texas for a bird-watching expedition. Sarah's hapless boyfriend is soon murdered, and Sarah turns to Dr. Alex McKenzie, another bird-watcher, for help in solving the murder. Subsequent novels in the series find Sarah and Alex back on home ground in New England. In *The Student Body* (St. Martin, 1988), Sarah is a teaching fellow when she finds herself involved in a perplexing academic mystery. In the latest, *Dude on Arrival* (St. Martin, 1992), Sarah and Alex spend Christmas vacation on an Arizona dude ranch as a gift from one of Sarah's eccentric relatives, and they become embroiled in another murder. Borthwick has a leisurely writing style; she unfolds her stories deliberately and carefully. Sarah and Alex are an appealing couple, and their combined expertise in literature and medicine makes them a formidable sleuthing duo.

Readers who have enjoyed Borthwick might try the work of Sally Gunning, Susan Kenney, Jane Langton, B. J. Morison, and Katherine Hall Page, all of whom have made effective use of New England settings. Readers looking for more about bird-watching should try the work of English writer Ann Cleeves.

Boylan, Eleanor. Few contemporary American mystery writers (other than Sue Grafton, perhaps) have the pedigree belonging to both Boylan and her series character, Clara Gamadge. Boylan is the niece of the late Elizabeth Daly, whom Dame Agatha Christie once proclaimed her favorite American mystery writer. Daly's detective was the bibliophile Henry Gamadge, and Boylan has adopted Gamadge's wife, Clara, now widowed, as her detective. In her late sixties, Clara Gamadge is an active, intelligent, and attractive character. Surrounded by her children and grandchildren, and a beloved cousin her own age, Clara first appeared in *Working Murder* (Henry Holt, 1990). Delving into a mystery that involves friends from the past, Clara proves herself as capable as her dear, departed Henry in getting to the bottom of things. This first novel was a nominee for an Agatha Award for Best First Novel. In a recent outing, *Murder Machree* (Henry Holt, 1992), Clara and her cousin Charles "Sadd" Saddlier travel to Ireland to aid an old friend who may fall victim to a murderous deception. Harking back to the classic mystery tradition so beautifully practiced by her aunt, Boylan holds up the family tradition quite well.

Other writers who feature older women detectives are Mary Bowen Hall, Corinne Holt Sawyer, Gallagher Gray, and E. X. Ferrars. Readers unacquainted with the work of Elizabeth Daly might also enjoy seeking out these tales of Clara and her beloved Henry, in many ways an American cousin of Lord Peter Wimsey.

Braun, Lilian Jackson. Braun began writing about newspaperman Jim Qwilleran and his two talented Siamese cats in 1966. She wrote *The Cat Who Could Read Backwards* (Dutton, 1966) and two more Cat Who . . . novels, then took a break from writing books for eighteen years. Her first mystery in the revived series was *The Cat Who Saw Red* (Jove, 1986), which was nominated for an Edgar award. In the earlier books in the series, Braun's main character, Qwill, lives in a Midwestern city and works as a journalist at the *Daily Fluxion*. The extravagantly mustachioed Qwill is grumpy, crotchety, and a confirmed bachelor. In *The Cat Who Played Brahms* (Jove, 1987), he inherits the Klingenschoen fortune, which is contingent upon his living in rural Pickax City in Moose County. Qwill retires and moves north, but he continues to produce columns for a local newspaper and to become involved (along with his cats) in local crime-solving. Pickax City is described as 400 miles north of anywhere, and the later books in the series have a distinctly upper Midwest ambience. The other main characters in the series are Qwill's cats, Koko and Yum Yum, who have extraordinary powers of perception and a close bond with Qwilleran, while he spoils them shamelessly. Each cat, too, has a firmly established personality: Koko is notedly psychic, intelligent, and curious, while Yum Yum is coy, playful, and affectionate. Koko especially noses out evidence and clues, and thus sends Qwill hints on crimes that have been committed. In each book, Qwill eventually understands what the cats are trying to communicate to him and thus is able to solve a mystery.

Braun also has written a collection of feline-centered short stories, *The Cat Who Had 14 Tales* (Jove, 1988).

Other writers who have created lively animal characters include Carole Nelson Douglas, Rita Mae Brown, Susan Conant, and Melissa Cleary.

Brod, D. C. Quint McCauley is the private eye created by Brod for her series of novels. Quint is a PI very much in the style of Philip Marlowe—laconic, principled, and sardonic. In Brod's first novel, *Murder in Store* (Walker, 1989), Quint, a former policeman, is in charge of security for a Chicago department store that seems rather akin to Marshall Field. Quint's life is complicated because he has been dumped by his girlfriend for a younger man and then has been reprimanded for catching his boss's wife shoplifting. When his boss is murdered, Quint, in the tradition of Marlowe, pursues truth doggedly while trying to keep his principles intact. In later novels, Quint moves to Foxport, a mythical suburb of Chicago on the Fox River. Even when everyone in Foxport (including the chief of police) is against him, Quint is persistent in solving mysteries. Inevitably, Quint gets beaten up, threatened, and car-bombed in the pursuit of truth. Brod's prose is unadorned and hard-boiled; her stories are tightly plotted.

Brod's readers might also be interested in the writings of Nancy Baker Jacobs, M. K. Wren, and Sara Paretsky.

Brown, Rita Mae. Already a well-established novelist with a string of successful books to her credit, Brown recently, with the aid of her tiger cat, Sneaky Pie Brown, turned to writing mysteries. The setting for this series is the small town of Crozet, Virginia, near Charlottesville, and Brown has filled the town with engaging and believable characters, both animal and human. Mary Minor "Harry" Haristeen, the town's young postmistress, is the central human character. Watched over lovingly by Mrs. Murphy and Tee Tucker, her cat and dog, the central animal characters, Harry learns to live with the aftermath of divorce in a small and close-knit community. Her ex-husband, "Fair" (for

Pharamond), is the town's veterinarian. In the first of the series, *Wish You Were Here* (Bantam, 1990), Harry starts noting strange postcards that are heralds to murder. Prodded when necessary by Mrs. Murphy and Tee Tucker and other animal characters, Harry solves the mystery. Brown intersperses the narrative from the human point of view with engaging and amusing conversations among the animals (presumably these are the contributions of Sneaky Pie), which enhance the plot and offer another dimension of observation, with some quite satirical comments on the foibles of human behavior. Rich in character and small-town Southern ambience, the "Mrs. Murphy" mysteries are great fun. Each book includes illustrations by artist Wendy Wray.

For readers eager to enjoy the exploits of animal crime-solvers, *The Cat Who...* series of Lilian Jackson Braun remains the most popular, though the works of canine experts Susan Conant, Melissa Cleary, and cat fancier Carole Nelson Douglas are fast gaining an audience. Readers who like the Southern settings of Brown's work might also try the work of Charlaine Harris, Deborah Adams, Sarah Shankman, or Sharyn McCrumb.

Burden, Pat. In this cozy series of English mysteries, retired policeman Henry Bassett has settled into a comfortable life in a Herefordshire cottage, tending his pigs and chickens and his garden. But a bizarre crime intrudes upon this rustic calm in *Screaming Bones* (Doubleday, 1990), the first novel in the series, and Bassett finds himself itching to become involved. Burden depicts the rural and village settings in Herefordshire with a loving eye and peoples her works with engaging descendants of the classic English mystery novel. There is a comforting sense of familiarity for the reader in Burden's novels, but rather than breeding contempt, familiarity in this case brings the cheering sense of recognition of yet another skilled practitioner of an established form. Burden's little corner of England is definitely part of the England of the 1990s but with recognizable ties to the past. *Screaming Bones* was an Agatha Award nominee for Best First Malice Domestic Mystery Novel.

Like Burden, June Thomson, Dorothy Simpson, and Susan B. Kelly infuse their works with a strong sense of rural and smaller-town England. Readers might also enjoy the work of Ann Granger and Ann Cleeves.

Butler, Gwendoline.   This veteran author has penned over fifty novels under her own name and as Jennie Melville since the late 1950s. As Butler, she began writing mysteries, most of which featured Inspector Winter and his sergeant, John Coffin; the first is *Dead in a Row* (Geoffrey Bles, 1957). Then Coffin became the main character in a long series of novels, through the mid-1970s. Butler abandoned him for awhile, writing instead historical novels with elements of mystery and suspense, like *Sarsen Place* (Coward McCann, 1974). Then, in 1986, she resurrected Coffin (in *Coffin on the Water;* St. Martin, 1989), re-created some of the details of his personal life, and the series was reborn. As Jennie Melville, she created policewoman Charmian Daniels, born and reared in Scotland, but working in Deerham Hills, near London. Daniels first appeared in *Come Home and Be Killed* (London House and Maxwell, 1964). Besides the Daniels books, Melville has written novels in the romantic suspense vein, like *Dragon's Eye* (Simon & Schuster, 1976). Both Charmian Daniels and John Coffin are intelligent, intense, and curious about their fellow human beings. Whether writing as Butler or Melville, the author has a style quite different from any of her peers. She creates a chilling sense of unease unlike anyone else, except perhaps Ruth Rendell. The murderer's presence is eerily tangible throughout each novel, like a goblin hovering on the periphery of vision. Readers looking for an unusual variation on the traditional English mystery will find Butler worth a visit.

Those who are familiar with Butler/Melville might try the Wexford novels of Ruth Rendell and the works of Minette Walters and S. T. Haymon. Readers looking for other writings of historical or contemporary romantic suspense might enjoy the work of Victoria Holt and her pseudonym Philippa Carr, Jean Stubbs, or Jessica Stirling.

C

Cannell, Dorothy. Cannell's first novel, *The Thin Woman* (St. Martin, 1984) has been a perennial favorite with mystery readers. In this charming, eccentric comedy-mystery, the heroine, Ellie Simons, is an overweight interior decorator who becomes embroiled in a romantic fantasy straight out of her dreams. The problem is that she has to lose weight (sixty-three pounds!) and find a hidden treasure in six months in order to inherit a castle and win her true love. The leading man, Ben Haskell, is an aspiring chef and writer of great literature who makes ends meet by writing trashy stories and working (innocently enough) for an escort service. Cannell's second novel, *Down the Garden Path* (St. Martin, 1985) introduces Hyacinth and Primrose Tramwell, elderly (and odd) sisters with a bent for duplicity and investigation. Later novels continue Ellie's adventures in life and crime, sometimes with the assistance (or perhaps it's the hindrance) of the Tramwells. All are set in England, except *Mum's the Word* (Bantam, 1990), which takes place in the hilariously described small Midwestern town of Mud Creek, Illinois. Cannell's characters are endearingly dotty, in the best tradition of English literary eccentrics.

Comedy-mysteries by Elizabeth Peters, Charlotte MacLeod, and Joan Hess also may be fun for readers of Cannell. *Aunt Dimity's Death* (Viking, 1992) by Nancy Atherton is a charming, gentle tale that may appeal to admirers of *The Thin Woman*.

Carlson, P. M. The P stands for Patricia. Carlson holds a Ph.D. in the psychology of language and has coauthored a textbook called *Behavioral Statistics*. Some of this background is evident in her mysteries, for Carlson has endowed her series character, Maggie Ryan, with her own interest and abilities in statistics. In the first of the series, *Audition for Murder* (Avon, 1985), set in 1967, Maggie is an undergraduate in a small college in upstate New York. Several professional actors are teaching at the college and starring in a production of *Hamlet*. Among the actors are Nick O'Connor and his wife Lisette, who has a troubled history of drug abuse. Maggie, lighting expert for the play, soon turns sleuth when someone seems bent on driving Lisette back to drugs with malicious pranks. In subsequent books, the relationship between Maggie and Nick grows, and by *Murder Unrenovated* (Bantam, 1988), they're married and expecting their first child. While Carlson constructs neat puzzles along with the best of them, the chief appeal in her series is the strong characterizations. Maggie Ryan, the centerpiece, is intelligent, intense, and fiercely loyal to her friends. Sometimes she seems like a superwoman, because she can handle just about anything thrown in her path, never ducking an emotion simply because it is painful. Strength of character is her long suit. With *Gravestone* (Pocket, 1993), Carlson introduces Marty Hopkins, a sheriff's deputy in southern Indiana. A working mother with an unreliable husband, Marty is bright and tough, like Maggie Ryan.

The characters of M. K. Lorens are also intense, though perhaps more eccentric than those of Carlson. Nevertheless, readers who enjoy one might well try the other. Another New York series with intriguing characters are the Sigrid Harald books of Margaret Maron. In addition, Carlson fans might also enjoy the works of Nancy Pickard, B. J. Oliphant, and Kate Wilhelm. Jane Dentinger and Anne Morice both have main characters who are actresses.

Caudwell, Sarah. Though she has only three books thus far to her credit, Caudwell has achieved a wide following for her mirthful tales of murder and mayhem. With an erudition and precision of language worthy of the late Dorothy L. Sayers, Caudwell does what she does quite unlike anyone else writing contemporary mystery novels. The narrator of Caudwell's work is the androgynous Oxford professor of law, Hilary Tamar. Though readers may claim to know whether Hilary is male or female, Caudwell smilingly refuses ever to settle the debate. The affairs that Hilary so amusingly relates concern five young London barristers, each of whom has her or his own particular talent for running into trouble. In the brilliantly funny *Thus Was Adonis Murdered* (Scribner, 1981), Julia Larwood, who knows the Finance Act inside out but who can't quite remember where she left her passport, becomes embroiled in murder while she's on holiday in Venice. Hilary, of course, must come to the rescue. The combination of wit, humor, and intelligence makes Caudwell's work a rare vintage. Caudwell's third novel, *The Sirens Sang of Murder* (Delacorte, 1989), won the Anthony Award for Best Novel from the Bouchercon.

Though few mystery writers currently writing quite approach the combination of Caudwell's elegant wit and humor, readers hungering for other highly individual or humorous writing styles might browse the work of Margery Allingham, Mollie Hardwick, Elizabeth Peters, Charlotte MacLeod, Patricia Moyes, and Dorothy L. Sayers.

Chaplin, Elizabeth. See **McGown, Jill.**

Charles, Kate. An American currently living in Bedford, England, Charles uses her experience as a former Anglican church administrator and her love of English ecclesiastical history and architecture to provide a fascinating background for a series of mysteries starring solicitor David Middleton-Brown. Middleton-Brown is himself an expert of a sort on church architecture, and in this role he sometimes finds himself involved in mysterious goings-on. In the first book of the series, *A Drink of Deadly Wine* (Mysterious Press, 1992), David must confront difficult secrets out of his own past when he is called upon for help by a charismatic priest, Gabriel Neville. Neville is being blackmailed, and, because of the peculiar circumstances, he knows David Middleton-Brown is the one person who can solve the puzzle. In the course of his investigation David meets the artist Lucy Kingsley, with whom he develops an unusual relationship that continues in later books. In *The Snares of Death* (Mysterious Press, 1993), David and Lucy agree to investigate the death of a prominent Evangelical minister who had a talent for rubbing people the wrong way. Full of church politics and intriguing characters, this series has much to offer the fan of the traditional English mystery.

Readers who enjoy mysteries with clerical settings or characters should try the work of D. M. Greenwood, Mollie Hardwick, and Barbara Whitehead. Those interested in American mysteries with clerical backgrounds could try the work of Isabelle Holland and Sister Carol Anne O'Marie.

Christmas, Joyce.   After writing several novels, some nonfiction books, and children's plays, Christmas turned to the mystery novel. Her series detective is Lady Margaret Priam, a genteel Englishwoman living in New York City. In her first appearance, *Suddenly in Her Sorbet* (Fawcett, 1988), Lady Margaret is attending a charity fund-raiser when someone poisons the organizer, a grande dame of New York Society. Aided by her young friend and fellow socialite, Prince Paul Castrocani, Lady Margaret dives into the case. Along the way she becomes interested in the investigating police officer, detective Sam de Vere, and in subsequent novels the two pursue a romantic relationship. Christmas handles the intriguing social world of New York City with deft skill, her slightly ironic eye yielding the reader quiet amusement at the foibles of the rich and often tasteless. Though much of the action in the series takes place in New York and its environs, Lady Margaret occasionally investigates farther afield. In one novel, *Friend or Faux* (Fawcett, 1991), she returns to England to help her brother, the Earl of Brayfield, solve the murder of one of his guests.

Female English aristocrats are scarce among today's crime-solvers, although former Member of Parliament Michael Spicer has written several novels about Lady Jane Hildreth. Evelyn E. Smith is writing a series about Miss Susan Melville, a well-bred American woman who just happens to be a hired assassin, based in New York City. Other entertaining series set in New York City are the works of Gallagher Gray and Annette Meyers.

Churchill, Jill. Churchill's books are charming and unpretentious. Jane Jeffry, a widowed homemaker and mother, lives in the suburbs of Chicago. Jane has three kids, nosy neighbors, and a network of friends who do volunteer work for charities and help each other out of jams. And of course they get involved in local murders. Jane and her friends solve murders by deduction and the application of common sense. They confound the police, especially Detective Mel VanDyne, with conclusions drawn from their everyday knowledge of housework and neighborhood customs. In *Grime and Punishment,* for example, Jane makes a crucial deduction by knowing how women typically vacuum a room. Churchill uses the traditional format: The murders occur in a small town among a closed circle of suspects, and the puzzle is solved by the use of well-hidden clues and logical deductions made by the amateur sleuth. Jane is a younger Miss Marple figure. She observes human nature, suburban life, and people, and then combines her observations with her inborn intelligence to solve crimes. Aside from the mystery plot, the books are brimful of Churchill's wry comments on motherhood, carpooling, living in suburbia, raising teenagers, and other conditions of modern life.

The first Jane Jeffry book is *Grime and Punishment* (Bantam, 1989). It won an Agatha Award for Best First Mystery Novel.

Jill Churchill is a pseudonym of Janice Young Brooks, who also writes historical novels. Other crime novelists the reader might like include Charlotte MacLeod, Valerie Wolzien, Katherine Hall Page, and of course Agatha Christie, especially her Miss Marple books.

Clark, Mary Higgins. Clark's well-crafted novels of suspense have been making the best-seller lists since the 1970s. The books generally have attractive heroines or children in danger from a killer who is stalking them. Positively portrayed authority figures—police officers, doctors, lawyers, and detectives—help find the criminal and protect the vulnerable. Clark's protagonists are mostly upscale, sophisticated, and articulate people. She provides vividly realized settings, and wintry scenes of Northeastern cities and their suburbs abound. Her first novel, *Where Are the Children?* (Simon & Schuster, 1975), is set on Cape Cod, with a villain who kidnaps two small children in order to frame their mother, who had been accused earlier in her life of killing two other children. In this and subsequent novels, Clark slowly builds suspense with her clear prose and measured evocation of daily life, as the killer hovers and events move out of the control of the innocent. Incidents move inevitably toward a terrifying crisis, which must occur before order can be restored at the end of the story. Meanwhile, Clark has given the reader a strong sense of the danger that can lurk even in the most protected and affluent lives.

Clark also has written a volume of short stories, *The Anastasia Syndrome and Other Stories* (Simon & Schuster, 1989), and she moved away a bit from the suspense novel to write a mystery in the classic format, *Weep No More, My Lady* (Simon & Schuster, 1987).

She received the French Grand Prix de Litterature Policiere in 1980.

Other novelists of suspense include Judith Kelman, T. J. MacGregor, Nancy Baker Jacobs, Rochelle Majer Krich, Patricia Cornwell, D. F. Mills, and Kate Green.

Clarke, Anna. The literary world and its denizens hold strong interest for Clarke, for in many of her novels central characters are writers, sometimes of mystery fiction of some sort. An early example is *Plot Counter-Plot* (Walker, 1975), in which a successful, older woman novelist takes under her wing a brash, unsuccessful young man, also a novelist. Their relationship, both literary and amorous, leads them down the path to destruction, and Clarke cleverly keeps the reader guessing all the way. Another novel, *The Lady in Black* (McKay, 1978), has a Victorian setting and revolves around a mysterious woman who has penned a suspenseful tale of murder and remorse that may be fact rather than fiction. Only recently has Clarke developed a series character. When she first appears in *Last Judgement* (Doubleday, 1985), University of London English professor Paula Glenning is actually a minor character, but she soon moves to the forefront, as in *Murder in Writing* (Doubleday, 1988). Clarke's interest in psychology and the myriad quirks of human behavior makes the best of her work suspenseful; she can take clichés of the genre and make them seem refreshingly new. *Letter from the Dead* (Doubleday, 1981), along with *Plot Counter-Plot,* demonstrate this very well.

Those who have enjoyed the work of Clarke might try the novels of E. X. Ferrars, Margaret Yorke, and Celia Fremlin.

Cleary, Melissa. The central character in Cleary's series of dog-lovers' mysteries is Jackie Walsh, who has recently divorced her husband and forsaken her life as a suburban housewife and mother to move back into the city and take up her career once again. Living with Jackie is her son Peter, ten years old. In the first book of the series, *A Tail of Two Murders* (Berkley, 1992), Jackie and Peter find an Alsatian shepherd with a bullet wound in his leg, and they adopt the dog and name him Jake. Jake turns out to be a retired police dog whose owner has been mysteriously murdered. An instructor in the Rodgers University film department, Jackie finds her department chairman dead in the film library one day. Lieutenant Michael McGowan is officially in charge of the case, and he elicits Jackie's help. Their relationship continues in further books in the series, edging a little closer to romance all the time. The presence of Jake the retired police dog involves Jackie and Peter in danger, for the murder of Jake's former master is still unsolved, and someone considers Jake a threat. This is an enjoyably cozy series, with an attractive single mother, her son, and their adopted dog as the centerpieces.

Readers acquainted with Cleary might try as well the series by Susan Conant and Dana Stabenow, in which dogs play important roles in the crime-solving.

Cleeves, Ann. The distinctive feature of one of the two series that Cleeves writes is the prominence of bird-watching and related environmental issues. The main character, former Home Office official George Palmer-Jones, is an avid bird-watcher, and the murders with which he becomes involved generally occur around some activity connected with bird-watching. For the uninitiated, Cleeves explains the enthusiasms of the activity well, though readers with no interest in the subject might prefer Cleeves's other series. The second series features Inspector Stephen Ramsay as the detective, and the setting is Northumberland. This series follows conventional lines for the modern British police detective mystery. Both series fit comfortably into the traditional or cozy mold. First in the Palmer-Jones series is *A Bird in the Hand* (Fawcett, 1988); first in the Inspector Ramsay series is *A Lesson in Dying* (Fawcett, 1990).

No other writers have made bird-watching such a prominent feature of their series, except perhaps J. S. Borthwick, though bird-watching characters do appear rather often in many English series. Other writers who touch upon environmental and animal rights issues with frequency are Gwen Moffat and Susan Conant.

Cody, Liza. Until recently, it has been unusual for British women to write hard-boiled crime fiction, but Liza Cody has done so successfully and has added a distinctly English and feminist twist to a largely American art form. Cody's heroine is Anna Lee, an operative with Brierly Security in London. Anna's boss doesn't think much of women investigators, so he tends to assign her "female" cases, like hunting for a missing daughter or providing security for a department store (in spite of Anna's five years' experience in the police department). Anna is certainly the low person on the totem pole and her position is not improved by the perception in the agency that she handles her assignments in ways different from the male agents. Somehow she gets involved with the people in her cases, even when doing security for a difficult rock star in *Under Contract* (Scribner, 1987). In the tradition of fictional private eyes, Anna tends to be a self-reliant lone wolf. When she has a day off, she's likely to spend it cleaning the spark plugs and tuning up the engine on her old Triumph. Anna does have friendly and eccentric neighbors, Bea and Selwyn Price, who leave her little privacy or quiet. Like Sue Grafton, Cody is interested in the routine minutiae of the investigator's day. Her books are set in a grimy London; details of the traffic, the tube system, and the daily challenges of urban life are abundant.

Cody has also written *Rift* (Scribner, 1988), a novel about a naive young woman's harrowing trip through a drought-stricken Ethiopia in 1974. Her novel *Bucket Nut* (Doubleday, 1993) is a virtuoso character study of Eva Wylie, a female wrestler, petty criminal, and security guard. Anna Lee appears briefly in this novel, but the focus is on Eva, the "London Lassassin," and her daily struggle for survival and independence.

Cody's first Anna Lee novel, *Dupe* (Scribner, 1980), won the British Crime Writers' Association John Creasey Award for Best First Novel. *Bucket Nut* won the Silver Dagger Award from the British Crime Writers' Association.

Gillian Slovo and Sarah Dunant also write novels set in London with hard-boiled investigators Kate Baeier and Hannah Wolfe, while Val McDermid uses Manchester as a backdrop.

Cohen, Janet. See **Neel, Janet.**

Conant, Susan. All those dog-lovers tired of seeing cats get all the cover art in pet-centered mysteries found a welcome new voice in Conant. Her series detective is Holly Winter, columnist for the magazine *Dog's Life* and malamute enthusiast. In between writing her column and training her malamute Rowdy, Holly stumbles upon crimes, usually involving dogs in some way, in and around Cambridge, Massachusetts. Sparked by a sense of humor with a strong streak of irony, Holly has a pithy narrative voice and little patience for those who fail to treat animals with respect. In addition to giving man's and woman's best friend a share of the spotlight, Conant also manages to raise the consciousness of her readers with her plots, which often involve issues relating to animal welfare. These issues sometimes make the books perhaps less cozy than some readers might prefer, but Conant, like Nancy Pickard, has the knack of blending trenchant social comment with an entertaining story. The series begins with *A New Leash on Death* (Berkley, 1990).

Dogs are still in the minority when it comes to appearances in mystery novels, but Melissa Cleary has recently debuted with a new series of dog-lover's mysteries with *A Tail of Two Murders* (Berkley, 1992). Joan Hess's novel, *Roll Over and Play Dead* (St. Martin, 1991), is a strong comment on some of the same issues that concern Conant. Barbara Moore wrote two books about a crime-solving veterinarian, and both Susan Kelly and Kathryn

Lasky Knight write about Cambridge and its environs in their series.

Cooper, Natasha. Cooper is a pseudonymous British author of romantic mysteries featuring Willow King, a civil servant who leads a double life as a romance novelist. Willow works three days a week in the Department of Old Age Pensions as an administrator and lives in a scruffy south London flat on a tight budget. But in her second life as Cressida Woodruffe, she spends Friday through Monday writing romance novels and living in a lavishly decorated apartment with a gourmet cook-housekeeper. The success of this strange existence is threatened when she encounters murderous events. In *A Common Death* (Crown, 1990), the Minister of State in charge of Willow's department is killed, she meets Chief Inspector Tom Worth, who is investigating the murder, and she is threatened by an attacker who burglarizes and befouls her luxurious Cressida Woodruffe flat. Cooper establishes Willow as a person who possesses great self-control and personal fortitude, but who also has built an emotional wall around herself. As the series progresses, that personal armor slowly breaks down, and she begins to admit other people behind her defenses. For example, she comes at once to the aid of a former lover accused of murder in *Bloody Roses* (Crown, 1992). Cooper's novels are entertaining, light reading; the improbable double life plot twist becomes less important as Willow develops into a sympathetic and three-dimensional character.

Janet Neel and Ruth Dudley Edwards also use the British civil service system as a backdrop for their mysteries. Dorothy Cannell, Elizabeth Peters, and Nancy Atherton have written romantic mysteries.

Cooper, Susan Rogers. A writer who describes herself as half fifth-generation Texan and half Yankee, Cooper has let the Texas half prevail in her two series set in the Southwest. The first series features chief deputy Milt Kovak of the Prophesy

County, Oklahoma, Sheriff's Department. In his first recorded case, *The Man in the Green Chevy* (St. Martin, 1988), Milt has to deal with a rapist and murderer of little old ladies, and the whole county is horrified. Cooper describes her territory well, and she manages to convey the atmosphere of rural and small-town Oklahoma with the ease of a veteran. She also makes Milt Kovak sound like a completely believable, somewhat irascible, forty-eight-year-old-man. In a voice that is wry, reflective, and occasionally raunchy, Milt narrates these tales of murder and misbehavior with a definite Southwestern inflection. These same strong qualities carry over into Cooper's second series, which features housewife and romance novelist, E. J. (Eloise Janine) Pugh. Debuting in *One, Two, What Did Daddy Do?* (St. Martin, 1992), E. J. and her husband Willis, residents of the small community of Black Cat Ridge, Texas, solve the murders of their next-door neighbors.

Those readers for whom the Southwestern setting has an appeal might try the two Texas Panhandle series of D. R. Meredith, the Oklahoma series of Jean Hager and Eve K. Sandstrom, or B. J. Oliphant's series about a Colorado rancher, Shirley McClintock.

Cornwell, Patricia D. Having spent a number of years working as a computer analyst in the office of the chief medical examiner of the Commonwealth of Virginia, Cornwell uses her knowledge of forensic pathology and the methods of contemporary crime-solving to give her fiction a compelling realism. The main character in the series is Dr. Kay Scarpetta, Virginia's chief medical examiner. Tough and intense, Scarpetta makes an effective centerpiece for the series. She develops a strong working relationship with Richmond homicide cop Pete Marino, who complements the prickly Scarpetta well. The settings of the series are Richmond and its environs. Cornwell has a strong sense of pace; the action rarely lags in her work. She also has a knack for explaining the complexities of forensic pathology to the ignorant. She sometimes includes details that the squeamish might quickly skim over, but, for the most part, Cornwell treats matter-of-factly the details that some novelists tend to sensationalize for mere effect. Cornwell understands that the commonplace or ordinary can become quite sinister in the hands or mind of a killer. For example, when Scarpetta comes to understand the link among the victims of the serial killers in *Postmortem* (Scribner, 1990) and *Body of Evidence* (Scribner, 1991), the reader will never take some relatively mundane things for granted ever again. The first novel in the series, *Postmortem,* has won a host of prestigious awards for first novels, including the Edgar, the Creasey, the Macavity, and the Anthony. Cornwell's combination of suspense and unusual professional setting for her protagonist has propelled her rapidly onto the best-seller lists.

D. J. Donaldson currently writes a series featuring a medical examiner who works in New Orleans. Susan Dunlap's Kiernan O'Shaughnessy is a former medical examiner turned private investigator. Readers looking for other fast-paced series with tough-minded main characters should try the work of Sue Grafton, J. A. Jance, T. J. MacGregor, and Sara Paretsky.

Craig, Alisa. See **MacLeod, Charlotte.**

Crane, Caroline. Agatha Christie knew that one secret of writing a good mystery novel was seeking out the sinister in the commonplace. Crane makes good use of this technique in her low-key novels of suspense, which generally involve ordinary people in difficult situations beyond their control. For example, in *Woman Vanishes* (Dodd, Mead, 1984), a young wife and mother finds herself on the run from a vicious loan shark when her husband disappears after defaulting on his loan. How will she save herself and her young daughter from harm? In another novel, *Someone at the Door* (Dodd, Mead, 1985), Crane takes an intriguing premise and spins it into a good yarn. A pregnant woman in labor calls her sister to come look after her young autistic son while she drives herself to the hospital. The pregnant woman interrupts the conversation, saying there's someone at the door. When the sister arrives at the house later, the door is open, and her pregnant sister is missing. She never turned up at the hospital, and the police at first can find no trace of her. The answer to this puzzle is a chilling one. Readers looking for quietly effective tales of suspense will find pleasure with Caroline Crane's work. Crane has written a number of novels for children and young adults. Her first adult novel was *Summer Girl* (Dodd, Mead, 1979).

Those who have enjoyed Crane might try Mary Higgins Clark, Velda Johnston, and Phyllis A. Whitney. Valerie Wolzien and Katherine Hall Page also write engagingly about the suburban Northeast.

Crane, Hamilton. See **Mason, Sarah J.**

Crespi, Trella. Simona Griffo is the protagonist in Crespi's series of *The Trouble With . . .* mysteries. Simona has emigrated from Italy to New York in search of a new life after a difficult divorce; now she works as an art buyer in an advertising agency. Simona loves to cook and to eat. The books are full of descriptions of food, especially Italian food (and the author does give recipes). Simona also likes, as she says, to stick her Roman nose into trouble, which naturally turns out to be murder. In the series, she is confronted with crimes on a film set with an Italian director, in her own advertising office, and at Club Med in Guadeloupe. Simona is not a completely independent woman; she is aware that, for her, happiness depends on having a man around. However, she is curious, emotional, talkative, and an interesting personality study.

The first Simona Griffo novel is *The Trouble With a Small Raise* (Zebra, 1991).

Readers also may like Carole Berry's Bonnie Indermill novels. Other mystery writers who are adept at descriptions of gustatory delights include Virginia Rich, Janet Laurence, and Diane Mott Davidson. For mysteries set in ad agencies, try *Strangle Hold* (Harper, 1951) by Mary McMullen and *Murder Must Advertise* (Harcourt Brace, 1933) by Dorothy L. Sayers.

Crombie, Deborah. Native Texan Crombie is following somewhat in the footsteps of fellow American writers Elizabeth George and Martha Grimes, in that she is writing a series of mysteries set in England, featuring English police detectives. Otherwise, Crombie's books are quite different from those of George and Grimes. Crombie's main characters are Superintendent Duncan Kincaid and Detective Sergeant Gemma James. Kincaid, in his mid-thirties, is a little younger than most men of his rank, but his intelligence and skill in his job have brought him promotion early. Gemma James is a young, divorced mother of a toddler named Toby; she is bright, somewhat impulsive in her thinking, but altogether an appealing character. Kincaid is cast in the mold of the sensitive, thinking detective, like Adam Dalgliesh and Thomas Lynley, but Kincaid is not constantly riven by soul-wrenching angst as are his peers. Kincaid and James make an effective and interesting duo. Their first appearance is *A Share in Death* (Scribner, 1993). Crombie has taken the conventional English detective story and updated it pleasantly; fans of the traditional English mystery will find much to enjoy here.

Readers who have already encountered the work of Crombie might try as well the series of Anthea Fraser, Susan B. Kelly, Elizabeth Lemarchand, Susannah Stacey, Medora Sale, and Clare Curzon.

Cross, Amanda. When she made her debut on the mystery scene in 1964, Columbia English professor Carolyn G. Heilbrun masked her identity with the pseudonym Amanda Cross to safeguard her academic reputation. The choice of the first name for her pseudonym turned out to be a propitious one (Amanda, loosely translated from the Latin, means "one who is to be loved''), for Cross has become a well-loved writer, and her detective, English professor Kate Fansler, is the epitome of the feminist sleuth. Kate comes from a wealthy and socially prominent New York family, but she finds her values much at odds with those of the rest of her family, with one or two exceptions. Having invested Kate Fansler with her own academic, if not her social and financial, background, Cross has made her detective the most literate and literary since Dorothy L. Sayers's Lord Peter Wimsey. In a career that has spanned nearly thirty years, Kate has solved several crimes with a literary bent, such as *The James Joyce Murder* (Macmillan, 1967) or *The Players Come Again* (Random House, 1990). Acclaimed by her fans and critics alike for the richness of her dialogue, Amanda Cross always provides a veritable feast for the lover of the English language. Perhaps her most interesting novel is *Death in a Tenured Position* (Dutton, 1981), which involves Kate in the murder of the only woman to have received tenure in the Harvard English department. First in the series is *In the Last Analysis* (Macmillan, 1964).

Like Cross, Sara Paretsky also brings a distinct moral and political stance to her fiction, though Paretsky's V. I. Warshawski and Kate Fansler come from very different social and economic backgrounds. B. J. Oliphant's series character, Shirley McClintock, holds very strong opinions as well, and she is not shy about sharing them with those around her. For enjoyable academic mysteries, Dorothy L. Sayers's *Gaudy Night* (Harcourt Brace, 1936) is the epitome. Readers should also try the works of Nora Kelly and Sophie Belfort.

Curzon, Clare. After writing a series of mysteries in the 1960s under the name of Rhona Petrie, Curzon turned away from crime for awhile, until the publication of *A Leaven of Malice* (Collins Crime Club, 1979). Eight Curzon novels were published in England before the ninth, *Three-Core Lead* (Doubleday, 1990), was published in the United States. Most of the Curzon novels feature the Thames Valley Serious Crimes Squad under the direction of Detective-Superintendent Mike Yeadings. Yeadings much of the time is the central character in this series, but in true police procedural fashion, Curzon aims her spotlight on various members of the team, like Detective Inspector Angus Mott, Yeadings's right-hand-man, throughout the books. Curzon weaves authentic details of ordinary police procedure into her tales, which feature solid plotting and engaging series characters as well. Curzon's world of the Thames Valley Serious Crime Squad is very much contemporary England, but occasionally there are echoes of the England of the classic detective novel. Curzon's work is an effective and entertaining blend of both, as demonstrated in the recent *First Wife, Twice Removed* (St. Martin, 1993).

Other writers of contemporary British police procedurals similar to Curzon are Susannah Stacey, Anthea Fraser, Marjorie Eccles, Deborah Crombie, and Jill McGown.

Daheim, Mary. A Seattle native who is an award-winning writer of historical romances, Daheim has recently added two mystery series to her repertoire. The first series features Judith McMonigle, who has turned her family home into a bed-and-breakfast named Hillside Manor Inn. The city that serves as the setting in this series is never named but is otherwise a thinly veiled Seattle. Judith, a widow with one college-age son, operates the bed-and-breakfast despite the ill-natured interference of her mother, Gertrude, who lives with her. In the first of the series, *Just Desserts* (Avon, 1991), a fortune-teller meets an unforeseen end at Hillside Manor Inn. Aided by her cousin Renie, Judith solves the mystery. In Daheim's second series, which begins with *The Alpine Advocate* (Ballantine, 1992), the main character is Emma Lord, journalist turned newspaper owner, in the small town of Alpine, Washington, in the foothills of the Cascade Mountains. Both series characters have much in common, including troubled relationships with old lovers who reappear to complicate their lives. While one series is written in third person (Judith) and the other in the first person (Emma), Daheim's voice in both series is wry, ocassionally ribald, and often sarcastic. Both series have a pleasant, cozy feel, and readers looking for conventional mystery reading will find good entertainment value with Daheim.

Like Mary Daheim, Joan Hess writes humorously of the tribulations of single parenthood in her Claire Molloy series. Otherwise, readers might try the work of Jill Churchill, Celestine Sibley, Joyce Christmas, Gloria Dank, and Katherine Hall Page. Readers looking for Seattle and Pacific Northwest settings might try the work of J. A. Jance and Janet L. Smith, although both writers are somewhat harder-edged than Daheim.

Dain, Catherine/Garwood, Judith. Her first mystery, *Make Friends with Murder* (St. Martin, 1992) was published under her own name, Judith Garwood. Garwood tells the story of Morgan Reeves, a writer of magazine articles and former television newscaster, who finds murder in a winery near Santa Barbara. Garwood's later mysteries appear under the pseudonym of Catherine Dain. Her series stars Freddie O'Neal, a Reno private investigator. Freddie is a hard-boiled private eye and licensed pilot, who carries a gun in her cowboy boot and can disarm a knife-wielding attacker by kicking him where it hurts the most. She is a loner who has grown up in Reno, and the sense of place in the stories is strong. Freddie is addicted to playing keno in the casinos, and she pals around with Deke, a retired cop who is now a casino security guard. In the first book, *Lay It on the Line* (Jove, 1992), Freddie takes on a simple stolen car recovery that turns into a case involving drug sales and multiple murder. *Sing a Song of Death* (Jove, 1993), is set mostly in Lake Tahoe, where Freddie takes a job as a bodyguard to Vince Marina, a charming alcoholic singer. When Vince is killed, everyone except Freddie assumes the obvious suspect, his ex-wife, is the murderer.

Readers also may enjoy the hard-boiled stories of Sue Grafton, Judith Van Gieson, Janet Dawson, and Karen Kijewski. Deborah Valentine has written a mystery series set in Lake Tahoe.

D'Amato, Barbara. D'Amato has created freelance Chicago reporter Cat Marsala, who often investigates social problems like gambling and prostitution. The first Cat Marsala novel is *Hardball* (Scribner, 1990). In each of the novels, Cat's research for her current assignment leads her into a murderous situation. D'Amato obviously researches each topic extensively herself. In *Hard Tack* (Scribner, 1991), for example, she manages to fit into the story just about everything anyone could want to know about sailing on the Great Lakes. *Hard Women* (Scribner, 1993) uses the device of Cat doing research for her television assignment on the lives of hookers to bring the reader into the everyday worlds of different kinds of prostitutes, from street hookers to high-priced call girls. Cat investigates the crimes she encounters as carefully as she does her basic research; her interviewing techniques help get the story plus solve the murder. The part of each book that is strictly mystery plot is tightly constructed and well-planned, and a small group of suspects is typically identified and analyzed wittily. Before she began the Cat Marsala series, D'Amato also wrote two puzzlers in the classic mode: *The Hands of Healing Murder* (Charter, 1980) and *The Eyes on Utopia Murder* (Ace, 1981). D'Amato also has written *On My Honor* (Windsor, 1989) under the pseudonym of Malacai Black; it was nominated for an Anthony award.

D'Amato's Chicago settings are somewhat cheerier than Sara Paretsky's. Other resourceful reporters and writers appear in Sarah Shankman's amusing Samantha Adams books, and in Mickey Friedman's Georgia Lee Maxwell stories.

Dank, Gloria. Snooky Randolph is the bane of many people's existence. Despite his wealth, Snooky has no job and no home of his own, and thus has the disconcerting habit of descending upon his sister and her husband with little warning. Snooky (whose real name is Arthur) is particularly irritating to his brother-in-law Bernard, an eccentric writer of children's books. But the garrulous, effortlessly charming Snooky and the taciturn, often misanthropic Bernard make a surprisingly effective detective team, especially with Snooky's sister—Bernard's wife—Maya there to smooth the troubled waters. Set in New England, generally in the town where Bernard and Maya live, the series has a charming cozy feel, and Dank's gently satiric sense of humor lends a nice twist to what otherwise might be commonplace. The series began with *Friends Till the End* (Bantam, 1989). The text of each novel is illustrated with line drawings, presumably by Dank herself, reminiscent of those Jane Langton provides for her own work.

For other charmingly eccentric characters, readers might try the work of M. K. Lorens (though her work has greater emotional intensity), the wacky whimsy of Dorothy Cannell, the eccentric small Tennessee town of Deborah Adams, or the numerous offbeat characters of Charlotte MacLeod and Alisa Craig.

Davidson, Diane Mott. The biographical information included on the dust jacket of her first book claimed that Davidson is "addicted to cooking." If that be the case, Davidson has put her addiction to good use in her series of culinary crimes featuring caterer Gertrude "Goldy" Bear. In the first novel, punningly titled *Catering to Nobody* (St. Martin, 1990), Goldy is catering a wake for her eleven-year-old son's favorite teacher. Her ex-father-in-law almost dies from something he ate at the wake, and Goldy scrambles to redeem her reputation as a caterer and to save herself from jail. Along the way she has to cope with her physically abusive ex-husband, a nastily charming doctor prominent in their Aspen Meadow, Colorado, hometown. Davidson mixes mouthwatering recipes and descriptions of food with complex plotting. In addition, she explores the life of a single mother who is trying to rear her son while fending off the psychotic behavior of an ex-husband. Goldy is a courageous character, whose offbeat sense of humor and compassionate heart carry her through. *Catering to Nobody* was nominated for the

Agatha, Anthony, and Macavity Awards for Best First Novel.

The late Virginia Rich laced her plots with recipes, and Amy Myers includes descriptions of Victorian dishes in her series. Janet Laurence writes a series about an Englishwoman who is a gourmet cook.

Davis, Dorothy Salisbury. Davis was awarded the Grand Master Award by the Mystery Writers of America in 1984, and she has received multiple Edgar nominations for her books. Davis is known for creating a mean streets atmosphere in her psychological mysteries, many of which are set in New York City. *A Gentle Murderer* (Scribner, 1951) uses a parallel construction, with a young priest, Father Duffy, and Detective Sergeant Goldsmith of the New York City police each searching separately for the same murderer. The murderer has confessed anonymously to Duffy, and the priest wants to find him in order to save his soul. The background and psychology of the killer is slowly revealed as Goldsmith and Father Duffy each talk to the people they find in their searches. Davis also uses a Catholic priest as a main character in *Where the Dark Streets Go* (Scribner, 1969), and many of her mysteries have a decidedly Irish-American atmosphere.

Davis has written several mysteries with series characters Mrs. Norris and Jasper Tully. The first is *Death of an Old Sinner* (Scribner, 1957), which tells the story of the mysterious death of a retired general who has gotten mixed up with New York gangsters. Mrs. Norris is his Scottish housekeeper; Jasper Tully is an investigator for the District Attorney's office.

Davis's newest series character is Julie Hayes. The first mystery in this series is *A Death in the Life* (Scribner, 1976). Julie is married to an older man who travels a great deal, and she finds herself insecure and at loose ends. On impulse, she sets up a storefront fortune-telling establishment and bills herself as Friend Julie. She encounters crime and hostility in the seedy neighborhood, but also discovers that she can investigate murder successfully. In the later novels in the series, Julie grows and changes as she gains confidence and skills, and even a paying job.

Davis's first novel was *The Judas Cat* (Scribner, 1949).

Readers looking for psychological mysteries and suspense novels might try Elizabeth George, Celia Fremlin, Patricia Highsmith, and B. M. Gill. Dorothy Uhnak and Lillian O'Donnell write effectively of the New York underworld, while the late Mary McMullen added a distinctly Irish atmosphere to her mysteries.

Davis, Lindsey. Davis has taken the world of first-century A.D. Rome and made it her own. Her series character, public informer Marcus Didius Falco (pun most definitely intended, *falco* being Latin for *falcon*), is the ancient Roman ancestor of Philip Marlowe and Sam Spade. Falco's voice makes the first novel in the series, *Silver Pigs* (Crown, 1990), seem almost anachronistic in the early pages, but then the reader watches the streets and the people of ancient Rome come vividly alive and forgets about the modern world. The plebeian Falco is an ardent republican in the days of the Flavian emperors, and, to his own disgust, he often finds himself working for the emperor Vespasian, or his son, Titus. In *Silver Pigs,* Falco meets the patrician Helena Justina, and the sparks fly between them, for Helena Justina is just as strong-willed as Falco. These lovers' path to each other is not an easy one, for the barriers of social class and wealth are difficult to breach, but Davis makes the struggle an enjoyable and involving one. She is a fine historical novelist, and she's no mean mystery writer, either. Davis stands alongside Ellis Peters and Anne Perry, other writers who make their respective historical periods lively and unforgettable.

Other writers who write mysteries set in ancient Rome are Steven Saylor, whose fine debut, *Roman Blood* (St. Martin, 1991), is a worthy peer of Davis's work, Joan O'Hagan, John Madox Roberts, and Ron Burns.

Dawson, Janet. Dawson writes hard-boiled mysteries set in Oakland, California and the Bay Area. Her first mystery, *Kindred Crimes* (St. Martin, 1990), introduces Jeri Howard, an Oakland private eye. Jeri is hired to find a woman who has abandoned her child and disappeared. As she is fired and rehired by various clients in the same family, Jeri begins to peel away layers of deception and abuse that hide the true story of an old crime. Jeri is very close to her father, a history professor, and he is responsible for involving her in a new case in *Till the Old Men Die* (Fawcett, 1993). A Filipino history professor has been murdered, and her father asks Jeri to look into the circumstances behind his friend's death. Jeri's investigations draw her into the local Filipino-American community, and she learns a great deal about the politics and recent history of the Philippines. Dawson provides richly detailed urban landscapes for her novels, and Jeri Howard is a persistent and courageous investigator.

Marcia Muller, Linda Grant, and Margaret Lucke write mysteries with women private eyes that are set in the Bay Area.

Dentinger, Jane. Not only has Dentinger worked as an actor, director, and mystery bookstore manager, she also has written a series of mysteries featuring Jocelyn (Josh) O'Roarke, a New York actress. Dentinger's novels are traditional in form, with a lively theatrical ambience and a wealth of backstage detail. In the first novel, *Murder on Cue* (Doubleday, 1983), Josh meets and is attracted to NYPD Detective Phillip Gerrard during a murder investigation. Their relationship, however, is far from easy, and Josh values her independence and her career. In *Death Mask* (Scribner, 1988), Josh directs a revival of Shaw's *Major Barbara* to raise money and save an old theater; crime, of course, interferes with the production. *Dead Pan* (Viking, 1992) is set in Los Angeles, as Josh goes west to work in television with her old friend, writer Austin Frost. Josh is knowledgeable and wise about the craft of acting and the turbulent lives of actors. She also is garrulous, and the novels are replete with quotes from classic plays. Josh's lively observations and her friendships with eccentric secondary characters make these mysteries entertaining experiences.

Readers may also appreciate the theatrical mysteries of Ngaio Marsh, Anne Morice, and Barbara Paul, the Maggie Ryan series of P. M. Carlson, and the Michael Spraggue mysteries by Linda Barnes.

Dominic, R. B.   See **Lathen, Emma.**

Douglas, Carole Nelson.   In addition to her romance and science fiction novels, two very different series of mysteries are emerging from the talented pen of Carole Nelson Douglas. She has bravely taken on the task of adding to the Sherlock Holmes canon by writing stories from the point of view of Irene Adler ("THE woman"). The novels are Holmesian in their technique and storytelling, with beautifully re-created Victorian backgrounds. They are narrated by Penelope (Nell) Huxleigh, a typist and impecunious parson's daughter, who functions as Adler's Dr. Watson. The first book, *Good Night, Mr. Holmes* (Doherty, 1990), is an expanded version of the story "A Scandal in Bohemia." *Good Morning, Irene* (Tor, 1991), the second novel, continues the adventures of Irene and Nell in Paris and Monte Carlo. In each book, Irene, Nell, and Godfrey Norton match wits with Sherlock Holmes himself in their investigations. Douglas has begun a second series of mystery novels with *Catnap* (Tor, 1992), a light romp told by Temple Barr, a Las Vegas publicist, and Midnight Louie, a large Runyonesque black cat. The feline narrative of Midnight Louie is in the hard-boiled tradition (somewhat reminiscent of archy the cockroach's observations in the archy & mehitabel stories of Don Marquis). Both of Douglas's series are fun to read and well worth the time of mystery lovers.

Readers who relish the Victorian atmosphere of the Irene Adler novels may want to try Anne Perry's series of novels. L. B.

Greenwood and Marian J. A. Jackson have written mysteries that make use of the Sherlock Holmes tradition. Elizabeth Peters has written an outstanding series of Victorian mysteries with the unforgettable Egyptologist Amelia Peabody. Amy Myers has also written a series of Victoriana. For fans of the Midnight Louie stories, Lilian Jackson Braun's *The Cat Who . . .* novels and Rita Mae Brown's tales of Mrs. Murphy are enjoyable feline mysteries.

Douglas, Lauren Wright. Douglas writes about the adventures of lesbian detective Caitlin Reece. Caitlin is a private eye on Vancouver Island in Canada, and she is especially concerned with solving crimes committed against women, children, and animals. She is strong, courageous, and very certain that she knows what is wrong and what is right. Douglas has created a group of clearly drawn secondary characters to help Caitlin with her sleuthing. They include Maggie, a doctor who had her license lifted for doing an abortion when they were illegal; Gray Ng, a mysterious Vietnamese woman who is an animal psychologist; Sandy the cop; Lester the electronics expert; and Francis the Ferret. *The Always Anonymous Beast* (Naiad, 1987) is the first book in the series. Two lesbians are being blackmailed and Caitlin is called in to investigate. In *Ninth Life* (Naiad, 1989), animal rights activists hire Caitlin to look into a murder and a cosmetics company that is supposedly cruelty-free, but secretly conducts gruesome tests on cats and rabbits. Douglas's mysteries feature good writing, a strong social agenda, and violent denouements. They are action-filled, with contemplative moments in which Caitlin reflects on her life and her Celtic heritage.

Elisabeth Bowers has a series of private eye novels set in Vancouver, British Columbia. Other writers about lesbian private investigators include Sandra Scoppettone and Ellen Hart.

Drake, Alison. See **MacGregor, T. J.**

Dreher, Sarah. Offbeat humor and quirky characters highlight the series of mysteries written by Dreher. Her detective is Stoner McTavish, a travel agent in the Boston area. In her debut, *Stoner McTavish* (New Victoria, 1985), Stoner gets hooked into investigating a strange situation by her eccentric Aunt Hermione, a psychic. Raised by emotionally distant parents, Stoner fled her home as a teenager when her parents couldn't cope with her attraction to other girls. Aunt Hermione gave her a home and the emotional support she needed, though Stoner, now in her thirties, continues to battle with the demons raised by her parents' neglect. Besides Aunt Hermione, Stoner has the love and support of her straight partner in the travel agency, Marylou, who'd rather eat than travel. In her first outing, Stoner encounters love and danger in Grand Teton National Park as she tries to prevent a murder. Subsequent adventures take Stoner on unconventional paths, through a story redolent of Hopi mysticism in *Gray Magic* (New Victoria, 1987) and even into the nineteenth century in *A Captive in Time* (New Victoria, 1990). Unconventional is a good word to describe Dreher's work and her characters. Dreher experiments with the conventional forms of the mystery novel, and she provides unusual entertainment with her efforts.

Those looking for other lesbian detectives might try the work of Ellen Hart, Barbara Wilson, Vicki P. McConnell, and Val McDermid.

Dunant, Sarah. British television journalist Dunant writes literate, reflective novels. *Snowstorms in a Hot Climate* (Random House, 1988), her first novel, is not as much a mystery as a novel of the chase. Marla Masterson, a British professor of Anglo-Saxon literature, comes to America in response to a message from her friend Elly, to find Elly mentally and physically in thrall to her slick drug-dealer lover. Marla feels compelled to try to get her friend away from this man without an eruption of violence. The novel centers around the cocaine culture and trade, and follows the drug trail from Colombia to New York to California to Scotland. Dunant provides sharp renditions of the seduction of the drug and the maneuverings of the dealers. She shows each character's version of the truth about Elly, and each character's self-interest and weakness.

Dunant's novel *Birth Marks* (Doubleday, 1992) is a British version of the hard-boiled detective story, and it is well done indeed. The sleuth is Hannah Wolfe, who does contract work for a London private eye agency. The victim, a missing ballet dancer, is clearly and sympathetically drawn. Dunant makes references (both literal and metaphorical) to Raymond Chandler's novel *The Big Sleep* (Knopf, 1939); most of the Chandler influence, however, is in the language and attitude of her detective, with little of Chandler's violence. Much of the book also discusses aspects of parenthood and child-parent relations.

Other British private eyes appear in the works of Liza Cody, Lesley Grant-Adamson, and Gillian Slovo. Elisabeth Bowers writes about PI Meg Lacey, who works in Vancouver, Canada.

Dunlap, Susan. Sue Dunlap has written three sets of novels featuring female sleuths Vejay Haskell, Jill Smith, and Kiernan O'Shaughnessy. In the first series, Haskell is an executive dropout turned meter reader in Russian River, California. *The Last Annual Slugfest* (St. Martin, 1986) is one of Dunlap's best, with its vivid descriptions of the small settlements among the redwoods in northern California. The second series features Berkeley homicide detective Jill Smith. Smith is cool and persistent, determined to solve crimes in spite of departmental constraints and sexism. The unique and slightly crazed nature of the city of Berkeley and its inhabitants creates suitably oddball crimes for Jill to investigate, such as the murder of a guru in *Karma*. *Death and Taxes* (Delacorte, 1992) is a sharp, funny story of the murder of an IRS agent and Jill Smith's investigation of his many enemies and financial victims.

Dunlap's newest protagonist, Kiernan O'Shaughnessy, is a

former (read: fired) medical examiner and gymnast, now a private eye. She specializes in cases with medical oddities, charges enormous fees, and lives an unashamedly opulent life with a young male housekeeper in a beach house in La Jolla.

Dunlap's style is spare and humorous; her protagonists are curious, bright women with a cynical eye for the absurdities of the large corporate entities with which their lives are intertwined.

If possible, readers may want to read these series in order. The first Vejay Haskell is *An Equal Opportunity Death* (St. Martin, 1984); the first Jill Smith is *Karma* (Severn House, 1984); the first Kiernan O'Shaughnessy is *Pious Deception* (Villard, 1989).

Readers who like Dunlap may enjoy Margaret Maron's police procedurals with Lt. Sigrid Harald; Marcia Muller; Patricia Cornwell; L. V. Sims; or Jaqueline Girdner's stories of New Age life in Marin County, California.

Dunnett, Dorothy. Scottish writer and painter Dorothy Dunnett began to contribute a female voice to the overwhelmingly male world of espionage novels in the late 1960s. Her thrillers center around two continuing elements: the portrait painter and British agent Johnson Johnson, and his yacht, *Dolly*. The first Johnson Johnson novel was *The Photogenic Soprano* (Houghton Mifflin, 1968), also published with the author's name as Dorothy Halliday and the title as *Dolly and the Singing Bird* (London: Cassell, 1968). In each book the narration is provided by a different woman (the "bird" of the titles) who becomes involved in a crime. Each woman has a distinct personality and career of her own, and is a vibrant character in contrast to the bland and shadowy Johnson. The imperious and strong-willed Madame Tina Rossi of *The Photogenic Soprano,* for example, is a very different character study from Sarah Cassells, the impecunious but blue-blooded young caterer of *Murder in the Round* (Houghton Mifflin, 1970), also published as *Dolly and the Cookie Bird* (London: Cassell, 1970). Dunnett's stories often unfold at a leisurely pace, with an abundance of descriptive prose about the novel's location (Scotland, Ibiza, the Bahamas, and other picturesque locales). *Send a Fax to the Kasbah* (Harcourt Brace Jovanovich, 1992), however, sends its players in the game of multinational business intrigues through the souks and mountains of Morocco at a fast clip.

Dunnett also has become famous for her lengthy historical novels, including the Francis Crawford of Lymond cycle and the House of Niccolo series.

Readers also may enjoy the thrillers of Susan Moody, Janice Law, Dorothy Gilman, and Jessica Mann.

Early, Jack. See **Scoppettone, Sandra.**

Eccles, Marjorie. Eccles wrote a number of romance novels in her native England before turning to a life of crime, and the mystery lover's gain may well be the romance world's loss. Her series features Detective Chief Inspector Gil Mayo, a Yorkshireman now transplanted farther south. In the first of the series, *Cast a Cold Eye* (Doubleday, 1988), Mayo investigates the death of a prominent architect. In the five novels in the series published thus far, Eccles demonstrates a quietly effective hand with both plot and character. The focus in each novel is the cast of characters whom the murder most directly affects; Mayo and his supporting cast from the police are developed slowly as the series progresses. Working within the classic traditions of the British mystery, Eccles takes an old form and makes it both contemporary and entertaining. A standout in the series is the recent *More Deaths Than One* (Doubleday, 1991), which easily puts Eccles on a par with such favorites as Dorothy Simpson and June Thomson.

Other good "village" English police procedural writers are

Anthea Fraser, Clare Curzon, Catherine Aird, Susan B. Kelly, and Erica Quest (whose lead character is a woman).

Edwards, Ruth Dudley. Edwards is an Irish writer living in London, and a former civil servant. In her first mystery, *Corridors of Death* (St. Martin, 1982), a much-disliked senior civil servant is murdered. Police Superintendent James Milton uses Robert Amiss as his mole in the affected department, in order to get information on the suspects. Although he is only a very junior civil servant, Amiss's inside knowledge eventually solves the crime. As with several of Edwards's books, the mystery is set against a backdrop of incompetence and mismanagement in the British civil service system. *St. Valentine's Day Murders* (St. Martin, 1985) begins hilariously with Amiss temporarily seconded to a purchasing department that is a corporate Siberia for fallen bureaucrats. These bureaucrats scheme against each other endlessly and their intrigues inevitably escalate into murder. In *Clubbed to Death* (St. Martin, 1992), Amiss finally has left the civil service in disgust. Superintendent Milton asks him to go undercover as a waiter at an old-fashioned London gentlemen's club, the ffeatherstonehaugh Club (pronounced *fanshaw*). The club secretary has been killed, and further deaths follow while Amiss works there. The members are unrepentantly racist and sexist and the club atmosphere exudes the worst kind of English snobbishness, so Amiss is even worse off than he had been in the civil service. In her novels, Edwards has brought a satirical view of English institutions to the traditional mystery format.

Janet Neel and Natasha Cooper have provided other views of the British civil service system in their mysteries. Sarah Caudwell's crime novels about barristers are slyly witty. M. C. Beaton, Nancy Livingston, and Marian Babson write gently humorous mysteries.

Egan, Lesley. See **Linington, Elizabeth.**

Eyre, Elizabeth. See **Stacey, Susannah.**

Fallon, Ann C. Fallon has taken the traditional English mystery and given it an agreeable Irish brogue with a series of novels about young Dublin solicitor James Fleming. A bachelor with a comfortable income, an upper–middle class background, and a passion for railways all over the world, James Fleming makes an attractive character for a series set in contemporary Ireland. Through his law practice, James encounters some odd cases that call for using his skills as a lawyer in more creative ways. In *Dead Ends* (Pocket, 1992) James goes to a beautiful country inn near Sligo to draw up a will for the inn's owner, an old friend of a colleague. A mysterious death occurs at the inn while James is there, and soon he finds himself working to solve the puzzle to save the owner of the inn from arrest. Fallon's writing style is leisurely, spinning out the thread of the narrative in the fashion of mysteries from the Golden Age. While the pace is not fast, the plot is usually neatly and fairly constructed. The series begins with *Blood Is Thicker* (Pocket, 1990).

Other writers who have set their work in Ireland are Eilis Dillon and Nigel Fitzgerald. Readers who enjoy lawyers as sleuths might also try the work of Sara Woods, Frances Fyfield, M. R. D. Meek, or E. X. Giroux.

Femling, Jean. Femling's first book, *Backyard* (Harper & Row, 1975), is a suspense novel about Alma, a woman who is suddenly awakened late at night by the police and arrested for a murder she didn't commit. It's a dark tale of innocents whose lives are ruined because of a mistake. Femling then began a series of mysteries set in Orange County, California, featuring Martha "Moz" Brant, an auto insurance claims investigator. Although Moz is actually half-Filipino, most people assume she is Mexican and she encounters prejudice regularly. Moz is a recovering alcoholic and a loner who is persistent in her investigations of crimes among the moneyed elite of southern California. In *Hush, Money* (St. Martin, 1989), she inquires into the death of a friend in an arson case. Also dead is the wealthy Arnie Tenhagen, whose unhappy family react badly to being suspects. *Getting Mine* (St. Martin, 1991) is about a car wreck insurance scam, in which Moz finds a fraud ring run by supposedly respectable, affluent men.

Other writers who set their mysteries in Orange County, California include Maxine O'Callaghan, A. E. Maxwell, and Noreen Ayres.

Ferrars, E. X. Known in her native England as Elizabeth Ferrars, this grande dame of the English mystery novel has been steadily producing a novel or two a year for just over fifty years. Her first few novels, with series detective Toby Dyke, followed closely in the classic tradition of the upper-class, gentleman sleuth. Dyke first appeared in *Give a Corpse a Bad Name* (Hodder and Stoughton, 1940). These books are adequate representations of the genteel English mystery, but it was not until Ferrars abandoned Dyke that she found a better and fresher voice. Ferrars writes convincingly about civilized people faced with that most uncivilized of crimes, and each novel unfolds like a small but elegantly presented movie. In recent years Ferrars has adopted two sets of series characters. One series features Virginia Freer and her estranged, but not-quite-divorced husband Felix, who has a gift for staying on the right side of the law—just barely. They appear first in *Last Will and Testament* (Doubleday, 1978). The other series features Andrew Basnett, retired professor of botany (supposedly modeled upon Ms. Ferrars's husband). Basnett, who debuts in *Something Wicked* (Doubleday, 1984), serves as an effective tool for Ferrars to write simply and affectingly about life in old age. Ferrars is a special vintage, one that connoisseurs of the English mystery will always enjoy.

Like Ferrars, Anna Clarke until recent years eschewed a series character, and her novels of mystery are much in the Ferrars vein, as are the works of Celia Fremlin. American Corinne Holt Sawyer writes an entertaining series about two elderly women sleuths. Other entertaining English cozy writers are Sarah J. Mason and Catherine Aird.

Forrest, Katherine V. Forrest has written a series of police procedurals with protagonist Kate Delafield, a detective in the Los Angeles Police Department. Kate is a lesbian in an occupation notable for its homophobia, so she has kept her private life a secret from her coworkers. Her partner is Ed Taylor, an older man who seems to exemplify the prejudices of many LAPD officers in the novels. Kate is a good police officer: thoughtful, sensitive, and scrupulous about the details of her work. Above all, she has integrity. She deals fairly with suspects in interviews and is painstakingly careful in her examinations of crime scenes. Forrest writes extensively about the details of murder investigations, and the scenes in which Kate questions suspects are especially effective. There usually is an explicit sex scene or two per novel. The first mystery in the series is *Amateur City* (Naiad, 1984), a story of murder in an office design firm in Los Angeles. Kate has lost her lover of many years a few months earlier in a car wreck; she meets a woman here who reminds her of her dead lover and who is a witness to the murder. *Murder at the Nightwood*

Bar (Naiad, 1987) revolves around the murder of a young woman at a lesbian bar who is a bisexual hooker. A gay-bashing murder occurs in *Murder by Tradition* (Naiad, 1991) and Forrest follows it from Kate's investigation through the trial.

Other writers of effective police procedurals include Lillian O'Donnell, Faye Kellerman, Teri White, and Susan Dunlap. Other mystery writers with lesbian protagonists are Claire McNab, Sandra Scoppettone, Barbara Wilson, Mary Wings, Ellen Hart, Deborah Powell, Lauren Wright Douglas, and Sarah Dreher.

Fraser, Anthea. She began her writing career with short stories and had her first novel published in 1970, going in turn from romantic fiction to paranormal fiction and finally to crime fiction. With *A Necessary End* (Walker, 1986) and *A Shroud for Delilah* (Doubleday, 1986) Fraser commenced a series of police detective mysteries starring Inspector David Webb. The viewpoint of several of the early novels is a young woman character, different in each book, of course, but nevertheless similar in some respects. Often estranged from her husband or family, the young woman is in a vulnerable position in which murder threatens. In the more recent books, however, Fraser has shifted toward the telling of her stories mostly from the viewpoint of Webb, and this has added considerable strength and variety to her plotting. With *The Nine Bright Shiners* (Doubleday, 1988) Fraser began taking her titles from the old folk tune, "Green Grow the Rushes-O." One of the strongest in the series is *Six Proud Walkers* (Doubleday, 1989). Fraser's work falls well within the conventions of the contemporary British police procedural, using engaging characters, deftly constructed plots, and regional English settings.

Readers of Fraser would also enjoy the work of Dorothy Simpson, Clare Curzon, June Thomson, and Susan B. Kelly, all of whom expertly use the various regions of England as their settings, proving that London is not the only setting for good police procedural work.

Fraser, Antonia. Well-known for her popular biographies of British historical figures, Antonia Fraser also writes mysteries. Her series character is Jemima Shore, a television journalist. Jemima does documentaries on social problems, and she is known to the public as Jemima Shore, Investigator. Her primary attribute is curiosity; she is also elegant and wry. Fraser's first Jemima Shore novel was *Quiet as a Nun* (Viking, 1977). A young nun from a wealthy family dies mysteriously in the convent where Jemima was educated, and the Reverend Mother calls in Jemima to investigate. *The Wild Island* (Norton, 1978) is set in the Highlands of Scotland, where Jemima has rented a cottage on an island for a month of quiet away from her frenetic career. She becomes involved, willy-nilly, in the batty activities of a group of islanders who think the local laird is the legitimate descendant of Bonnie Prince Charlie and the rightful king of Scotland. *A Splash of Red* (Norton, 1982) is set in the Bloomsbury section of London, where Jemima's old friend Chloe has disappeared after lending Jemima her penthouse flat. Most of the characters in Fraser's novels are affluent professionals or aristocrats, and the settings are generally affluent ones as well.

Fraser also has written two volumes of short stories about Jemima Shore, *Jemima Shore's First Case* (Norton, 1986) and *Jemima Shore at the Sunny Grave* (Bantam, 1993).

Fraser's biographical works include the well-received *Mary, Queen of Scots* (Delacorte, 1969), and *The Wives of Henry VIII* (Knopf, 1992).

Readers also may enjoy the works of British crime novelists Lesley Grant-Adamson and Joan Smith.

Frazer, Margaret. See **Pulver, Mary Monica.**

Fremlin, Celia. English novelist Fremlin struck gold her first time out, winning the Edgar for Best Novel with *The Hours Before Dawn* (Lippincott, 1959). This tale of suspense exhibits many of the qualities that inform Fremlin's later work. A young housewife and mother, trying her best to tend to a husband, two small daughters, and a constantly crying infant son, thinks there is something odd about their new lodger. But, then again, maybe she's just groggy from lack of sleep. Fremlin takes these very ordinary circumstances and turns them into a fascinating tale of suspense. This knack for taking ordinary, domestic details, weaving them in with the oddities and frailties of ordinary human beings, and producing quietly suspenseful tales makes Fremlin rather unusual among her peers. Novels such as *The Long Shadow* (Doubleday, 1976) and *The Parasite Person* (Doubleday, 1982) are excellent examples of her work. If there may be said to be a cozy psychological suspense novel, then Fremlin is its premiere practitioner.

Those who have enjoyed Fremlin's work might try the novels of Margaret Yorke, Anna Clarke, Barbara Vine/Ruth Rendell, Dorothy Salisbury Davis, E. X. Ferrars, Sheila Radley, or Frances Hegarty.

Friedman, Mickey. Friedman's first novel, *Hurricane Season* (Dutton, 1983), is not only a mystery, but a fine evocation of the people and landscape of a small Florida fishing town in the early 1950s. She draws the reader completely into a world dominated by moonshining, local politics, and the ever-present heat and humidity. This is not the Florida tourists see; it is rural, red-neck, and poverty-stricken swampland. *Venetian Mask* (Scribner, 1987), offers a detailed look at Venice during Carnival. A game that turns to murder occurs among a group of self-absorbed acquaintances. The story is dark, brooding, and full of sexual tensions. Friedman has recently turned to writing a series of books with protagonist Georgia Lee Maxwell, an expatriate journalist in Paris. Her cases involve stories that she starts to research and write, which then turn into mysteries. Georgia Lee wants the story, and she must investigate the murder to get it. Friedman's writing in these books is lucid and suspenseful. Georgia Lee is a believable, rounded character, especially in the first series novel, *The Magic Mirror* (Viking, 1988).

Investigative journalists who also solve mysteries include Jessica James, created by Meg O'Brien; Cat Marsala, invented by Barbara D'Amato; and Chris Martin, created by Annette Roome.

Fyfield, Frances/Hegarty, Frances. Hailed as a star already in the tradition of her fellow Englishwomen P. D. James and Ruth Rendell, Fyfield uses her own extensive background as a solicitor specializing in criminal law to lend authenticity to her writing. In an Edgar- and Agatha-nominated debut, *A Question of Guilt* (Pocket, 1989), Fyfield's series characters, Crown Prosecutor Helen West and Detective Superintendent Geoffrey Bailey, demonstrate with quiet effect the often opposing goals of the law courts and the police. Fyfield's great strength as a writer comes from the assurance with which she delineates character. Her plots are always meticulous in their construction, but her ability to conjure fully fleshed and compelling characters makes for powerful reading. Fyfield also possesses the saving grace of a sense of humor, realizing—unlike some of her peers—that her characters need not be relentlessly morose to be believable. As Frances Hegarty (her real name), Fyfield has followed the lead of Ruth Rendell and Rendell's alter ego Barbara Vine by writing a somewhat different kind of novel. In *The Playroom* (Pocket, 1991), Hegarty demonstrates considerable skill with the type of psychological novel that Rendell/Vine regularly produces, proving herself a worthy peer of the better-known writer.

Those who enjoy Fyfield's work should try Jill McGown, whose strengths are also those of character and plot; other suggestions are Ruth Rendell's long series of novels about Inspector Wexford, M. R. D. Meek's series about lawyer Lennox Kemp, and Sheila Radley's series about policeman Douglas Quantrill. For the more psychological side, readers might try the work of Minette Walters, Margaret Yorke, or Margaret Millar.

Garwood, Judith. See **Dain, Catherine.**

George, Elizabeth. George is a novelist from Southern California who is, nevertheless, clearly at home writing classic mysteries set in Great Britain. In a distinguished series of novels, George charts the emotional lives of her detectives as well as those of the murder victims and suspects. She has created a memorable group of continuing characters: Scotland Yard Inspector Thomas Lynley, the eighth earl of Asherton; his unflinchingly working-class partner, Sergeant Barbara Havers; forensic pathologist Simon Allcourt–St. James and his wife Deborah, a photographer; and Lady Helen Clyde, St. James's laboratory assistant. The lives of Lynley, Simon, Deborah, and Lady Helen have been intertwined for years; they carry with them emotional baggage from the past that affects their current investigations. Each novel then becomes a chapter in the ongoing saga of the investigators' personal lives; each murder case moves the relationships onward and causes the characters to reflect on some part of their emotional makeup. A recurring theme in the books is living with a physical difference or disability. This theme is personified by St. James, who is partially disabled after a car crash (inevitably, the car was driven by a drunken Lynley, St. James's best friend), and the theme is central to the plot of *For the Sake of Elena* (Bantam, 1992), in which the murder victim is deaf. George's style is psychological and intense, with vividly detailed settings and many strands of plot artfully pulled together in the end. She uses traditional English mystery formats, like the locked-room mystery in *Payment in Blood* (Bantam, 1989), and brings new life and power to the genre.

George's first novel was *A Great Deliverance* (Bantam, 1988), which won both the Anthony and the Agatha Awards for Best First Novel. *A Suitable Vengeance* (Bantam, 1991), although published later, tells of events in the lives of George's characters that occur before the time of *A Great Deliverance.*

Readers who admire George's writing may also like P. D. James, Dorothy L. Sayers, B. M. Gill, and Ruth Rendell. American novelists who also may prove enjoyable for readers include Faye Kellerman, Audrey Peterson, and Julie Smith (especially Smith's Skip Langdon mysteries).

Gill, B. M. Gill is a pseudonym for Welsh novelist Barbara M. Trimble; before beginning her career as a mystery novelist, she wrote romantic thrillers under the name of Margaret Blake and romance novels as Barbara Gilmour. Gill is expert at providing grim psychological motivations for her characters. Her dark tales revolve around the motivations and reactions of people in crises such as during a criminal trial, the breakup of a marriage, or the addition of foster children to a family. Gill won the Gold Dagger for *The Twelfth Juror* (Scribner, 1984), a strong exploration of the characters of a juror and a defendant in a murder trial, whose lives cross in and out of the courtroom. *Seminar for Murder* (Scribner, 1986) and *The Fifth Rapunzel* (Scribner, 1991) feature a rather detached but observant police inspector, Tom Maybridge. *Dying to Meet You* (Doubleday, 1990) is a somber view of a doomed romantic triangle. *Time and Time Again* (Scribner, 1990) is a story of a middle-class woman who is jailed after inadvertently injuring a policeman during a peace demonstration. Jail changes her so completely that, on her release, she cannot fit back into her comfortable marriage and home. Like many of Gill's novels, this one is as much a character study as a mystery. *Nursery Crimes* (Scribner, 1987) is an Edgar-nominated tour de force psychological novel about the crimes of a psychopathic child during and after World War II.

Other writers of psychological crime novels include Ruth Rendell, P. D. James, Elizabeth George, Patricia Highsmith, S. T. Haymon, and L. R. Wright.

Gilman, Dorothy. Gilman is known best for her tales of Mrs. Emily Pollifax, who, bored with widowhood and retirement, decided to apply one day for a job with the CIA, in *The Unexpected Mrs. Pollifax* (Doubleday, 1966). After initial demurs, the CIA hired Mrs. Pollifax under the assumption that no one would *ever* suspect such a grandmotherly figure of being a spy. Mrs. Pollifax has trotted around the globe to such exotic places as Mexico, Albania, Switzerland, and Africa on various errands for the CIA, all of them proving highly dangerous, of course. In more recent years, with the cooling down of the Cold War, Mrs. Pollifax has had several adventures in the Orient. Whatever the reader's reservations about the plausibility of Mrs. Pollifax as a spy, the novels provide terrific escape to various exotic locales. In addition to the Pollifax novels, Gilman has written a number of other very entertaining works, including two recent adventure/suspense novels, *Incident at Badamya* (Doubleday, 1989) and *Caravan* (Doubleday, 1992). One of her most popular nonseries novels is the suspense tale, *The Tightrope Walker* (Doubleday, 1979); another is *A Nun in the Closet* (Doubleday, 1975). Gilman has also written numerous children's books.

The recent novel by Serita Stevens and Rayanne Moore, *Red Sea, Dead Sea* (St. Martin, 1991), features a character, Jewish grandmother Fanny Zindel, who has much in common with Emily Pollifax. Other entertaining elderly sleuths can be found in the work of Corinne Holt Sawyer, Eleanor Boylan, Margot Arnold, Gallagher Gray, and Kate Morgan.

Girdner, Jaqueline. The heroine of Girdner's mystery series is Kate Jasper, who lives in Marin County, California. Kate owns Jest Gifts, a company that makes humorous mail-order gifts such as shark ties for lawyers. Kate is also a fanatic vegetarian, non-dairy, non-caffeine, non-sugar, non-everything person. Her friends in Mill Valley are psychics, software developers, artists, trendy restaurateurs, and other yuppie entrepreneurs. A former drug dealer is murdered at the office of Kate's chiropractor in *Adjusted to Death* (Diamond, 1991), the first book in the series. Everyone in the office at the time, including Kate, is a suspect. *The Last Resort* (Diamond, 1991) is set in southern California in a spa that is being restored. The girlfriend of Kate's ex-husband, Craig Jasper, is killed, and Craig asks Kate to help prove that he didn't do it. *Murder Most Mellow* (Diamond, 1992) is set in Marin County, where a computer programmer and robot designer, who is also a member of Kate's study group, is killed. Girdner's plots are developed as her characters take part in typically New Age, Marin County kinds of activities—sitting in hot tubs, eating tofu, designing robots, and talking about their chakras.

Detectives created by Kate Green, Shelley Singer, and Susan Dunlap also find crime among California's New Age populace.

Giroux, E. X. Canadian novelist Doris Shannon adopted the Giroux pseudonym for a series of English mysteries featuring barrister Robert Forsythe and his secretary, Abigail Sanderson. The first novel in the series, *A Death for Adonis* (St. Martin, 1984), offers a complex plot that smacks of Agatha Christie in its construction, if not in its subject matter. Throughout the series, Forsythe and Sandy, as she is affectionately called, have shared almost equal billing, and in at least two of the novels, *A Death* *for a Doctor* (St. Martin, 1986) and *A Death for a Dietitian* (St. Martin, 1988), Sandy does most of the detecting herself. The warm relationship between Forsythe and Sandy, who is almost old enough to be, and indeed often seems like, Forsythe's mother, adds a charming touch to a series notable for the cleverness of the plots. In a recent case, *A Death for a Dancing Doll* (St. Martin, 1991), the intrepid duo leaves England for British Columbia, Giroux's home turf. Readers who still enjoy puzzles constructed in the classic vein will find much that appeals in Giroux's work.

Other English legal detectives of interest include Sara Woods's long-running series about barrister Antony Maitland, Ann Fallon's series about Irish solicitor James Fleming, and M. R. D. Meek's series about Lennox Kemp.

Gordon, Alison. Gordon was the first woman journalist to cover major-league baseball. It seems inevitable, then, that her mysteries are set in that world, with Toronto sports writer Kate Henry as Gordon's protagonist. Kate covers the fictional Toronto Titans, much as Gordon covered the Toronto Blue Jays in her newspaper career. Kate is a completely professional, mature woman, with the inquisitive bent of a reporter and an amateur sleuth. As one would expect, Gordon gives the reader an insider's view of baseball and the experience of touring with a team. She has a crisp, journalistic style and creates distinctive Toronto settings. Her first novel was *The Dead Pull Hitter* (St. Martin, 1989). Two players are murdered and Kate finds herself involved in the crimes as she covers the story. She meets Staff Sergeant Andy Munro of Homicide, who is in charge of the case, and they begin a relationship. In *Safe at Home* (St. Martin, 1990), young boys are being murdered by a serial killer. There is an interesting subplot about the difficulties encountered by a ballplayer who decides to come out of the closet with the news of his homosexuality. Gordon depicts the homophobia present in major-league sports. *Night Game* (St. Martin, 1993) is set in Florida, at the

Titans' spring training camp. A sexy woman journalist is killed on the beach, and Kate investigates. In all of her mysteries, Gordon provides a principled, positive view of the media, and she shows how a working journalist gets her daily stories and works with her sources.

Other novelists who use Canadian settings include L. R. Wright, Alisa Craig, Medora Sale, Elisabeth Bowers, and Lauren Wright Douglas. Linda Mariz and Julie Robitaille write sports mysteries.

Gosling, Paula. American born and bred, Gosling moved to England permanently in 1964, and in 1979 she launched a full-time writing career after *Fair Game* (Coward, McCann, 1978; English title, *A Running Duck,* Macmillan, 1978) was published and received the British Crime Writers' Association John Creasey Award for Best First Novel. In this first novel Gosling offered an entertaining variation on the woman-in-jeopardy novel set in San Francisco. Other action-packed suspense novels followed, like *Solo Blues* (Coward, McCann, 1980; English title, *Loser's Blues,* Macmillan, 1980), about a musician named Johnny Cosatelli whose involvement with the wrong woman leads to a deadly situation. With *Monkey Puzzle* (Doubleday, 1985), which won the CWA Gold Dagger, Gosling launched her first series. This combination academic mystery and police procedural is set in the American midwestern city of Grantham, and the main characters are homicide cop Jack Stryker and English professor Kate Trevorne. They appear as supporting characters in the hilarious *Hoodwink* (Doubleday, 1988), which demonstrates Gosling's knack for writing deliciously funny physical comedy scenes. Two further novels have featured Stryker and Trevorne as central characters. In *The Wychford Murders* (Doubleday, 1986), Gosling introduced English cop Luke Abbott, who reappeared in a supporting role in *Death Penalties* (Mysterious, 1991). Gosling creates strong, likable characters. Her wicked sense of humor is an important element in many of the novels, and she has a knack for writing vivid and believable action scenes.

Readers who have enjoyed Gosling's crime novels might try the humorous suspense novels of Elizabeth Peters, the Sigrid Harald novels of Margaret Maron, the Tamara Hoyland novels of Jessica Mann, or the British police mysteries of Cynthia Harrod-Eagles, Caroline Graham, Susan B. Kelly, and Jill McGown.

Grafton, Sue. The daughter of the late lawyer and mystery novelist C. W. Grafton, Sue Grafton has written numerous screenplays, in addition to two novels and her series of best-selling mysteries starring Kinsey Millhone. In the decade since her debut (in *"A" Is for Alibi;* Holt, Rinehart, Winston, 1982), private eye Kinsey Millhone has become one of the most popular characters in current mystery fiction. In her early thirties, Kinsey is something of a loner. Twice-divorced, she lives in a small apartment with few possessions and even fewer emotional attachments. One of Kinsey's most important emotional ties, however, is to her octogenarian landlord, Henry Pitts, a retired baker who supplements his income by devising crossword puzzles. Henry serves as something of a father figure and emotional anchor for Kinsey. Tough, stubborn, but with a healthy sense of humor as a saving grace, Kinsey is definitely a descendant of the wise-cracking, hard-boiled male private eye who has been a staple of American detective fiction for seventy years. The fictional California town of Santa Teresa, where Kinsey lives and works, is a thinly veiled Santa Barbara, home to one of Grafton's important influences, the writer Ross MacDonald. Though she is part of an established tradition, Kinsey nevertheless remains an individual. Grafton's style, which moves easily between action and introspection, from grim reality to humorous aside, demonstrates the range of an author well in command of her voice. Kinsey's yearly progress toward the end of the alphabet is usually a much-anticipated event for mystery fans.

Grafton fans unacquainted with the work of Ross MacDonald might enjoy these older works which are, in many ways, the epitome of southern California detective fiction. Otherwise, readers might try the work of Marcia Muller, Linda Barnes, Patricia D. Cornwell, or Janet Dawson.

Graham, Caroline. With her first novel published in the United States, the Agatha-nominated *The Killings at Badger's Drift* (Adler & Adler, 1988), Graham quickly became a favorite among English mystery fans. Her traditional style harks back to the Golden Age classics, but her subject matter and the frank treatment she gives it make her work thoroughly contemporary. Those who love the work of James and Rendell will appreciate the psychological acuity with which Graham delineates her characters and the flashes of wit with which she leavens the mixture. Her detective, Chief Inspector Barnaby, is a likable and intelligent figure in his two appearances to date; the second is the theatrical mystery, *Death of a Hollow Man* (Morrow, 1990). Here the author uses her own experience with theater and television to construct a complex and engaging story. Graham's third novel, the funny *Murder at Madingley Grange* (Morrow, 1991), offers a contemporary twist on the classic country-house scenario. Powerful and compelling at her best, Graham is a fine new voice in the English mystery tradition.

Readers of Graham might also enjoy the Inspector Bone mysteries of Susannah Stacey, the work of Frances Fyfield, Paula Gosling, P. D. James, Patricia Moyes, Janet Neel, or the American writer of English mysteries, Martha Grimes.

Granger, Ann. Like her heroine, Meredith Mitchell, Granger has worked in the diplomatic service in various parts of the world. In the first novel of the series, *Say It with Poison* (St. Martin, 1991), Meredith is visiting her glamorous actress cousin, Eve, on the night before Eve's daughter's wedding. Weddings are always an occasion for drama, but soon Meredith finds herself mixed up with murder and blackmail and a certain divorced Chief Inspector Alan Markby. Markby, an avid gardener, is drawn to the aloof but appealing Meredith, and as he investigates the crime, the two of them edge toward some sort of relationship. Meredith uses her diplomatic skills to help in the investigation. Granger uses the Cotswolds and the village atmosphere to advantage in this series. The relationship between Meredith and Markby is the cornerstone of the series. Meredith is prickly and uncertain, while Markby definitely knows that he wants to get married. But will Meredith give up her career for domestic life, leavened with crime-solving? Readers who enjoy the English village whodunit will find an able practitioner in Granger, who handles characters, plots, and settings, with consistent skill.

Other enjoyable English village cozy series are those of June Thomson, Susan B. Kelly, Ann Cleeves, Hazel Holt, Elizabeth Lemarchand, and Kay Mitchell.

Grant, Linda. Catherine Sayler, Grant's protagonist in a series of mysteries, is a private investigator in San Francisco. Catherine has her own firm (with a partner in later books), and she specializes in financial crime. She deliberately has tried to avoid taking cases where she might have to deal with violent and habitual criminals; she prefers to work only with white-collar crime. Somehow Catherine's cases aren't always as straightforward as she would like, as in *Blind Trust* (Scribner, 1990), and she is forced into dangerous and volatile confrontations. Catherine is, however, adept at aikido, and she uses her skills in some physical showdowns. One character who brings a somewhat different perspective to this series is Catherine's assistant, Jesse, an African-American computer whiz who eventually becomes her partner in the firm. Grant's novels also portray Catherine as an independent and thoughtful woman, and she has given readers a welcome addition to the ranks of female private eyes.

The first Catherine Sayler novel is *Random Access Murder* (Avon, 1988).

Admirers of Grant's novels also may enjoy Janet Dawson, Catherine Dain, and Sarah Dunant. Other contemporary mysteries set in San Francisco have been written by Margaret Lucke, Marcia Muller, Lia Matera, Gloria White, and Elizabeth Atwood Taylor.

Grant-Adamson, Lesley. A veteran British journalist, Grant-Adamson has written several different kinds of crime novels. She has explored the psychological mystery in *The Face of Death* (Scribner, 1985), the cozy English village mystery in *Death on Widow's Walk* (Scribner, 1985), and the private eye genre in *Too Many Questions* (St. Martin, 1991). London gossip columnist Rain Morgan is Grant-Adamson's protagonist in many of the mysteries. Rain is curious and persistent, with an instinct for discovering an oddity that may turn into a good story for her newspaper column. The first Rain Morgan novel is *Death on Widow's Walk*, which was published in the United Kingdom under the title *Patterns in the Dust* (Faber, 1985). It is a fairly typical English village mystery, updated to the 1980s with new technology as an essential part of the plot element. *Wild Justice* (St. Martin, 1987) is set in the offices of the fictional London *Post,* and it reeks with newsroom ambience. Grant-Adamson provides an insider's view of how a megalomaniacal businessman might run a British newspaper. Grant-Adamson has a new series, starting with *Too Many Questions,* which was published in Great Britain as *Flynn* (Faber, 1991). Laura Flynn, a private investigator, is the heroine. Laura comes from a large Irish family and grew up in a close-knit Irish community in London. In this novel, she deals with multiple cases simultaneously: looking into her own father's disappearance many years ago for her dying grandmother, investigating a possible business outlet for a dress designer, and looking for a lost cat. Laura is sardonic, single, and persistent. Grant-Adamson creates literate, compelling, well-crafted plots and effective settings in her varied mysteries.

Other British mystery writers of note include Liza Cody, Gillian Slovo, Antonia Fraser, B. M. Gill, and Joan Smith. Annette Roome writes about a British journalist-sleuth.

Gray, Gallagher. The morning after he has retired as personnel manager of a prestigious Wall Street bank, T. S. Hubbert receives a telephone call, seeking his help in solving the murder of one of the bank's partners. With the people skills honed from thirty years in personnel selection and management, T. S. wades into the fray, assisted by his octogenarian aunt, Lillian Hubbert. Auntie Lil, as she is affectionately called, spent over sixty years in the fashion industry, and she has a flair for the dramatic that Bette Davis would have envied. Together, T. S. and Auntie Lil make a formidable detective duo. As the series progresses, they gain assistance from secondary characters, such as Herbert Wong, a retired messenger for T. S.'s old firm, and Lilah Cheswick, the widow of the murder victim in the first book. The pseudonymous Gray, who is in reality Katy Munger, has created vivid and interesting characters for her series. Readers will enjoy the books as much for keeping up with the exploits of Auntie Lil as they will for solving the intricately designed whodunit puzzles that Gray has created. The first book in the series is *Hubbert & Lil: Partners in Crime* (Donald I. Fine, 1991).

Readers acquainted with Hubbert and Lil might try also the series by Emma Lathen and Annette Meyers, both of whom use the Wall Street and New York City milieu to great effect. Readers looking for other sleuths of retirement age might try the work of Eleanor Boylan, Stefanie Matteson, M. K. Lorens, and Corinne Holt Sawyer.

Green, Kate. Green writes suspense novels that often contain elements of the occult. Her first book, *Shattered Moon* (Dell, 1986), introduces a California psychic who keeps seeing visions of horrible killings; she then helps the police find victims of a serial murderer. The positive (if New Age) orientation of the psychic is counterpointed by the madness of the killer in the narrative, and both characters are well depicted by Green. *Shattered Moon* was nominated for an Edgar Award for Best Paperback Original. In her second book, *Night Angel* (Delacorte, 1989),

Green portrays a group of old friends who lived together in Berkeley in the 1960s and are reunited after a mysterious death within the circle. Maggie Shea, now a psychologist in Minneapolis, returns to California, and the surviving friends try to come to terms with the unexpected death. Maggie discovers that mysterious events that happened twenty years ago in their house in Berkeley may have contributed to the recent murder. The setting is atmospheric and nostalgic (especially for readers of the sixties generation), but not overly sentimental. Green's third novel, *Shooting Star* (HarperCollins, 1992), is about an actress who thinks she's being stalked by a crazed admirer. Violent events in the scripts of her films are duplicated in her real life, and Green keeps the level of suspense high and the inside look at filmmaking absorbing.

Other suspense writers of interest to the reader may include Mary Higgins Clark and T. J. MacGregor (who also writes as Alison Drake and Trish Janeshutz). Authors who have created characters who are psychics include Mignon Warner, Jaqueline Girdner, and Dorothy Gilman (in her novel *The Clairvoyant Countess* [Doubleday, 1975]).

Greenwood, D. M. The author describes herself as an ecclesiastical civil servant, and she uses to advantage her knowledge of the workings of the hierarchy and institutions of the Church of England in her series of ecclesiastical mysteries. Her series character is Deaconess Theodora Braithwaite, who stands over six feet tall and comes from a distinguished English clerical family. In her first appearance, in *Clerical Errors* (St. Martin, 1991), the Deaconess delves into a murder that takes place within the precincts of Medewich Cathedral. In *Unholy Ghosts* (St. Martin, 1992), Theodora is on holiday in a Norfolk village, when the mysterious death of the parish priest once again involves her in murder. Greenwood observes with a keen eye the lives of those whose vocation is the care of souls, and she writes novels that are bound to interest those who enjoy mysteries with clerical settings. The politics of cloister and cathedral can be no less vicious than those of statehouse or university, and Greenwood ably employs Theodora Braithwaite, committed but clear-eyed in her vocation, to sort out the trouble.

Fans of mysteries with clerical settings might try the Claire Aldington novels of Isabelle Holland, the series by Veronica Black, Sister Carol Anne O'Marie, Kate Charles, Mollie Hardwick, and Barbara Whitehead. Those looking for clerical mysteries with a different twist might try Ellis Peters's tales of her twelfth-century Benedictine sleuth, Brother Cadfael.

Greenwood, L. B. One testament to the unfailing popularity of Sir Arthur Conan Doyle's creation, Sherlock Holmes, is the steady number of new novels featuring that great detective over sixty years after Doyle's death. Greenwood is one of the few women to take up the mantle of Sir Arthur. Her first Holmes story is *Sherlock Holmes and the Case of the Raleigh Legacy* (Atheneum, 1986). Here Greenwood employs Holmes and Watson, at a very early stage in their careers as detectives, in a tale mixing murder with a missing historical treasure left by that Elizabethan gentleman, Sir Walter Raleigh. The third book, *Sherlock Holmes and the Thistle of Scotland* (Simon and Schuster, 1989), involves a missing jewel that once belonged to the hapless Mary, Queen of Scots. All three of Greenwood's Holmes pastiches to date follow well in the conventions established by Holmes's creator. Readers can enjoy the atmosphere of the late Victorian settings, the amiable byplay between Holmes and Watson, and neatly constructed puzzles that Holmes works out in the accustomed manner.

Those who have read Greenwood certainly might like to seek out the original Holmes stories, if they have not yet done so. Otherwise, they might try the work of Carole Nelson Douglas, whose books featuring Irene Adler give a decidedly feminist slant to the Holmes era.

Grimes, Martha. Her debut novel, *The Man With a Load of Mischief* (Little, Brown, 1981), was greeted by American fans of the traditional English mystery with a warm reception. Grimes's next two novels, *The Old Fox Deceiv'd* (Little, Brown, 1982) and *The Anodyne Necklace* (Little, Brown, 1983), followed in much the same vein, Agatha Christie and Dorothy L. Sayers blended with the early P. D. James. Subsequent books began to take on something of a different flavor and demonstrated, perhaps, the cross-breeding of an American, albeit a devout Anglophile, writing the traditional British mystery. Critics, particularly the English ones, have taken Grimes to task for elementary errors of fact, such as having trains leaving London from the wrong station. Most fans have been willing to overlook such details for the rich rewards of character and setting. Grimes's moodiness and flair for the eccentric have made her chief characters, the policeman Richard Jury and the aristocrat Melrose Plant, an unusual and somewhat unlikely duo. Grimes is also possessed of a wicked sense of humor, which surfaces in many of the books, perhaps most notably in *I Am the Only Running Footman* (Little, Brown, 1986), with the creation of the Warboys family, a dangerously inept crew running a country pub. In her most recent work, *The Horse You Came In On* (Knopf, 1993), Grimes aims her guns at literary theft with humorously entertaining results. But the intensity of her plots and the emotional appeal of her characters have made Grimes a great favorite with the American reading public, who have put Grimes onto the best-seller list. The recent *The End of the Pier* (Knopf, 1992), a nonseries book, is set in America and shows Grimes attempting a more psychological vein. The titles of all the Jury books are taken from the names of English pubs.

Like Grimes, the American writer Elizabeth George also writes "English" mysteries, though George is much more the "English" of the two, closer to P. D. James or Ruth Rendell than is Grimes. Grimes fans might also enjoy the work of Frances Fyfield, Caroline Graham, and Deborah Crombie.

Gunning, Sally. The central character in Gunning's series is Peter Bartholomew, who is owner of a business called Factotum. Pete and his partner, Rita Peck, and their changing cast of employees literally do just about anything in their setting of the Cape Hook island of Nashtoba, Massachusetts. In addition to the run-of-the-mill odd jobs that anybody would need doing, Pete often finds himself playing detective, because murders just seem to keep happening in this small community. Pete, who's in his mid-thirties and comfortable with his job and his island, is an amiable, attractive character, and Gunning renders the small-town setting well. The reappearing cast of minor characters is reminiscent of the denizens of television's Cabot's Cove, Maine on "Murder, She Wrote"; there's a special flavor to the Down East type of murder, which Gunning seems to have captured. Complicating Pete's life is the return of his ex-wife Connie, and their tortured rapprochement serves as a subplot through the books in the series published thus far. The first in the series is *Hot Water* (Pocket, 1990); subsequent entries in the series also have "water" in their titles.

Readers looking for other New England series might try the work of J. S. Borthwick, Susan Kenney, Charlotte MacLeod, B. J. Morison, and the work of an older writer, Phoebe Atwood Taylor, whose Asey Mayo might be considered something of a literary grandfather to Peter Bartholomew.

Haddam, Jane/Papazoglou, Orania. Under her own name, Papazoglou has written a series of mysteries featuring writer Patience "Pay" Campbell McKenna. In the first novel, *Sweet, Savage Death* (Doubleday, 1984), Pay is a writer of respectable articles in national magazines, and she also writes category romance novels (under a pseudonym, of course). Some of the major figures in romance publishing are murdered, and Pay and her friend and fellow novelist Phoebe investigate the crimes. Papazoglou provides plenty of satire on the romance publishing business. In the succeeding books in the series, Pay is writing true crime books for a living. Papazoglou also has written a psychological suspense novel, *Charisma* (Crown, 1992), about a succession of killings of former nuns in New Haven, Connecticut.

For another series of mysteries, Papazoglou adopted the pseudonym of Jane Haddam. Her protagonist is Gregor Demarkian, a retired FBI agent, and the series is set around the celebration of holidays. The novels are strongly imbued with the atmosphere of the Armenian-American community of Philadelphia, and Demarkian eventually becomes famous for his sleuthing and known as the Armenian-American Hercule Poirot. The series begins with a Christmas mystery, *Not a Creature Was Stirring* (Bantam, 1990), set in Philadelphia and its wealthy Main Line suburbs. Gregor is assisted in his cases by Father Tibor Kasparian, an Armenian Orthodox priest, and by Bennis Hannaford, a rich and intelligent writer of fantasy novels. Demarkian is an expert in poisons and the behavioral analysis of serial killers, and the crimes he solves are traditional cozy puzzle mysteries.

Readers who enjoy the Patience McKenna novels should try Elizabeth Peters's *Die for Love* (Congdon & Weed, 1984) and the Ben and Carrie Porter mysteries by Elizabeth Travis. Aficionados of the Demarkian series might want to look for books by Agatha Christie, Carolyn G. Hart, Jennifer Rowe, Dorothy Sucher, and Betty Rowlands. Gillian Roberts also gives her mysteries a Philadelphia backdrop.

Hadley, Joan. See **Hess, Joan.**

Hager, Jean. The books in Hager's first series of mysteries are police procedurals, with a background of Cherokee lore and medicine. They are set in Oklahoma, with a continuing protagonist in Police Chief Mitch Bushyhead. Bushyhead is half Cherokee, but he is an outsider to the tribe since he was raised as a white man and married a white woman. His wife is dead, and now he has to cope with raising a teenage daughter by himself. Another continuing character in the books is Crying Wolf, a Cherokee medicine man. Bushyhead dispenses the white man's justice; Crying Wolf uses his medicine to work problems out in the historic Cherokee way. Among the Cherokee characters in the stories are the Nighthawks, who are devoted to traditional tribal learning and don't want to lose the language and customs of their ancestors. The first novel in the series is *The Grandfather Medicine* (St. Martin, 1989). Hager also has introduced a new series with *Ravenmocker* (Mysterious, 1992), in which the heroine is Molly Bearpaw, an investigator for the Native American Advocacy League. Molly works out of Tahlequah, Oklahoma and deals with cases in which members of the Cherokee tribe may have been denied their civil rights.

Eve K. Sandstrom, D. R. Meredith, and Susan Rogers Cooper also write mysteries set in Oklahoma and Texas. Dana Stabenow and Chelsea Quinn Yarbro write series with Native American investigators.

Hall, Mary Bowen. The Emma Chizzit series written by Hall represents a recent twist on the classic practice of using an observant older woman as an amateur sleuth. Elderly sleuths of the past, like Miss Marple, tended to be more mentally than physically active. In this series, however, Emma is a feisty, self-sufficient, and energetic woman who owns a salvage business in Sacramento. (She has made up the name of Emma Chizzit as a joke about her business; customers naturally would ask, "How much is it?") To supplement her social security check, Emma cleans out old buildings, keeps anything worthwhile, and sells the salvage. She does the hard physical labor herself, and she also gardens and does other chores in order to pay her rent. Emma likes to fit crime-solving into her busy schedule, and she and her more conventional friend, Frannie, investigate murder, rape, and missing manuscripts.

The first novel in the series is *Emma Chizzit and the Queen Anne Killer* (Walker, 1989).

Other mysteries that feature dynamic women of a certain age include B. J. Oliphant's Shirley McClintock novels, Stefanie Matteson's series about Charlotte Graham, and Virginia Rich's Mrs. Potter books.

Hardwick, Mollie. Hardwick's mysteries are quintessential English cozies, with a spot of evil spreading through each book. The heroine is Doran Fairweather, who owns an antique business and lives in a beautiful old house in the village of Abbotsbourne in Kent. In the first book, *Malice Domestic* (St. Martin, 1986), Doran begins a close personal and investigative relationship with the local vicar, Rodney Chelmarsh. At the beginning of the series, Doran is an uncertain, vulnerable young woman; she matures into an interesting, thoughtful woman with a group of loyal friends and family. A strong vein of religion and literature runs through all of Hardwick's mysteries. Crimes take place against the backgrounds of the antique trade, the art world, and the Anglican church. Hardwick's writing is charmingly erudite and chock-full of quotes; she will often use an individual English artist or writer for a thematic background—including Keats, Lewis Carroll, Gilbert and Sullivan, and Dante Gabriel Rossetti.

Hardwick has also written many historical novels, and she is perhaps best known for writing the Upstairs, Downstairs series of books.

Those interested in mysteries with an Episcopalian church setting may enjoy Isabelle Holland, D. M. Greenwood, and Barbara Whitehead.

Harris, Charlaine. For the setting of her first mystery novel, *Sweet and Deadly* (Houghton Mifflin, 1981), Harris used her native Mississippi Delta and the fictional town of Lowfield. The heroine of this novel, Catherine Linton, has the characteristics that are hallmarks of Harris's creations. Catherine, like Nickie Callahan of *A Secret Rage* (Houghton Mifflin, 1984), is intelligent, independent, and attractive. Catherine Linton is delving into the mysterious deaths of her parents while working as a society editor for the Lowfield *Gazette.* Nickie is a former New York model who has tired of the glamorous life and has returned to the South for a college education. The small town of Knolls, Tennessee, is being terrorized by a rapist, and Nickie falls prey to him. Writing with sensitivity and compassion, Harris handles a difficult subject well. Lately Harris has begun a series starring Aurora "Roe" Teagarden, a diminutive librarian with a sassy tongue and an affinity for true crime. In the Agatha-nominated *Real Murders* (Walker, 1990), Roe finds herself investigating the murders of fellow members of her "real murders" club. All the victims have died in a way reminiscent of some famous true crime. Roe's adventures continue in *A Bone to Pick* (Walker, 1992). Wit, humor, intelligence, and Southern settings grace Harris's accomplished work.

Readers who have enjoyed the work of Harris should try Sharyn McCrumb, Margaret Maron, Carolyn G. Hart, and Sarah Shankman. Those looking for other librarian detectives may seek out the Jacqueline Kirby novels of Elizabeth Peters.

Harrod-Eagles, Cynthia. The prolific Harrod-Eagles penned over thirty historical and fantasy novels before turning to the crime novel with *Orchestrated Death* (Scribner, 1992), which introduced London policeman Bill Slider. Slider is a Detective Inspector, and he is content with his rank, though his wife keeps nagging him to work for promotion. Promotion, however, would take Slider away from the work of detection into the world of administration, and he fights against it, though it could cost him his marriage. In *Orchestrated Death,* Slider is investigating the case of a murdered female, left naked and unidentifiable, the only clues at the scene a priceless Stradivarius and a giant tin of olive oil. From this, Harrod-Eagles fashions a complex and engaging police procedural novel. Her London cops are earthy, often ribald, and tough when necessary. Readers who have watched the "Prime Suspect" dramas aired on "Mystery!" on PBS will identify easily with the characters in this series, though there is no highly ranking female detective in the series.

Readers who enjoy English police procedurals might try the work of Paula Gosling, Jennie Melville, P. D. James, the Wexford novels of Ruth Rendell, the private eye series of Sarah Dunant, and the Canadian police procedural series of Medora Sale.

Hart, Carolyn G. Hart writes tightly plotted mysteries in the classic tradition. Her first series features Annie Laurance, and the initial novel is *Death on Demand* (Bantam, 1987). Annie owns Death on Demand, a mystery bookstore on Broward's Rock Island off the coast of South Carolina. She has an encyclopedic knowledge of crime novels and a strong bent for detection. Annie is assisted in her sleuthing by Max Darling, with whom she has a relationship that develops throughout the series. Hart shows particular strength in her creation of memorable secondary characters like Max's dotty mother, Laurel, who enjoys a succession of dubious enthusiasms, and Henny Brawley, a bookstore customer who knows even more about mysteries than Annie and never lets her forget it. *The Christie Caper* (Bantam, 1991), one of Hart's best works, is a classic puzzle novel set at a convention in honor of the one hundredth birthday of Agatha Christie. Hart pays homage in her novels to other honored mystery writers, especially those from the Golden Age of crime fiction. In *A Little Class on Murder* (Doubleday, 1989), for example, Annie teaches a class on three of the great women mystery writers: Agatha Christie, Dorothy Sayers, and Mary Roberts Rinehart. Hart also builds upon the traditional styles of mysteries for her books. *Southern Ghost* (Bantam, 1992), to cite one instance, uses many of the conventions of the Southern gothic suspense novel, but in a fresh and noteworthy fashion. Hart is especially good in this novel at chronicling the family traditions and emotional baggage with which a contemporary generation of Southerners feels burdened.

Hart has started a new series of mysteries whose heroine is Oklahoma journalist Henrietta (Henrie O) O'Dwyer Collins. The first novel in the series is *Dead Man's Island* (Bantam, 1993).

Hart has won both the Agatha and the Anthony Awards for Best Novel for *Something Wicked* (Bantam, 1988), an Anthony Award for *Honeymoon with Murder* (Bantam, 1988), and a Macavity Award for Best Novel for *A Little Class on Murder.*

Fans of Hart should try the mysteries of Agatha Christie, Jill Churchill, Dorothy Cannell, Jennifer Rowe, and Betty Rowlands. The adventures of other bookseller-sleuths have been chronicled by Joan Hess, M. K. Wren, and Sheila Simonson.

Hart, Ellen. The main character in this series set in Minneapolis is lesbian restaurant owner Jane Lawless, who is in her mid-thirties, recovering from the death of her longtime lover a few years before as the series begins. Jane's restaurant, The Lyme House, reflects part of Jane's heritage—her mother was English, and Jane spent a considerable part of her childhood and adolescence in England. Jane's father, Raymond Lawless, is a well-known criminal lawyer in Minneapolis, and he and Jane have an uneasy relationship, which grows and changes as the series progresses. Jane's "Watson" in the series is her old college friend Cordelia Thorn, who is artistic director of a well-known theater in St. Paul. Cordelia, also a lesbian, has a deliciously theatrical manner that contrasts humorously with the much more sober and self-effacing character of Jane. Together, the two make an enjoyable detective duo in the time-honored tradition of Holmes and Watson, but with a decidedly feminist twist. Hart follows the format of the traditional mystery closely, and she weaves in her feminism as integral and understated parts of her plots. The first in the series is *Hallowed Murder* (Seal Press, 1989), in which Jane becomes involved with the murder of a member of her old college sorority.

Seal Press founder Barbara Wilson is currently writing two series about lesbian amateur detectives; those acquainted with Hart's work will find Wilson's books of great interest. Other lesbian mystery writers include Katherine V. Forrest, Claire McNab, Sandra Scoppettone, and Sarah Dreher.

Haymon, S. T. Haymon's first mystery novel has perhaps one of the most distinctive and curious titles in contemporary mystery fiction. *Death and the Pregnant Virgin* (St. Martin, 1980), besides introducing policeman Benjamin Jurnet, Norwich-born and bred, to modern detective fiction, signals the author's taste for the baroque. The characters and relationships in Haymon's work are never commonplace. Her central character sets the tone of the series. Somewhat in the mold of Adam Dalgliesh, Jurnet is introspective, often moody, and Haymon uses the setting of Norwich and Norfolk effectively to reinforce her characterizations. In addition to solving crimes, Jurnet also pursues the love of Miriam, a beautiful Jewish woman who refuses to marry outside her faith. Jurnet therefore determines to convert to Judaism, and thus the reader is often witness to Jurnet's struggles of faith and conscience as well as to his methods of detection. Haymon does not flinch to present human behavior at its nastiest or most depraved, though her prose, as stylish as that of James or Rendell, does not sensationalize the subject matter. Though very much a part of the modern school of British psychological detective fiction, Haymon nevertheless is a distinctive, if sometimes disturbing, voice.

Readers who appreciate the psychological acuity of Haymon's work might also try the works of P. D. James, Gwendoline Butler, Minette Walters, Ruth Rendell, Frances Fyfield/Frances Hegarty, Sheila Radley, B. M. Gill, and Margaret Yorke.

Hegarty, Frances. See **Fyfield, Frances.**

Hess, Joan/Hadley, Joan. Hess currently is writing two series of books under her own name. One series, known as the Ozarks murder mysteries, is set in the small town of Maggody, Arkansas, with protagonist Police Chief Arly Hanks. Arly has returned to her childhood hometown reluctantly, after a bitter divorce in New York. Somehow she manages to keep her sanity in the eccentric, rural community, while surrounded by bizarre townsfolk. For example, there's Arly's mother Rubella Belinda Hanks, who runs Ruby Bee's Bar & Grill and tries to solve crimes while swopping rumors with her buddy, beautician Estelle Oppers. Then there's Brother Verber, the pastor of the Voice of the Almighty Lord Assembly Hall and a busy reader of pornography, and upright (if a trifle crooked) citizens like Hizzoner Mayor Jim Bob and his sanctimonious wife Mrs. Jim Bob (Mizzoner). And the county is full of members of the inbred, illiterate Buchanon clan (like good ole boy Raz Buchanon, who likes to watch television with his pig, Marjorie). The first Maggody novel is *Malice in Maggody* (St. Martin, 1987).

Hess's other series is set in a college town in Arkansas, and its continuing characters are amateur sleuth and bookstore owner Claire Malloy and her obnoxious teenage daughter Caron. Claire persists doggedly in her sleuthing on local crimes despite the constant hindrance of Caron, her pimply friend Inez, and attractive (if jaded) local cop Peter Rosen. The first Claire Malloy mystery is *Strangled Prose* (St. Martin, 1986).

Hess also wrote two novels under the name of Joan Hadley. The protagonist in these is Theo Bloomer, a retiree who loves plants and has exotic adventures in crime. The first Theo Bloomer book is *The Night-Blooming Cereus* (St. Martin, 1986).

The tone of Hess's work is sarcastic, biting, and hilarious. The Maggody series especially is pretty much off the wall. Readers will enjoy these novels if they like slapstick humor, strong regional description, eccentric Southern writing, or redneck satire. Hess is a winner of the American Mystery Award for *A Diet to Die For* (St. Martin, 1989).

Readers who like Joan Hess also may enjoy Carole Berry, whose sleuth, Bonnie Indermill, has an ironic and sharp mind; Charlotte MacLeod, whose humor is gentler; Taylor McCafferty; and Sharyn McCrumb. Annette Roome's Chris Martin novels should be fun to read for admirers of the Claire Malloy books.

Highsmith, Patricia. Highsmith is American by birth but lives in Europe, where many of her novels are set. Her first work was *Strangers on a Train* (Harper, 1950), which Alfred Hitchcock filmed, though in altering the ending he deprived the story of much of its punch. In *Strangers on a Train,* two seemingly normal people meet accidentally; one is quickly revealed to be corrupt, and the other withdraws, only to be caught up in the other's criminality in spite of himself. Highsmith's leading characters are often the criminals, and their victims come across as frightening and villainous. Robert Forester, in *The Cry of the Owl* (Harper, 1962), is a peeping tom who is caught by the young woman he's been watching through her window, introduces himself, makes friends, and steals her from her fiancé, who comes after Robert with murderous intent. Robert ruins lives and families from beginning to end, yet somehow the reader sides with him and against the people he harms. Highsmith's stories usually include a strong dose of paranoia, complex relationships, and sexual ambiguity; her lead characters are usually men drawn into criminal difficulties by their failure to take advantage of potential ways out which are apparent to the reader. The mix of comedy and killing in Highsmith's books; the mood darkening from an initial everyday calm into terror; and the amoral acceptance by characters of their and others' crimes will remind readers of the noir writer Jim Thompson.

Highsmith's best-regarded crime novels are the series involving Tom Ripley, beginning with *The Talented Mr. Ripley* (Coward, 1955) and continuing through the most recent in the series, *Ripley Under Water* (Knopf, 1992). Tom Ripley is a young man, fired from his job and supporting himself through minor forgery, who's commissioned by a concerned father to go to Europe and persuade the man's expatriate son, with whom Tom is slightly acquainted, to return to America and the family business. Seeing a chance for a free vacation, Tom goes to Italy, looks up the son, and makes himself a part of his life. Eventually, he assumes the son's identity, his income, even his clothing. When the man's friends start to question events, he can think of no solution other than to murder them. Through the Ripley series, Tom forges, impersonates, murders, and yet lives an increasingly luxurious life, free of guilt and penalty, improvising his escapes from the police who are always suspicious of his lengthening list of dead associates, yet never quite smart enough to pin anything on him.

Highsmith also wrote *The Price of Salt* (Coward-McCann,

1952), a novel about a lesbian relationship, under the pseudonym of Claire Morgan.

Highsmith received the Silver Dagger Award in 1964 for *The Two Faces of January* (Doubleday, 1964).

Joyce Carol Oates writes psychological suspense novels under the pseudonym of Rosamond Smith, and Barbara Paul writes mysteries that are noted for their strong vein of black comedy and memorable villains.

Holland, Isabelle. Holland has written both romantic suspense novels and mysteries. Her investigator in a series of mysteries is the Reverend Claire Aldington, an assistant rector of St. Anselm's Episcopal Church in Manhattan. Claire's position is somewhat anomalous, as she is a psychologist as well as a priest. Throughout the series, she often has to justify her work in the church to others, especially those who don't think churches should offer psychological assistance. Claire's private life is troubled as well; she is a widow with a difficult teenage stepdaughter. Holland provides the reader with plenty of insider details about the running of a parish and Episcopal Church traditions. St. Anselm's is an inner-city church, but one with wealthy white parishioners; the church members and the clergy (including Claire) struggle with the ever-present urban issues of racism, homelessness, and alcoholism. Holland has also written *Bump in the Night* (Doubleday, 1988), not a series book, but a suspense novel dealing with the problems of alcoholism and missing children. It was filmed for a television movie in 1991.

The first Claire Aldington book is *A Death at St. Anselm's* (Doubleday, 1984).

Mollie Hardwick and Veronica Black both write clerical mysteries. D. M. Greenwood has a series with protagonist Deaconess Theodora Braithwaite. Annette Meyers uses interesting New York City settings, similar to Holland's.

Holt, Hazel. Known before her forays into crime fiction as the friend and literary executor of English novelist Barbara Pym, Holt is now becoming known as the creator of Sheila Malory, writer of literary criticism and occasional amateur sleuth. The widowed Sheila Malory lives in the seaside village of Taviscombe, and this is where her first case occurs, in *Mrs. Malory Investigates* (St. Martin, 1989; entitled *Gone Away* in England). A brash young woman is marrying an old friend of Sheila's, and the whole village whispers that she is marrying him for his money. Though Sheila secretly agrees, she cannot fail to help her old friend when his fiancée disappears. In her second outing, Sheila is in Oxford, doing research at the Bodleian Library in *The Cruellest Month* (St. Martin, 1991). Who murdered the blackmailing spinster librarian in the stacks of the Bodleian? Sheila Malory makes an engaging narrator, and Holt keeps her busy with puzzles in the traditional vein.

Those who have read Holt might try the work of Ann Granger, Betty Rowlands, Mollie Hardwick, Kay Mitchell, the Paula Glenning novels of Anna Clarke, E. X. Ferrars, and Nora Kelly.

Hooper, Kay. The author of a number of romance novels, Hooper has recently begun a mystery series starring an unconventional female private eye, Lane Montana, who lives and works in Atlanta. Though she has all the credentials of other Georgia private eyes, Lane has a particular specialty; she's a finder of lost objects. These objects can be such things as misplaced jewelry, missing heirlooms, even people, occasionally. She has a twin brother who is a successful artist, and the sibling relationship is important to the series and the characters. And, cat-lovers take note, Kay has an irascible Siamese named Choo. In *Crime of Passion* (Avon, 1991), Lane finds herself mixed up in a murder case involving a very prominent, wealthy Atlanta family. During the course of the investigation, she meets Lieutenant Trey Fortier, and the sparks begin to fly. Hooper handles the romantic element of the series with understated aplomb; the relationship between Lane and Trey is an effective underpinning. The plots demonstrate deft execution, and the Southern setting rings true. In the second novel, *House of Cards* (Avon, 1991), Lane takes Trey to meet her unusual family, and Hooper offers an entertaining variation on the "eccentric Southern family" convention.

Other writers who use Atlanta settings are Celestine Sibley, Patricia H. Sprinkle, Kathy Hogan Trocheck, and Sarah Shankman. Sherryl Woods also writes a series of mysteries with a strong component of romance between the two lead characters. Female private eye writers on the softer-boiled menu include Dorothy Sucher and Taylor McCafferty (whose character is a man).

Hornsby, Wendy. The first two mysteries written by Hornsby featured southern California policeman Roger Tejeda and professor Kate Teague. Tejeda and Teague meet in *No Harm* (Dodd, Mead, 1987) and investigate the murder of her uncle; their relationship, and the results of the earlier investigation, continue in *Half a Mind* (New American Library, 1990). These are hardboiled police procedurals, with a fair amount of violence and strong Orange County coastal settings. Tejeda and Teague are an interesting study in contrasts: Tejeda comes from a middleclass Latino background, while Teague is an heiress from an old money family. Hornsby has started a new series with *Telling Lies* (Dutton, 1992). Maggie MacGowen, a documentary filmmaker from San Francisco, is the protagonist. Maggie comes to Los Angeles in response to an urgent message from her sister, a physician and former radical, only to find her murdered. Maggie and her family have many ties back to the antiwar activism of the sixties, and this murder seems to be a part of those linkages. Hornsby is good at building suspense and describing the dark underside of Los Angeles, and her plot twists keep the reader engrossed until the very end.

Readers looking for Orange County settings should try A. E. Maxwell, Jean Femling, and Maxine O'Callaghan. Mysteries with old sixties radicals include Kate Green's *Night Angel* and the Willa Jansson novels of Lia Matera.

Jackson, Marian J. A. Miss Abigail Patience Danforth is an American heiress with considerable strength of mind and of purpose. Spurred on by the example of the exploits of Sherlock Holmes, Miss Danforth vows to become the world's first female consulting detective in this series set circa 1900. In her debut, *The Punjat's Ruby* (Pinnacle, 1990), Miss Danforth goes so far as to inveigle a meeting with Sir Arthur Conan Doyle to ask his advice. Not dampened by Conan Doyle's discouraging response, Miss Danforth takes on the case of the Punjat's missing ruby, all the while keeping a titled English suitor at bay. The action moves from England back to Abigail's native New York, where the story is resolved. From there Abigail journeys west across America with her new companion, Maude Cunningham, and the two find themselves in a real Western adventure with *The Arabian Pearl* (Pinnacle, 1990). Jackson's stories about her turn-of-the-century detective are a mixture of adventure, mystery, and a dash of romance.

Those who have read Jackson might try the Irene Adler novels of Carole Nelson Douglas, which are even more Holmesian in flavor than Jackson's.

Jacobs, Nancy Baker. Jacobs is one of the few writers of private eye novels who actually has been a private investigator herself. Her series with Devon MacDonald, a private eye in Minneapolis, thus has the detail and feel of authenticity. Jacobs's first novel in the series, *The Turquoise Tattoo* (Putnam, 1991), is an engrossing story about a boy dying of leukemia who needs a bone marrow transplant. His natural father, a Jewish doctor, also donated his sperm many years ago to a sperm bank. Devon finds the half-brother conceived from that donation, but the adoptive father is an Aryan supremacist. Devon and her partner Sam Sherman investigate the inevitable murder. Devon has lost a child of her own to a drunk driver, and this case engages her emotions as well as her skills. The second Devon MacDonald novel, *A Slash of Scarlet* (Putnam, 1992), is about a middle-aged Lothario who courts and then robs gullible women. As well as her series mysteries, Jacobs also has written suspense novels. *Deadly Companion* (Dell, 1986) tells the story of a twisted nurse who murders elderly patients and steals their possessions. *See Mommy Run* (Penguin, 1992) is a particularly strong tale of a mother on the run with her preschool daughter, who has been sexually abused by her father. There are interesting descriptions of an underground network that helps abuse victims, and details of how the mother gets a new identity and stays ahead of the police and private detectives. In her novels, Jacobs is clearly engaged with social issues that affect women and children, and she uses these concerns as effective elements in her well-constructed plots.

Readers also may want to try private eye mysteries by Maxine O'Callaghan, Karen Kijewski, and Liza Cody. Sara Paretsky's investigator, V. I. Warshawski, is often involved with social problems, as is lawyer Neil Hamel in Judith Van Gieson's series of crime novels. Other suspense writers include Mary Higgins Clark and Judith Kelman.

James, P. D. In private life, she is Phyllis Dorothy White, who worked as a civil servant for many years. In 1991, she was awarded a life peerage as Baroness James of Holland Park, and she now sits in the House of Lords. James is considered by many critics and readers to be one of the best crime writers of her generation. Her protagonists in two different series are Commander Adam Dalgliesh of the Metropolitan Police, and private investigator Cordelia Gray. James's first novel was *Cover Her Face* (Scribner, 1966). The format is that of a typical English village cozy, but with some Jamesian trademarks: acutely observed characters, an atmosphere of menace, medical details, and a loving attention to architectural details. The detective here is Dalgliesh, who is a poet as well as a policeman. Dalgliesh is rather an omniscient and morose detective, known for his exactitude and objectivity. In 1972, James created a female private eye, Cordelia Gray, thus predating a comparable trend by American crime writers. Cordelia has been trained as a private investigator by Bernie Pryde, who commits suicide at the beginning of *An Unsuitable Job for a Woman* (Scribner, 1972), leaving Cordelia his agency and his gun. Cordelia is less confident and controlled a detective than Dalgliesh.

James is known for her extensive use of literary quotations and symbolism, as well as her adroit plotting. For example, *The Skull Beneath the Skin* (Scribner, 1982) has many allusions to Shakespeare and the Jacobean revenge playwrights. In both this novel and *A Taste for Death* (Knopf, 1986), James's skill in using detailed architectural and interior descriptions of houses and churches to further her plot and character analysis is fully realized. Both novels are rather gothic and brooding, with the crimes deftly foreshadowed, and each character carefully delineated. These novels show James at the height of her powers. Her elegant prose and psychological acuity lift her work far above the standard crime novel.

James also has written nonseries books, including *Innocent Blood* (Scribner, 1980), a suspense novel. It is the macabre and sensational story of a young girl, Philippa Palfrey, who gains access to her adoption records and discovers that her birth parents were a rapist and a murderer. *The Children of Men* (Knopf, 1993) is a beautifully written novel set in the future. James tells the story of Theo Faron, cousin to Xan Lyppiatt, the dictator and Warden of England in the year 2021. No children have been born in the world for twenty-five years, and society is in decline. James handles her vision of the near future adroitly, not by inventing new technologies, but by writing in general terms about objects like houses and cars, while concentrating on human emotion and motivation.

James won Silver Dagger Awards for both *The Black Tower* (Scribner, 1975) and *Shroud for a Nightingale* (Scribner, 1971). She won a Macavity Award for Best Novel and a Silver Dagger Award for *A Taste for Death.* She won a Diamond Dagger Award for lifetime achievement from the British Crime Writers' Association in 1986, and was awarded the Order of the British Empire by the Queen in 1983.

Readers who admire James also may enjoy the works of Elizabeth George, Ruth Rendell, B. M. Gill, and Jennifer Rowe.

Jance, J. A. The author has established a large following for her series of novels featuring Seattle homicide cop J. P. Beaumont. Beau, as he is known to his friends, is a bit of a maverick, lover of junk food and booze, in the best tradition of the freewheeling cop of mystery fiction. In the first book of the series, *Until Proven Guilty* (Avon, 1985), Beau's on the trail of a child killer with his new partner, Detective Ron Peters. During the course of the investigation, Beau meets and falls for a mysterious, wealthy woman, whom he marries. Police procedurals by form, the series is fast-paced and generally full of action. Beau, though stubborn and irascible, demonstrates that he's capable of change as the series progresses. He's willing to rethink some of his prejudices and ideas, though he remains steadfast in others. The Seattle setting is an important component of the books, and

Jance makes the city a living entity, much in the way Sara Paretsky makes Chicago integral to her work or Julie Smith makes New Orleans in her Skip Langdon books. Recently Jance has begun a new series with a female character in *Desert Heat* (Avon, 1993). Joanna Brady is the widow of a sheriff's deputy in Cochise County, Arizona. Like the Beaumont books, this series promises fast action and a tough, yet appealing, central character. Jance has, in addition, penned one novel of psychological suspense, *Hour of the Hunter* (Morrow, 1991).

Those who have enjoyed the Beaumont series might try the work of Anne Wingate, who writes also as Lee Martin and Martha G. Webb, M. J. Adamson, the Skip Langdon books of Julie Smith, and the many novels of Elizabeth Linington, who wrote also as Lesley Egan and Dell Shannon.

Janeshutz, Trish. See **MacGregor, T. J.**

Johnston, Velda. A veteran suspense novelist, with more than thirty novels to her credit, Johnston began her work in the heyday of romantic suspense with *Along a Dark Path* (Dodd, Mead, 1968). Though Johnston's work features most of the characteristics of the romantic suspense, or gothic novel as it was called then, Johnston is so skilled at the suspense half of the recipe that many readers quite often forget that they are reading a gothic. The heroines of Johnston's fiction, whether contemporary or nineteenth-century, are independent, often stubborn, resourceful, and intelligent. Two of Johnston's early period settings, *The Late Mrs. Fonsell* (Dodd, Mead, 1972) and *Masquerade in Venice* (Dodd, Mead, 1973), rank alongside the best work of Victoria Holt and Phyllis A. Whitney. A more recent work, *The House on Bostwick Square* (Dodd, Mead, 1987), shows Johnston's skill at blending unusual and suspenseful elements into a not-so-traditional romantic suspense novel. *The Etruscan Smile* (Dodd, Mead, 1977), with its vividly etched foreign setting and intriguing plot, is one of the author's best contemporary suspense novels.

Readers acquainted with the work of Johnston will also enjoy the work of Barbara Michaels and her alter ego Elizabeth Peters, Phyllis A. Whitney, Caroline Crane, D. F. Mills, and Jane Aiken Hodge.

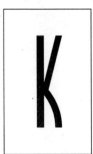

Kallen, Lucille. Kallen was a writer for such television comedies as Sid Caesar's classic "Your Show of Shows" before she began writing novels. Her first effort was *Outside There, Somewhere—!* (Macmillan, 1964), a comic feminist novel. She then turned to writing mysteries, and her first effort was *Introducing C. B. Greenfield* (Crown, 1979). It was a popular success and was nominated for The American Book Award (TABA). Kallen's series sleuths are Maggie Rome, a weekly newspaper reporter, and C. B. (Charlie) Greenfield, her editor and publisher. Their newspaper is the Sloan's Ford *Reporter,* and most of the books are located in the affluent suburban town of Sloan's Ford, Connecticut. The novels are narrated by Maggie, and she plays the Archie Goodwin role to Greenfield's Nero Wolfe. Maggie is the legman for Charlie; he is the grouchy, acerbic man of ideas. Inevitably, they argue a lot, and their version of the war of the sexes becomes an important part of the plot in each book. Classical music is also important to these characters, for C. B. and Maggie play together in a chamber music group. *C. B. Greenfield: The Tanglewood Murder* (Wyndham, 1980), for example, is set at the

Tanglewood Music Festival in the Berkshires. Kallen does take Maggie and Charlie out of Sloan's Ford occasionally. *C. B. Greenfield: The Piano Bird* (Random House, 1984) is set on a Florida island, and *C. B. Greenfield: A Little Madness* (Random House, 1986) is set in a women's peace camp and has a political bent. Kallen's novels are classic American puzzle mysteries, with strong lead characters.

Readers also may enjoy Diane K. Shah's Paris Chandler series (Paris is another newspaper legman) and Annette Roome's Chris Martin books. Gloria Dank, Melodie Johnson Howe, and Dorothy Sucher have created other amusing teams of investigators.

Kellerman, Faye. Kellerman's crime novels are both exciting police procedurals and windows into the little-known world of Orthodox Judaism. The protagonists are Rina Lazarus and Peter Decker. Rina is a widow with young sons; Peter is an LAPD cop in the Foothill Division. They meet in the first novel, *The Ritual Bath* (Arbor House, 1986), and their relationship deepens throughout the series. Peter discovers and learns about Judaism after being raised as a Baptist by his adoptive parents. Rina is Orthodox; each book in the series, especially *The Ritual Bath* and *Day of Atonement* (Morrow, 1991), gives details of the customs and rites of the Orthodox community. The murders Peter investigates, and Rina assists him with, are often gory and emotionally disturbing. There is quite a bit of graphic realism in these police stories, and it is contrasted with the security, faith, and love that Rina offers to her family.

Kellerman has also written a historical mystery, *The Quality of Mercy* (Morrow, 1989), about Rebecca Lopez, a Jewish woman who lives in sixteenth-century London and becomes the model for Shakespeare's Dark Lady in his sonnets. The novel is particularly good at creating the atmosphere of converso life in England for the hidden Jewish community.

Kellerman won a Macavity Award for Best First Novel for *The Ritual Bath.*

Wendy Hornsby and Teri White also write hard-boiled, gritty tales of Los Angeles cops. Rochelle Majer Krich, the team of Serita Stevens and Rayanne Moore, and S. T. Haymon also have written mysteries with backgrounds of Jewish culture.

Kelly, Nora. A historian in real life, Kelly has given her profession to her series sleuth, Gillian Adams, who ably demonstrates that the disciplined academic mind is well-suited to the rigors of mystery-solving. In the first novel, *In the Shadow of King's* (St. Martin, 1984), Gillian is on sabbatical in Cambridge, where she took her doctorate fifteen years earlier. The Regius Professor of Modern History is murdered, and Gillian, along with the policeman assigned to the case, Edward Gisborne of Scotland Yard, solves the case. Kelly describes the atmosphere of Cambridge in lucid, evocative prose. In its way, her first novel does for Cambridge what Dorothy L. Sayers's classic *Gaudy Night* (Harcourt Brace, 1936) did for the Oxford of half a century ago. In the second novel, *My Sister's Keeper* (St. Martin, 1992), the setting is the University of the Pacific Northwest in Vancouver, British Columbia. Feminism and the university's backwardness in women's rights issues are central to the plot of the book, and Kelly fashions a literate and compelling story from the mix.

Like Kelly, Amanda Cross and Sophie Belfort write literate and thought-provoking series of academic mysteries. Fans of Kelly might try the work of English feminist Joan Smith as well. Hazel Holt's Sheila Malory is an enjoyable academic-type sleuth as well.

Kelly, Susan. Kelly is a college English professor, with a Ph.D. in medieval literature. She has created an ongoing series of mysteries with the attractive heroine Liz Connors. Liz is a tall, redheaded former English professor, now a freelance writer who often concentrates on true crime stories. Her lover in the series is Jack Lingemann, a homicide detective. Liz is humorous, independent, and literate, while Jack is sensitive, thoughtful, and realistic about the violence he sees every day. Kelly provides Connors with finely detailed Cambridge, Massachusetts surroundings, and the crimes she encounters often are based on recent events. Thus, the first Liz Connors mystery, *The Gemini Man* (Walker, 1985), is the story of a serial killer and singles bars, and *Summertime Soldiers* (Walker, 1986), brings back old sixties radical terrorists, who resurface and begin to kill people they associate with the present high-tech military-industrial complex. An especially memorable novel in the series is *Out of the Darkness* (Villard, 1992), in which Connors assists a famous true-crime writer in his research on a brutal serial killer, while events in her own life go awry. Kelly is particularly good at building suspense from a quiet recounting of the daily events in her protagonist's life.

Kathryn Lasky Knight also uses a Cambridge setting for her mysteries. Readers of Kelly may enjoy Julie Smith's Paul McDonald books, in which the main character is a freelance writer.

Kelly, Susan B. The American publisher has added the initial B to this Susan Kelly's name to distinguish her from the American writer Susan Kelly. The British Susan Kelly is writing a series of police detective mysteries set in the Hop Valley. In the first novel, *Hope Against Hope* (Scribner, 1991), rich, intelligent, and attractive businesswoman Alison Hope moves her computer software business from London to the remote Hop Valley, where she soon encounters Detective Inspector Nick Trevellyan of the Hopbridge CID. When Alison's cousin and former business partner turns up dead, Alison becomes a prime suspect, and Nick has to fight a growing attraction to her in order to solve the case. The second novel in the series, *Time of Hope* (Scribner, 1992), chronicles further developments in the relationship of Nick and Alison. Kelly has created likable, realistic characters as the focus of her series. The plots are neatly constructed and should give pleasure to those looking for good whodunits. This is an attractive series that should build a strong following.

Other writers of English police detective series whom readers of Kelly might like are June Thomson, Dorothy Simpson, Clare Curzon, Marjorie Eccles, Cynthia Harrod-Eagles, and Anthea Fraser.

Kelman, Judith. Kelman writes chilling novels of psychological suspense, with plots involving women and particularly children in jeopardy from crazed serial killers. The psychology of the murderer is explored, as he stalks his victims through their daily lives. The books are often set in the suburbs, and the graphic violence and horror of a madman pursuing innocent children is contrasted with their ostensibly safe surroundings. *The House on the Hill* (Bantam, 1992), for example, has a maniacal sociopath, a missing child, and an attractive woman parole officer as key elements in an archetypal suspense story. In *Someone's Watching* (Bantam, 1991), the villain commits hit-and-run attacks, as well as kidnapping and killing neighborhood kids. In *Where Shadows Fall* (Berkley, 1987), Kelman tells the story of a mother investigating her son's alleged suicide at a distinguished university. As with other Kelman novels, it is notable for her effective scene-setting, research, and an atmosphere of lurking evil.

Kelman's first novel was *Prime Evil* (Berkley, 1986).

Readers also may want to try the novels of Mary Higgins Clark, T. J. MacGregor, D. F. Mills, and Nancy Baker Jacobs's *See Mommy Run.*

Kenney, Susan. Novelist and college professor Kenney has created a series of mysteries about Roz Howard, professor of English, whose specialties are medieval literature and women's studies. In her first appearance, *Garden of Malice* (Scribner, 1983), Roz is in England to work on the papers of Lady Viola Montfort-Snow, a well-known gardener and writer. While staying at Montfort Abbey, Roz encounters murder and mystery about Lady Viola's work, and she also meets Alan Stewart, an attractive and wealthy man of many talents, with whom she becomes romantically involved. In the second novel, *Graves in Academe* (Viking, 1985), Roz is teaching at Canterbury College in Maine, where someone has begun murdering faculty in ways straight out of the classics of English literature. *One Fell Sloop* (Viking, 1990) finds Roz and Alan at odds in their relationship while on a sailing vacation on the Maine coast. Murder intervenes, and they put aside their differences to focus on the solution of the crime. Kenney writes literate and leisurely mysteries that have much to offer to the fan of the traditional mystery and of the academic mystery novel. Roz Howard is a modern woman trying to balance the demands of a career where women have to work much harder to compete and of a relationship with a man who sometimes seems to have just too much to offer.

If readers find Kenney's work appealing, they might try the work of J. S. Borthwick, Amanda Cross, Sally Gunning, Sophie Belfort, and Jane Langton.

Kijewski, Karen. The sleuth in this series is Kat Colorado, PI, who operates out of Sacramento. Kijewski's writing is conversational and colloquial, with plenty of snappy dialogue. The secondary characters in the series, Kat's adopted grandmother, her best friend Charity, and her lover Hank, have their own well-developed styles and idiosyncracies. Kat is a tough, smart woman, but clients can appeal to her vulnerabilities, especially kids, the elderly, and people who apparently have nowhere else to turn. In many ways, Kat's persona follows the model of the hard-boiled shamus, but she brings a female perspective to these conventions; for example, she and her friends don't drink a lot of whiskey, but they certainly do eat, especially desserts. Kat is a former bartender (as is Kijewski), and this skill comes in handy when she goes under cover in *Copy Kat* (Doubleday, 1992). Kat takes her own risks, gets herself out of dangerous situations, and resents men in her life who try to protect her.

The first book in the series is *Katwalk* (St. Martin, 1989), which won the Best First Private Eye Novel Award (the "Shamus") from the Private Eye Writers of America.

Creators of other hard-boiled women private eyes include Janet Dawson, Catherine Dain, and Linda Barnes. Another view of Sacramento is given by Mary Bowen Hall's novels about Emma Chizzit. Marcia Muller also sets scenes from some of her Sharon McCone novels in the area.

Kittredge, Mary. Creator of two series of mysteries, Kittredge is a former respiratory therapist for a major urban hospital. Her first series features freelance writer Charlotte Kent. In *Murder in Mendocino* (Walker, 1988), Kent is living in California, teaching a writing class in a small town, and writing how-to books. She becomes involved with a troubled adolescent, whom she later adopts, and the two move to New Haven, Connecticut, when the adopted son, Joey Rosen, develops medical problems. This also allows Kent to be near her lover, surgeon Rob Solli. Kittredge's second series is also set in New Haven, often connected with the Chelsea Memorial Hospital, which figures in the other series. Edwina Crusoe, R.N., comes from a wealthy family and has a private income, which means she works only because she wants to. Her debut is *Fatal Diagnosis* (St. Martin, 1990). At the end of the book, she decides to leave the hospital and open her own agency for a combination of private nursing and medical investigation. Her boyfriend is Martin McIntyre, a cop whom she meets in the first book; his official status and expertise are often helpful. Both women characters are strong-willed and independent, and the medical backgrounds in the Crusoe books are vividly detailed.

Fans of mysteries with medical settings might try the work of English writer Stella Shepherd or the best-selling thrillers of Robin Cook. P. D. James has several times used a medical or scientific research background to excellent effect.

Knight, Alanna. A historical novelist and an expert on Robert Louis Stevenson, Knight has recently turned her talents to a series of mystery novels set in Victorian Edinburgh. Knight's series character is Detective Inspector Jeremy Faro, a widower with two young daughters (who live in Orkney with their grandmother) and a grown stepson, Dr. Vincent Laurie. Vince often provides unofficial assistance to Faro in his cases. In the first of the series, *Enter Second Murderer* (St. Martin, 1988), Faro investigates a gruesome murder in which one murderer has already been tried, convicted, and hanged. Faro believes, however, that another murderer is still at large. Knight's Victorian Edinburgh is an intriguing place, and the period detail makes an effective backdrop for the puzzles that Knight devises. Her writing style is somewhat lush, in the good Victorian manner, so readers might sometimes think they are reading actual Victorian prose. Faro and his stepson Vince are likable characters, serving as well-drawn centerpieces for a good historical mystery series.

Readers with a taste for Victorian murder and mayhem might try the two series of Anne Perry, the work of Amy Myers, or the American Victorian mysteries of Marian J. A. Jackson.

Knight, Kathryn Lasky. Calista Jacobs, a successful children's book illustrator, is the unusual heroine of Knight's series. Calista is earthy, bright, and imaginative, with an active sense of humor. She is widowed in the first book and begins her sleuthing career by discovering who killed her husband. Calista has able assistants in her investigations: her son Charley, who is precocious and enthralled by computers, and Archie Baldwin, an archaeologist for the Smithsonian. The books are set primarily in Cambridge, Massachusetts, although *Mumbo Jumbo* (Summit, 1991) is set in the Southwest at an archaeological site. The qualities that make Knight's books fun to read are the finely drawn characters of Calista and Charley, the absorbing descriptions of Calista's work as an illustrator, and the use of current issues like creationism and New Age cults as plot elements.

Knight has written many children's books under the name Kathryn Lasky. Her first adult mystery novel is *Trace Elements* (Norton, 1986).

Readers also might enjoy Susan Kelly and Jane Langton, who also have used Cambridge as a setting for mysteries. Judith Van Gieson sets her mysteries in the Southwest, with close attention to current social issues.

Kraft, Gabrielle. Screwball comedy-mysteries, like their film counterparts, flourished in the 1930s and 1940s. This classic American form returns in Kraft's series of novels starring Beverly Hills lawyer Jerry Zalman and his girlfriend Marie Thrasher. Diminutive, cigar-chomping Jerry somehow always gets clients with nutty problems, which then escalate into bizarre murders. A great deal of Kraft's writing is snappy, smart dialogue, filled with sarcastic remarks about southern California and its strange denizens. A zany atmosphere and loony characters abound in these novels. In *Let's Rob Roy* (Pocket, 1989), for example, a heavy metal rocker is being blackmailed by a psychic. The rock star's manager (Jerry's sister) is convinced that the singer will lose all his teenage fans if the psychic reveals that her client is really a mild-mannered English lad who likes to bake cakes and do needlepoint, rather than a Satan-worshipping headbanger. Naturally, Jerry tries to concoct a scheme to avert disaster; naturally, disaster strikes anyway.

The first Jerry Zalman novel, *Bullshot* (Pocket, 1987), was nominated for an Edgar award.

Kraft also has written *Hollywood Hills* (Pocket, 1993), a novel about an actress and agent, which spans fifty years of her Hollywood career.

Craig Rice's John J. Malone novels are classics of screwball humor. Joan Hess, Marissa Piesman, and Meg O'Brien write humorous mysteries.

Krich, Rochelle Majer. Krich's first book, *Where's Mommy Now* (Windsor, 1990), which won an Anthony Award, is a suspense novel about a young woman who has inherited millions. She has two children from her first marriage, and is now happily married to a doctor. Her comfortable life begins to unravel with the arrival in her household of an au pair babysitter from Switzerland. Krich's second book, *Till Death Do Us Part* (Avon, 1992), is a very different mystery about an Orthodox Jewish woman, Deena Vogler, whose ex-husband will not give her a religious divorce (a *get*). Without the *get,* Deena cannot marry again and resume a normal life. Krich sets her story of frustation and murder in an affluent neighborhood of Los Angeles, and she provides an indepth look at Orthodox life and customs.

Faye Kellerman's series of mysteries with Peter Decker and Rina Lazarus gives another view of Orthodox Judaism in a Los Angeles setting. Writers of suspense novels include Nancy Baker Jacobs, Judith Kelman, Susan Moody (in *Hush-a-bye*), and Meg O'Brien (in *The Keeper*).

Langton, Jane. Langton is a unique talent in the mystery world. Her lyrical, exuberant novels are more imaginative than puzzling, and she illustrates her books with witty pen-and-ink drawings. The reader generally knows all along who did the crime; the mystery lies in how and when justice will be done. Justice is not necessarily dispensed by human means; retribution is sometimes achieved through the vast impersonal workings of the universe. Homer Kelly, a Thoreau scholar and former lawyer and policeman, appears in most of Langton's novels. Homer worships at the shrine of New England transcendentalism, and his admiration is mirrored in many of the books. Most of these poetic, charming novels are set in historic Concord and Boston, and Langton brings the past, especially the nineteenth-century literary giants of Thoreau, Emerson, and Dickinson, to vibrant life. Langton's books also make excursions into the worlds of natural history, art, and music. Langton's descriptions of the natural world are graceful and memorable, especially in *Natural Enemy* (Ticknor & Fields, 1982) and *God in Concord* (Viking, 1992). Langton also writes jewel-like books for young adults.

The first Homer Kelly novel is *The Transcendental Murder*

(Harper, 1964), also published as *The Minuteman Murder* (Dell, 1976).

For other strong senses of place and environmental concern, readers may enjoy Janet LaPierre, Judith Van Gieson, and M. K. Wren. For settings in Cambridge and Massachusetts, try Kathryn Lasky Knight and Charlotte MacLeod. For elegance of writing, wisdom, and wit, read Sarah Caudwell, Mary Stewart, and Sharyn McCrumb.

LaPierre, Janet. The setting for LaPierre's novels is Port Silva, California, a fictional town based on the real Fort Bragg on the Mendocino coast. Meg Halloran, a local teacher, and the Port Silva Chief of Police, Vince Gutierrez, are featured characters in the mysteries. The Port Silva novels begin with *Unquiet Grave* (St. Martin, 1987); the second book in the series, *Children's Games* (Scribner, 1989), is a prequel that introduces Meg Halloran and her daughter. *The Cruel Mother* (Scribner, 1990) centers around Vince's bratty teenaged niece and Meg, who become kidnap victims. In *Grandmother's House* (Scribner, 1991), LaPierre shifts her focus to protagonists Charlotte Birdsong and her precocious son Petey, along with their tenant, Police Officer Val Kuisma. LaPierre is particularly good at depicting the parent-child relationship, especially with children who are smart and protective of their mothers. Other strengths include good psychological analyses of the main characters and a realistic North Coast atmosphere. The sense of threat and danger lurking in a small town is very well done. As much suspense novels as mysteries, these books are clearly and precisely rendered.

Readers of LaPierre may enjoy M. K. Wren's atmospheric North Coast novels, and the mysteries of Kathryn Lasky Knight, P. M. Carlson, and Isabelle Holland, all of whom write convincingly about mothers and children.

Lathen, Emma/Dominic, R. B. Since 1961, Mary Latsis and Martha Henissart have been publishing mystery novels under two pseudonyms: Emma Lathen and R. B. Dominic. Mysteries written under the Lathen name predominate; there have been more than twenty Lathen novels and eight Dominic novels as of this time. Latsis and Henissart guard their privacy, but it is known that they are, respectively, an economist and a lawyer, both living in Massachusetts. Under the Lathen name, they write financial and banking mysteries; under the Dominic name, they write political mysteries. In the Lathen books, the amateur sleuth is John Putnam Thatcher, senior vice president of the Sloan Guaranty Trust in New York. Thatcher has a lively team to assist him in his sleuthing: Miss Corsa, his loyal secretary, and fellow bankers Everett Gabler and Charlie Trinkham. The authors have a distinctive talent for writing clearly and entertainingly about complicated financial intrigues, and for combining these business matters with current events and a tightly plotted mystery to produce fascinating and civilized novels. The first Lathen novel was *Banking on Death* (Macmillan, 1961). The Dominic mysteries feature Ben Safford, a Democratic congressman from Ohio. As in the Lathen novels, the authors have created detailed and realistic backdrops for each book, and have surrounded Safford with a spirited group of professional colleagues and crime-solvers. The first Dominic novel was *Murder, Sunny Side Up* (Abelard-Schuman, 1968).

The authors were awarded the Gold Dagger Award in 1967 for *Murder Against the Grain* (Macmillan, 1967), and the Silver Dagger for *Accounting for Murder* (Macmillan, 1964). They also received the Mystery Writers of America Ellery Queen Award in 1982.

Fans of financial mysteries may enjoy Annette Meyers's Smith and Wetzon books and Margaret Logan's *A Killing in Venture Capital* (Walker, 1989). Readers of the Dominic mysteries may want to try the political crime novels of Margaret Truman.

Laurence, Janet. Making excellent use of her own background as a cooking instructor and contributor to cooking columns in English newspapers, Laurence has created as the heroine of her mystery series Darina Lisle, an expert cook. In her first outing, *A Deepe Coffyn* (Doubleday, 1990), Darina is assisting her detestable cousin Digby Cary, the golden boy of British gourmets, with the cooking for a meeting of the Society of Historical Gastronomes. Soon Darina is investigating Digby's murder to prove her own innocence. Amid mouthwatering descriptions—but no recipes, alas!—of elaborate medieval dishes, Laurence presents an engaging murder mystery. Darina also becomes acquainted with police sergeant William Pigram, an attractive man of good family, who appears in subsequent books trying to woo the staunchly independent Darina while also trying in vain to keep Darina out of harm's way. Though Laurence presents no recipes, she provides enough descriptions of good food to set the reader's mouth watering. She also delivers good entertainment in a time-honored form, the traditional British mystery.

The late Virginia Rich added many a recipe to her fiction, and newcomer Diane Mott Davidson is following well in her footsteps. Amy Myers writes a series about a Victorian master chef, and Katherine Hall Page's main character is also a caterer by profession.

Law, Janice. After writing nonfiction, Law turned to the suspense novel, and her first, *The Big Payoff* (Houghton Mifflin, 1976), received an Edgar nomination for Best First Novel. This book introduced Anna Peters, research assistant to an executive high in the ranks of the company, New World Oil. At the age of thirty, Anna had come somewhat to terms with some of the demons of her past life, including a brief but lucrative career as a blackmailer. When she suspects that her boss is part of a plot to sabotage profitable oil company dealings in the North Sea, Anna reluctantly becomes involved, and the results almost cost her her life and that of her boyfriend, Harry Radford. In subsequent books Anna undertakes various missions for New World Oil, all of which require her skills as an intelligent and resourceful investigator. In *The Shadow of the Palms* (Houghton Mifflin, 1980), Anna has left New World Oil and has opened her own agency, Executive Security. After a lengthy hiatus, the series has continued with *Time Lapse* (Walker, 1992). Anna Peters has much in common with many of her peers as a private eye. She is tough, undaunted in the face of physical danger, and Law has involved her in plenty of hair-raising situations, fast-paced and suspenseful. In addition to the series, Law has penned one other suspense novel, *Infected Be the Air* (Walker, 1991), and several historical novels.

Those familiar with Law and Anna Peters might try the work of Dorothy Dunnett, whose heroines also get involved in similar situations, the Tamara Hoyland novels of Jessica Mann, and the Mrs. Pollifax novels of Dorothy Gilman.

Lemarchand, Elizabeth. After retiring from a career as a school headmistress in England, Lemarchand embarked upon a second career as a crime writer. Her series of mysteries featuring Inspector Tom Pollard and Sergeant Gregory Toye of Scotland Yard began with the publication of *Death of an Old Girl* (London: Hart Davis, 1967; Walker, 1985). In this debut Lemarchand made excellent use of her considerable expertise in crafting an entertaining whodunit about the murder of an obnoxious "old girl," or alumna, of the Meldon School for Girls. Subsequent novels demonstrate a similar pattern; the two Yard men are called to various parts of England to take on cases somewhat beyond the ken of the local constabulary. *The Affacombe Affair* (London: Hart Davis, 1968; Walker, 1985) takes Pollard and Toye to a West Country village, and *Death on Doomsday* (London: Hart Davis, 1971; Walker, 1975) to the county of "Midshire" and murder in a stately home. Puzzles constructed in the classic Golden-Age vein are a hallmark of Lemarchand's work, and Pollard and Toye make an effective and engaging detective team, reminiscent in some ways of the team of Alleyn and Fox, created by the late Dame Ngaio Marsh.

Fans of Lemarchand might try the work of Ngaio Marsh, Catherine Aird, Marjorie Eccles, Patricia Moyes, and June Thomson.

Leon, Donna. Leon is an American who has lived for more than fifteen years in Venice, where she has taught English for the University of Maryland extension campus at a U.S. Air Force base. The setting of Leon's series of novels about policeman Guido Brunetti is the intriguing city of Venice, which Leon has woven so thoroughly into her novels that the city is as much a character in the books as are any of the people. Guido Brunetti is a principled, intelligent, and caring man, who has to steer his way carefully through the maze of Italian politics in order to see justice done. His wife comes from a very wealthy and prestigious Venetian family, and her connections are sometimes a hindrance, sometimes a help. In the first novel, *Death at La Fenice* (HarperCollins, 1992), which won Japan's prestigious Suntory Prize as best suspense novel of 1991, Brunetti is called to the renowned opera house, the Teatro la Fenice, to investigate the death of world-famous conductor-director Helmut Wellauer. In the second novel, *Death in a Strange Country* (HarperCollins, 1993), Brunetti is in charge of the investigation of the seemingly random murder of a young American from the nearby U.S. Air Force base. Leon uses the American military installation near Venice to give readers a glimpse of a setting rarely ever seen in most fiction.

Readers looking for other series with Italian settings should try the work of Magdalen Nabb, whose series is set in Florence. Other series that make effective use of setting are the York mysteries by Barbara Whitehead, the London series by Cynthia Harrod-Eagles, and the Australian books of Jennifer Rowe.

Linington, Elizabeth. With her various pseudonyms and numerous series of mysteries, the late Elizabeth Linington has legions of fans for her police procedurals. Under her own name, Linington, she began a series about policeman Ivor Maddox in *Greenmask!* (Harper & Row, 1964). The policemen in this series work out of the Hollywood section of the Los Angeles police force. As Lesley Egan, she created two series. The first Egan book, *A Case for Appeal* (Harper & Row, 1961) features policeman Vic Varallo and lawyer Jesse Falkenstein; both men went on to have their own separate series in subsequent books. Linington may be best known, though, under her pseudonym Dell Shannon, for the series featuring Lieutenant Luis Mendoza of the LAPD. Mendoza debuted in *Case Pending* (Harper & Row, 1960). Most of the books that Linington wrote share certain characteristics. She had rather an idealized view of the police; they were always the good guys. Readers won't find corruption in the LAPD in her novels. Also, Linington's cops do not get divorced, nor do they suffer from alcoholism, two fates which seem to befall many cops in the grittier police procedurals now in fashion. Despite this, Linington created characters whom readers came to know and care about, so that each new Linington, Egan, or Shannon promised further revelations about the lives of old and dear friends. In addition to her mysteries, Linington published a gothic suspense novel, *Nightmare* (Harper & Row, 1961), under the name Anne Blaisdell. A number of her books were published under the Blaisdell name in England. She also published several historical novels under various of her names.

Readers of the prolific Linington's series might find enjoyment with American writers J. A. Jance and Anne Wingate, who writes also as Lee Martin and Martha G. Webb, in addition to a number of the English writers of police procedurals, such as Dorothy Simpson, Marjorie Eccles, Clare Curzon, and Anthea Fraser.

Linscott, Gillian. Once a Parliamentary reporter for the BBC, Linscott now writes full-time. Her first mystery novel, *A*

Health Body (St. Martin, 1984), introduced ex-policeman Birdie Linnet, whose wife has left him for another man, one who can afford to take Birdie's former wife and his daughter on a trip to a holiday camp in France. Birdie follows them, and to his dismay, he discovers the camp is for nudists. Furthermore, he discovers his rival dead on the beach, and he must solve the murder to save his own skin. He appears in two further novels. With *Murder, I Presume* (St. Martin, 1990), Linscott penned her first historical mystery, revolving around British explorations in Africa after the death of David Livingstone. In *Sister Beneath the Sheet* (St. Martin, 1991), Linscott introduced Edwardian suffragette Nell Bray in an intriguing story about the murder of a fashionable courtesan in the resort town of Biarritz. Nell appears again in *Hanging on the Wire* (St. Martin, 1992), set in an unusual military hospital during the height of World War I. Linscott has a fine touch with setting, character, and plot. Nell Bray is perhaps her strongest creation, and Nell's political beliefs and the historical background against which she is portrayed are convincingly drawn.

Readers looking for mysteries set in the Victorian and Edwardian periods should try the works of Anne Perry, Carole Nelson Douglas, and Amy Myers. Those who have enjoyed Linscott's novels with contemporary settings might try the work of Paula Gosling or Lesley Grant-Adamson.

Livingston, Nancy. Connoisseurs of the humorous British mystery novel may place Livingston high on their must-read lists. Her series detective, retired tax inspector G. D. H. Pringle, on first glance seems a mild and singularly ineffective character. But those who have been on the receiving end of Mr. Pringle's expertise with both tax laws and crime know better. Along with his lady love, Mrs. Mavis Bignell, Mr. Pringle has ferreted out crime in numerous places, including England, Greece, Australia, and the United States. Mr. Pringle first appeared in *The Trouble at Aquitaine* (St. Martin, 1985). Two of his funniest adventures are *Death in a Distant Land* (St. Martin, 1989), which won an award for humor from the British Crime Writers' Association, and *Mayhem in Parva* (St. Martin, 1991), somewhat reminiscent of Colin Watson's devilishly offbeat novels. With *Death in Close-Up* (St. Martin, 1989), Livingston uses her own experiences as a production assistant in television land to offer a quirkily entertaining look at soap opera making, English style. Besides her mysteries, Livingston has written several historical novels.

Heron Carvic's Miss Seeton is another character who provides some of the funniest detection in crime fiction, and the series has been continued by Sarah J. Mason under the name Hamilton Crane. Less competent, but no less funny, than Mr. Pringle, is the late Joyce Porter's delightfully awful Inspector Dover. Readers might also enjoy the humor of Ruth Dudley Edwards and Gloria Dank.

Llewellyn, Caroline.   After the heyday of romantic suspense in the 1960s and 1970s, few besides the long-established practitioners (e.g., Victoria Holt, Mary Stewart, Phyllis A. Whitney, Barbara Michaels/Elizabeth Peters) are still writing in the genre. Llewellyn is an outstanding newcomer to the fold, and her three novels demonstrate a knack for suspense and an eye for setting that are reminiscent of Mary Stewart. Llewellyn's heroines are intelligent professional women who find themselves in dangerous circumstances through no fault of their own. Though they may have the assistance of an attractive male in extricating themselves from danger, they do so with courage, wit, and resourcefulness. *The Masks of Rome* (Scribner, 1988) is set in Rome during Carnival time, and *The Lady of the Labyrinth* (Scribner, 1990) is set in Sicily. Her latest novel, *Life Blood* (Scribner, 1993), is set in England. In all her work, Llewellyn makes effective use of setting.

Those who have read Llewellyn, but who are unfamiliar with Mary Stewart's early work, should look for such gems as *My Brother Michael* (Morrow, 1959) and *Nine Coaches Waiting* (Morrow, 1958). Also recommended are Velda Johnston, Elizabeth Peters, and Phyllis A. Whitney.

Logan, Margaret. In each of her mysteries, Logan satirizes her characters' social and work settings. The first book, *Death-ampton Summer* (Walker, 1988), is set on Long Island, with an elderly amateur sleuth, Tersh Trowbridge, investigating murder among his high society friends. Backbiting, adultery, gossip, and social climbing abound in this wealthy WASP enclave, along with sudden death by poison. In Logan's second book, *A Killing in Venture Capital* (Walker, 1989), Drew Lispenard, a venture capitalist, looks into the murder of his cousin's gay lover, a financial director of a biotechnology company. The setting is Boston, and Logan has created a high-tech, high-finance backdrop for her puzzle. Logan's third mystery, *C.A.T. Caper* (Walker, 1990), also takes place in Boston and its suburbs. This time she sets her mystery among troublesome teenagers and a group of English teachers who are responsible for correcting the College Aptitude Tests (obviously the SAT exams in disguise). The sleuth is high school English teacher Dodge Hackett, who tends to be sexist and politically incorrect. The victim is a shrill and ugly feminist who is universally disliked. Logan's novels have a strongly sardonic tone, and she takes aim at the contemporary icons of money, social status, and education.

Readers also may enjoy Barbara Paul, Annette Meyers, and Emma Lathen.

Lorens, M. K. Lorens's debut novel, *Sweet Narcissus* (Bantam, 1990), introduces one of the most eccentric, and oddly likable, casts of characters in current detective fiction. The centerpiece is Shakespeare professor Winston Marlowe Sherman, who writes mysteries of the Gilded Age as Henrietta Slocum about a character named Winchester Hyde. Winnie's longtime companion is Sarah Cromwell, a famous concert pianist, with whom he lives in Sarah's ancestral mansion in a small town not far from New York City. Sarah's younger brother David, much like a son to Winnie and Sarah, is a famous actor. Also part of the ménage is Winnie's retired colleague, Edward Merriman, who lives in one wing of the Cromwell mansion. Lorens's plots are generally complex, much in the traditional vein, but readers who adore unusual characters in their mystery novels will be fascinated by the adventures of Winnie Sherman and crew. The intensity of the emotions among the central characters in this series makes them seem startlingly real sometimes, eccentric though they be.

Readers who like the intense and eccentric characters of Lorens should try the work of P. M. Carlson, B. J. Oliphant (who writes also as A. J. Orde), Gallagher Gray, Mary Monica Pulver, and Kate Wilhelm, whose characters, though certainly less eccentric, are nevertheless intense and intriguing.

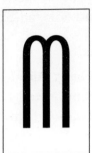

MacGregor, T. J./Janeshutz, Trish/Drake, Alison. Under three different names, this author has written three separate series of suspense thrillers set in south Florida. She began with two titles published under her unmarried name, Trish Janeshutz. In the first Janeshutz book, *In Shadow* (Ballantine, 1985), a killer stalks women on a Florida college campus, and this plot device is echoed in the recent MacGregor novel, *Spree* (Ballantine, 1992). As with other novels by this author, the occult is an integral plot element: The murder victim has developed a hallucinogenic drug that facilitates mind reading. The second series of books, written under the name Alison Drake, stars police detective Aline Scott. *Tango Key* (Ballantine, 1988), for example, is a lurid, brutal story of murder and smuggling set in the Florida keys. The third and most extensive series is written under the name T. J. MacGregor. In these books the sleuths are Quin St. James and Mike McCleary, who are married and partners in their own private eye firm. The novels are psychological suspense stories, with New Age and supernatural elements. *Death Flats* (Ballantine, 1991) depicts the murder of a psychologist who specializes in near-death experiences. A killer is stalking the widow, who is accused by the police of murdering her husband. The first MacGregor book is *Dark Fields* (Ballantine, 1986).

Other writers who may be of interest include Mary Higgins Clark, Wendy Hornsby, and Soledad Santiago.

MacLeod, Charlotte/Craig, Alisa. Under her own name, MacLeod writes two series of novels. One is set in Boston, with amateur sleuth Sarah Kelling and investigator Max Bittersohn, and the entire blue-blooded, eccentric Kelling clan as a supporting cast. The second series is set in rural Balaclava County, Massachusetts with a set of oddball academics from Balaclava Agricultural College, led by Professor Peter Shandy and his librarian wife Helen Marsh Shandy. MacLeod's work is humorous, often gently satirical, and imaginative. Her strong points are character development, a fondness for the stranger byways of the English language, and a charming New England setting. A few of the novels incorporate fantasy elements into their settings; the most unearthly of these is *Curse of the Giant Hogweed* (Doubleday, 1985).

MacLeod also writes two series of Canadian mysteries under the pseudonym of Alisa Craig. The Grub-and-Stakers series recounts the dizzy adventures of the Grub-and-Stake Gardening and Roving Club, in Lobelia Falls, Ontario. The chief characters include homemaker Dittany Henbit Monk, her husband Osbert Monk, who is a writer of Westerns, and his aunt Arethusa, a writer of swashbuckling romances. The second series of mysteries focuses on Royal Canadian Mounted Police officer Madoc Rhys, his wife Janet, and the eccentric, Welsh, and musical Rhys family.

The Family Vault (Doubleday, 1979) is the first Sarah Kelling book; *Rest You Merry* (Doubleday, 1978), one of the funniest ever Christmas mysteries, is the first Peter Shandy novel. The opening Grub-and-Stakers novel is *The Grub-and-Stakers Move a Mountain* (Doubleday, 1981); the first Madoc Rhys is *A Pint of Murder* (Doubleday, 1980). *The Corpse in Oozak's Pond* (Mysterious, 1987), a

Peter Shandy mystery, was nominated for an Edgar Award in 1987.

Readers who like Charlotte MacLeod also may enjoy Jane Langton, whose style is more literary but equally charming; Dorothy Cannell; Nancy Pickard's New England stories with Jenny Cain; Carolyn G. Hart; and Phoebe Atwood Taylor's Asey Mayo mysteries set on Cape Cod.

Mann, Jessica.   With degrees in archaeology and Anglo-Saxon from Cambridge University, Mann made both her women series characters archaeologists as well. The first of these is Professor Thea Crawford, who debuts in *Troublecross* (McKay Washburn, 1972; as *The Only Security* in England). Thea Crawford and her journalist husband Sylvester appear as the main characters in one other novel, and thereafter they often appear as minor characters in novels featuring Mann's second series detective, Tamara Hoyland, who was once one of Thea's students. Tamara first appears as a minor character in *Funeral Sites* (Doubleday, 1982), in which she aids a woman running from a vicious brother-in-law with political ambitions. Later, Tamara is recruited to work in the mysterious Department E as a spy, though she continues her work as an archaeologist for the Royal Commission on Historical Monuments as a cover. The plots often involve archaeology, English history, and politics. Tamara Hoyland is intelligent, tough, and efficient; she does not hesitate to kill in the line of duty. The stories featuring her are fast-paced, believable, and suspenseful. In addition to her crime novels, Mann has also written a valuable critical study, *Deadlier Than the Male* (Macmillan, 1981), which examines the work of English writers Margery Allingham, Agatha Christie, Ngaio Marsh, Dorothy L. Sayers, and Josephine Tey.

Fans of Jessica Mann might also enjoy the exploits of Dorothy Gilman's Mrs. Pollifax, an American spy, though there are considerable attitudinal and age differences. Otherwise, readers might try the works of Margot Arnold, Dorothy Dunnett, Paula Gosling, Liza Cody, and Susan Moody.

Maron, Margaret.   Maron has two series characters, cop Sigrid Harald and lawyer Deborah Knott. Harald, Maron's first character, features in a series of police procedurals in the traditional vein set in New York City; her debut was in the novel *One Coffee With* (Raven House/Worldwide, 1981). Knott, whose first novel-length appearance is the recent Agatha- and Edgar-winning *Bootlegger's Daughter* (Mysterious, 1992), lives and works in North Carolina, Maron's own home ground. Sigrid Harald is a tightly sealed-up character, efficient and seemingly emotionless as the series opens, but as the books progress, Sigrid slowly becomes less uninvolved with those around her, largely thanks to a relationship with a character introduced in the first book of the series. This series is a textbook example of how a writer can use a series for a natural and interesting development of a character who continues to grow and change. With Deborah Knott, Maron uses a different voice, writing in the first person, and through Deborah, Maron achieves perhaps her best work to date. The Southern setting seems effortlessly realized, and the dialogue is pitch-perfect. Maron won an Agatha Award for the story "Deborah's Judgment" in the collection *A Woman's Eye* (Delacorte, 1991), Deborah's debut.

For other series female police officers, try Lillian O'Donnell's novels about Norah Mulcahany; Erica Quest's novels about DCI Kate Maddox, Jennie Melville's long-running series about Charmian Daniels, or Susan Dunlap's funny series about Berkeley cop Jill Smith. Other writers of Southern mysteries are Sharyn McCrumb, Charlaine Harris, and Celestine Sibley.

Martin, Lee.   See **Wingate, Anne.**

Mason, Sarah J.   At the moment, Mason is perhaps better known by her pseudonym, Hamilton Crane, under which she has been continuing the Miss Seeton novels of the late Heron Carvic. Before his death in 1980, Carvic penned five novels about the English spinster Emily Dorothea Seeton, retired teacher of art and slightly unworldly catalyst of crime-solving. Hampton Charles wrote three novels more in the series before Mason took the helm as Hamilton Crane, and the series continues apace. Crane's first is *Miss Seeton Cracks the Case* (Berkley, 1991). The small village of Plummergen, with its eccentricities and gossip-mongering, much of it revolving around poor Miss Seeton, lives on, and Miss Seeton continues to be involved in humorous criminous escapades. With her umbrella firmly in hand, the "Battling Brolly" crosses paths with criminals, never quite realizing just how lethal a secret weapon she continues to be in the unorthodox arsenal of Chief Superintendent Delphick of Scotland Yard. Mason's sprightly style, with its attention to the oddities and quirks of the language, is well-suited to the unusual Miss Seeton. Under her own name, Mason wrote *Let's Talk of Wills* (St. Martin, 1985), a mystery in the traditional English vein. Beginning with *Murder in the Maze* (Berkley, 1993), Mason begins a second series featuring Detective Superintendent Trewley and Sergeant Stone of the Allingham constabulary. Many of the same qualities which are present in the Seeton books are present in this new series as well. Those with a taste for the eccentric English mystery novel will find Mason/Crane just their cup of tea.

Those who have enjoyed Mason's Miss Seeton novels might try the work of the late Gladys Mitchell, whose Dame Beatrice Bradley remains one of the most eccentric of all English detectives. Other suggestions are the work of writers like Catherine Aird, Marian Babson, Marjorie Eccles, Ann Cleeves, Anthea Fraser, or Nancy Livingston, whose Mr. Pringle books also feature that special brand of English humor.

Matera, Lia. Matera writes two series: one with Willa Jansson and one with Laura Di Palma, both of whom are San Francisco attorneys. Willa is the mixed-up daughter of aging leftist protesters who are still going strong, and she continues to live and work in her parents' milieu. She has a clear voice of her own, full of sardonic remarks about the political posturings of both left and right. We follow her through law school, first job, and then subsequent jobs, in all of which she becomes involved with murder. (Willa starts to worry about being Homicide Mary, as she is on the scene of so many killings.) The murders are investigated by Lt. Don Surgelato of the San Francisco Police Department, with whom Willa spars verbally.

Laura Di Palma is another kettle of fish: She is a high-powered defense attorney with a barracuda courtroom style. Di Palma can be an unlikable character, especially when she seems to be mired in materialism and the demands of her career. But her moments of self-awareness and honesty, coupled with her legal expertise, bring her alive for the reader. Matera is wonderful at skewering pretension and presenting eighties and nineties lifestyles with a strong, dry wit.

The first Willa Jansson novel is *Where Lawyers Fear to Tread* (Bantam, 1987); the first Laura Di Palma is *The Smart Money* (Bantam, 1988). Matera was nominated for Edgar Awards for *A Radical Departure* (Bantam, 1988) and *Prior Convictions* (Simon & Schuster, 1991).

Another wry look at the legal profession (British style) is offered by Sarah Caudwell. Readers may also enjoy Susan Wolfe's San Francisco legal mystery *The Last Billable Hour* (St. Martin, 1989) and the legal mysteries written by Carolyn Wheat, Chelsea Quinn Yarbro, and Janet L. Smith.

Matteson, Stefanie. Matteson has written a series of traditional mysteries starring Charlotte Graham, a noted Oscar-winning film and stage actress who lives in New York City. Charlotte is a finely detailed character who may remind the reader of Katharine Hepburn or Bette Davis. As well as being intelligent and observant in her sleuthing, Charlotte is a movie star of the old school: elegant, aristocratic, and strong-willed.

The first book, *Murder at the Spa* (Charter/Diamond, 1990), is set at a chic spa in upstate New York, where a client is murdered during treatment. Matteson provides a detailed background of the operations of a health spa, and she recounts the history of American spas as part of her scene-setting. *Murder at Teatime* (Diamond, 1991) is set on a secluded island off the coast of Maine; this novel includes plenty of herbal lore and information on rare books, especially early herbals. *Murder on the Cliff* (Diamond, 1991) takes place in Newport, Rhode Island and *Murder on the Silk Road* (Diamond, 1992) takes Charlotte to China for further adventures. These novels are notable for the research that Matteson has done to provide detailed backgrounds for each, and her skill in weaving her research into lively, interesting backdrops for her classic plots.

Other writers who portray active elderly sleuths include Kate Morgan, Virginia Rich, Dorothy Gilman, and Mary Bowen Hall.

Maxwell, A. E. (Ann and Evan). The Maxwells write fast, witty, and sharp suspense/action novels with philosophical undertones. The setting is southern California; the heroes are Fiddler and his brilliant ex-wife Fiora Flynn, an investment banker. They are assisted by Benny Speidel, Fiddler's buddy from Vietnam days, who is an electronics genius in a wheelchair and a setter of fiendish traps for bad guys. Fiddler is independently wealthy, so he is able to help people in trouble for free—but mostly for the excitement of the hunt and the violence. Fiora, of course, knows all the money angles and scams used by con men and international criminals. Fiddler got his wealth from a steamer trunk of used drug money left by his Uncle Jake, a drug runner; he says he got his taste for "the adrenaline life, the outlaw life" from him, too. The action in these novels zooms along as fast as Fiddler's Shelby Cobra sports car.

The first Fiddler and Fiora novel is *Just Another Day in Paradise* (Doubleday, 1985). Science fiction and romantic suspense novels appear under the name of Ann Maxwell, and Ann publishes romance novels under the pseudonym, Elizabeth Lowell.

The landscape and people of Orange County, California are also evoked in the mysteries of Jean Femling, Wendy Hornsby, and Maxine O'Callaghan.

McCafferty, Taylor. The small town of Pigeon Fork, Kentucky, is the venue for McCafferty's series of novels about Haskell Blevins, private eye. Though some residents of the town insist rather rudely that Haskell reminds them of Howdy Doody, Haskell himself can't see the resemblance, despite his red hair and freckles. Haskell grew up in Pigeon Fork, spent eight years as a cop in Louisville, then returned home after a divorce and job burnout to become a private eye in this town of about eleven hundred. In between cases, Haskell helps out his brother Elmo in his drugstore in return for office space above the drugstore. Haskell does a lot of this, since Pigeon Fork often seems not to have a pressing need for a private eye. The series begins with *Pet Peeves* (Pocket, 1990), in which Haskell investigates the problem of who killed an elderly lady, along with her parakeet and her cat. Delving into the case, Haskell discovers just how many secrets a small town can try to hide. McCafferty handles her small-town setting with ease and skill and describes her characters with affectionate humor. Haskell narrates his doings in a style reminiscent of his harder-boiled brethren, but overall the feel of this series is much cozier than the series of male PI writers. After all, a guy who has a dog with a phobia about stairs can't be all that hard-boiled.

Readers who have enjoyed McCafferty and her Southern settings might try the work of Deborah Adams, Kay Hooper, Sharyn McCrumb, or Mignon F. Ballard.

McConnell, Vicki P. Nyla Wade, a journalist and a lesbian, is the detective in McConnell's mystery novels. In her debut, *Mrs. Porter's Letter* (Naiad, 1982), Nyla, fresh from a divorce, has obtained a new job and a new life. She buys an old desk for her new apartment, and in the desk she discovers some mysterious love letters. These letters set her off on a quest of discovery, both of herself and of the writers of the letters. In *The Burnton Widows* (Naiad, 1984), Nyla has left Denver, her home base in the previous novel, for the Oregon coast. The third novel, *Double Daughter* (Naiad, 1988), finds Nyla back in Denver, where she investigates vicious assaults against gay teachers. Nyla Wade is compassionate and loyal, and her feminist beliefs are central to her character. McConnell spices the narrative with occasional, discreetly explicit sex scenes.

Readers interested in other lesbian/feminist detectives might try the work of Val McDermid, Barbara Wilson, Katherine V. Forrest, and Claire McNab. Barbara D'Amato, Mickey Friedman, and Sarah Shankman all have detectives who are journalists.

McCrumb, Sharyn. McCrumb is a wise and witty voice in contemporary mystery writing. She writes a series of books about forensic anthropologist Elizabeth MacPherson; a mystery–science fiction series with professors James Owen Mega (aka sci-fi author Jay Omega) and Marion Farley; and a third series of Appalachian novels with Sheriff Spencer Arrowood. The MacPherson books are the lightest in tone; although Elizabeth solves murders with her forensic knowledge, she also can succumb to imbecility in the expectation of attending a Royal garden party in *The Windsor Knot* (Ballantine, 1990). *Missing Susan* (Ballantine, 1991) is a funny tale of an accident-plagued bus trip through England, during which the guide keeps trying to kill an obnoxious tourist—and keeps missing her. The first Elizabeth MacPherson novel is *Sick of Shadows* (Avon, 1984).

In McCrumb's Jay Omega series, the Edgar Award–winning *Bimbos of the Death Sun* (TSR, 1988) is a bitingly hilarious satire of science fiction conventions; its sequel, *Zombies of the Gene Pool* (Simon & Schuster, 1992), is a more sober and thoughtful exploration of science fiction fans and their self-enclosed world.

In recent years, McCrumb has concentrated increasingly on

presenting acutely observed Appalachian backgrounds to her novels. *If Ever I Return, Pretty Peggy-O* (Scribner, 1990) begins her explorations of Appalachian life and mythology, and it is a splendid expansion of McCrumb's strength as a writer. *The Hangman's Beautiful Daughter* (Scribner, 1992) showcases McCrumb's full force as an elegant and powerful writer. In all of her mysteries, McCrumb makes trenchant observations on human behavior and thought patterns. Her writing is increasingly perceptive and lyrical; she has certainly matured as a writer with each book.

Other mystery writers that readers may enjoy include Joan Hess (for humor), Nancy Pickard, Margaret Maron, and Elizabeth Peters. Peters's novel *Naked Once More* (Warner, 1989) is also set in a sympathetically rendered Appalachia.

McDermid, Val. English journalist McDermid has created two separate series of mysteries. The first features journalist Lindsay Gordon, who, in her own words, is "a cynical socialist lesbian feminist." In her debut, *Report for Murder* (St. Martin, 1990), Lindsay finds herself embroiled in a murder in a girls' school, a bastion of privilege, which is just the type of setting Lindsay despises most. But Lindsay needs the work of writing a feature article about the school, so she goes for a weekend. Murder occurs, an old friend of Lindsay's is arrested, and Lindsay solves the crime. Lindsay reappears in *Open and Shut* (St. Martin, 1991), which is set in Glasgow. Lindsay is much as she describes herself, and McDermid weaves the politics of feminism and alternative lifestyles into her novels compellingly. With *Dead Beat* (St. Martin, 1993), McDermid introduces Manchester-based private eye Kate Brannigan. Kate lives next door to her lover, rock music journalist Richard Barclay. When a rock star, an old friend of Richard's, asks Kate to find an important person from his past, Kate has little idea that murder will be the result. Kate, like Lindsay, is intelligent, resourceful, and independent. Readers looking for strong women characters will find McDermid of great interest.

Other writers of series with lesbian detectives include Katherine V. Forrest, Sandra Scoppettone, Vicki P. McConnell (whose character Nyla Wade is also a journalist), Barbara Wilson, J. M. Redmann, and Pat Welch. Readers interested in other journalist detectives might try the series of Sarah Shankman, Lesley Grant-Adamson, and Annette Roome.

McGown, Jill.   Thanks to her standout police procedurals, McGown is fast earning an excellent critical reputation. Beginning with the enjoyable *A Perfect Match* (St. Martin, 1983), McGown has written, to date, five novels featuring the police detectives Lloyd (who maddeningly refuses to divulge his first name) and Judy Hill, his partner and lover. The relationship of Lloyd and Hill serves in these novels as an interesting counterpoint to the mystery plots, and McGown handles the relationship with skill, avoiding the clichés that some writers fall into with their series characters. The mystery plots of McGown's novels, moreover, are a marvelous fusion of the intricately knitted classic English school and the fully fleshed character novels of contemporary mystery fiction. For example, *Gone to Her Death* (St. Martin, 1990; *Death of a Dancer* in England) utilizes the setting of an English public school to great effect. McGown takes the conventions of the traditional English mystery and gives them a thoroughly modern interpretation. In addition to the Lloyd and Hill series, McGown has produced a number of suspense novels with memorable characters and settings, such as *The Stalking Horse* (St. Martin, 1988). These works feature excellent puzzles as well. McGown has recently published a novel as Elizabeth Chaplin, titled *Hostage to Fortune* (Mysterious, 1993), which is much like her nonseries novels as Jill McGown.

Those who have sampled McGown and liked her work should also consider the work of Frances Fyfield, Susan B. Kelly, Cynthia Harrod-Eagles, Jennie Melville, Sheila Radley, and Paula Gosling.

McNab, Claire.   McNab writes a series that features Detective Inspector Carol Ashton and is set in Sydney, Australia. Ashton is a blond, beautiful lesbian who is divorced and has a son. In the first mystery, *Lessons in Murder* (Naiad, 1988), a high school shop teacher has been killed by a Black & Decker drill driven through his skull. Carol is in charge of the investigation, and she falls in love with a suspect, Sybil Quade, who has always been heterosexual. *Cop Out* (Naiad, 1991) finds Ashton investigating the murder of Bryce Darcy, a member of an influential and wealthy local family. It is generally assumed that his sister, Charlotte, killed him. But Charlotte's confession is suspect because she is hooked on amphetamines. Ashton and Detective Sergeant Mark Bourke uncover family secrets and hidden animosities in their search for the truth. McNab's mysteries are mixtures of police procedurals and classic cozies, with some graphic sex scenes as well.

Katherine V. Forrest, Mary Wings, Lauren Wright Douglas, and Sandra Scoppettone write about lesbian detectives. Jennifer Rowe and Kerry Greenwood also set mysteries in Australia.

Meek, M. R. D.   A retired solicitor, Meek brings her knowledge of the law and the legal life to a series starring lawyer Lennox Kemp. In his American debut, *Hang the Consequences* (Scribner, 1985), Kemp is disbarred and working for McCready's Detective Agency. An earlier novel, *With Flowers That Fell* (Hale, 1983), not published in the United States, apparently tells the story behind Kemp's disbarment. In the next book in the series, however, Kemp has been reinstated at the bar, and the murders with which he becomes involved thereafter generally begin somehow with one of his legal cases. Meek, though British, displays an obvious affection for American detective fiction in her work, for the wry and cynical Kemp often has more in common with Archie Goodwin or Lew Archer than with Peter Wimsey or Hercule Poirot. Meek's prose is spare, yet often elegant, and her observations of the human character are penetrating and compassionate. This is a series rich in character, an especial treat for those who value characterization, as well as clever puzzles, which Meek also handles with dexterity.

Like Meek, Frances Fyfield uses her legal expertise to create an authentic background for her characters. Hannah Wakefield has recently begun a new series about a woman lawyer in London. Readers looking for other enjoyable English legal mysteries might try the work of the late Sara Woods, the series by E. X. Giroux, Janet L. Smith's series, or the funny and cleverly plotted novels by the late Anthony Gilbert, starring the unforgettable Cockney lawyer, Arthur Crook.

Melville, Jennie. See **Butler, Gwendoline.**

Meredith, D. R. The D stands for Doris. Meredith, a former librarian and bookseller, lives in Amarillo, Texas, and she has claimed the Texas Panhandle as her own in two mystery series. The first features Sheriff Charles Matthews of mythical Crawford County, Texas. In *The Sheriff and the Panhandle Murders* (Walker, 1984), Matthews investigates the case of the murders of a good ol' boy and a beautiful young Hispanic woman. Matthews is honest and courageous, a good man to have on your side. Meredith's second series is set in the real town of Canadian, Texas, near Amarillo, but her characters are fictional. The star of the series is lawyer John Lloyd Branson, a forceful, intense, and intelligent man who is a little like a Peter Wimsey in a bolo tie. Branson's assistant is Lydia Fairchild, a law student from Southern Methodist University in Dallas. Amid the solving of crimes, as in *Murder by Impulse* (Ballantine, 1987), the first in the series, John Lloyd and Lydia fight a wary but insistent attraction to each other. John Lloyd is a true Texas-style character, slightly outrageous in everything he does. Meredith has a grand time inviting the reader to have a sly laugh along with her as she involves John Lloyd and Lydia in intriguing and cleverly constructed plots. Meredith depicts with a loving eye her corner of the world, and between them, Charles Matthews and John Lloyd Branson do their best to keep the Panhandle a law-abiding area.

Readers who like their mysteries Southwestern-style might try the work of Susan Rogers Cooper, Lee Martin, and Mary Willis Walker. Jean Hager and Eve K. Sandstrom also use the Southwest, namely Oklahoma, to good effect in their series.

Mertz, Barbara. See **Peters, Elizabeth.**

Meyers, Annette/Meyers, Maan. Annette Meyers writes a series of novels with Wall Street headhunters Xenia Smith and Leslie Wetzon. Smith is a shallow, greedy, manipulative yuppie; Wetzon is a former chorus dancer and is warm, caring, and loyal. Wetzon is an amateur sleuth and the real star of the stories, and the reader (along with Wetzon herself) continually wonders why she puts up with Smith. As well as creating memorable characters in her mismatched duo, Meyers has devised vibrant settings in the diverse neighborhoods of New York City for her mysteries. The first Smith and Wetzon novel is *The Big Killing* (Bantam, 1989). The plots of the mysteries revolve around stockbroking and financial malfeasance, and Meyers brings an insider's view to her accounts of white-collar crime in the eighties and nineties.

Annette Meyers and her husband, Martin Meyers, also have written *The Dutchman* (Doubleday, 1992), under the name of Maan Meyers. The protagonist is Tonneman, the schout, or sheriff, for the community of New Amsterdam in 1664. He uncovers a murder that brings him into contact with Racqel Mendoza, a beautiful Jewish widow. This is the first novel in a projected series of mysteries set in historic New York.

Readers who appreciate Meyers might like Emma Lathen, the dean of financial mystery writers; A. E. Maxwell, who writes knowledgeably about banker Fiora Flynn; and Margaret Logan. Evelyn E. Smith, Kerry Tucker, and Carole Berry also bring the city of New York to life in their idiosyncratic crime novels.

Meyers, Maan. See **Meyers, Annette.**

Michaels, Barbara. See **Peters, Elizabeth.**

Millar, Margaret. The Canadian-born Millar grew up to become half of one of the world's most famous husband-and-wife teams. The late Kenneth Millar, perhaps better known as Ross MacDonald, actually turned to writing crime fiction after seeing the success of his wife. Margaret Millar began her career with three novels in the conventional detective vein featuring psychiatrist Dr. Paul Prye (beginning with *The Invisible Worm,* Doubleday, 1941). Prye's whimsical name is evidence of his creator's sense of humor, which is an underlying element in even the most hair-raising of her novels. Soon, however, Millar abandoned the detective story and concentrated on the mystery novel, and with such tales she found her greatest success. A prime example is the Edgar-winning *Beast in View* (Random House, 1955), often imitated, but never with the level of skill Millar brings to her work. Millar starts with some unusual event, a disappearance, a murder, a crime of some sort, then weaves a subtle tale of menace and suspense. Often the reader is never quite certain whodunit or whydunit until the last line of the novel. *The Listening Walls* (Random House, 1959) demonstrates this powerful technique beautifully. Late in her career, Millar created a new series character, the young Chicano lawyer Tom Aragon, who debuted in *Ask for Me Tomorrow* (Random House, 1976). Intelligent, compassionate, with a strong streak of unconventional humor, Aragon is an appealing sleuth. Standouts among the Millar oeuvre are *The Murder of Miranda* (Random House, 1979), *Beyond This Point Are Monsters* (Random House, 1970), and *How Like an Angel* (Random House, 1962). For her continued excellence in the field, Millar was named a Grand Master by the Mystery Writers of America in 1983.

Those who have enjoyed the work of Margaret Millar might try the psychological suspense novels of Ruth Rendell/Barbara Vine, Margaret Yorke, Rosamond Smith, Minette Walters, Anna Clarke, and Frances Hegarty.

Mills, D. F. Mills writes compelling novels of suspense that would have been called, once upon a time, romantic suspense. But in Mills's case, the emphasis in her work is definitely on the suspense, with romance only a small part of the entire picture. Mills takes women, often with some great difficulty to overcome, puts them into trying and terrifying situations, and lets the reader sweat to see how things will turn out. In *Deadline* (Diamond, 1991), the heroine is a writer, Tess Alexander, who is becoming well-known for her true crime works. She is asked by a former governor of Texas to write the true story of his innocence in the arson deaths of his wife, daughter, and grandchild. Tess agrees to write the book, on her own terms, though, and soon she is plunged into a terrifying situation that forces her to confront long-buried secrets in her own past. Another novel, *Freefall* (Diamond, 1992), offers an intriguing twist on the heroine-with-amnesia convention. Mills creates believable and often scary situations in her novels, which most readers will want to devour in a single sitting. Her first novel was *Darkroom* (Charter/Diamond, 1990).

Fans of the suspense novel are certainly acquainted with the current American queen of suspense, Mary Higgins Clark. Other suspense novelists of interest are Barbara Michaels, Phyllis A. Whitney, Judith Kelman, and Velda Johnston.

Mitchell, Kay. A former nurse and health visitor in England, Mitchell has lately turned her talents to writing crime fiction. Her series character is Chief Inspector John Morrissey of Malminster CID. In the first novel of the series, *A Lively Form of Death* (St. Martin, 1991) Morrissey investigates a death by poisoning in the nearby village of Little Henge, which is rife with secrets and seething passions. Mitchell's territory is in many ways the conventional English village of the traditional crime story, but though her work might appear cozy from a cursory look, the novels have thus far included crimes that were beyond the pale in the Golden Age. Mitchell has updated the cozy, old-fashioned English murder mystery in an effective and entertaining way. Her second novel, *In Stony Places* (St. Martin, 1992), demonstrates that a serial-killer book need not be gory and nasty to be suspenseful. Along with a number of other English women writing today, Mitchell shows that there is considerable life in a venerable form of entertainment.

Readers who have enjoyed Mitchell might try the work of Pat Burden, Ann Granger, Susan B. Kelly, and Erica Quest.

Moffat, Gwen. Landscape is an important component in the work of Moffat, for her series character, Miss Melinda Pink, is a dedicated mountaineer. Since her debut in *Lady with a Cool Eye* (Gollancz, 1973), Miss Pink has combined mountain climbing with sleuthing in twelve novels, about half of which have been published in the United States. In addition to her climbing, Miss Pink also finds the time to serve as a magistrate and to write novels. The settings of the books always involve mountain regions, either in Great Britain or the United States. In a number of her more recent works, such as *The Stone Hawk* (St. Martin, 1989) and *Rage* (St. Martin, 1990), Miss Pink has visited Utah canyon country and California, respectively. Miss Pink faces physical danger and harsh conditions with great equanimity, and she offers the reader her opinions, as a matter of course, on many issues regarding the environment. Moffat is a distinctive writer with a woman series character not quite like any other in mystery fiction.

Those acquainted with Miss Pink might enjoy the work of Judith Van Gieson, for whom environmental concerns form an important thread in her books. Otherwise, readers might look for the out-of-print works by Glyn Carr, whose character, Sir Abercrombie Lewker, is also a climber of distinction.

Monfredo, Miriam Grace. A writer and former librarian who lives in western New York State, Monfredo has utilized her interest in the history of her area to produce an unusual series set in nineteenth-century New York State. The central character of the series is Glynis Tryon, librarian in the city of Seneca Falls.

Determining early on that she wasn't too keen on the yoke of marriage, Glynis sets her sights on having a career at a time when very few women had such ideas. Her budding feminist ideas get her involved with Elizabeth Cady Stanton and the meeting on women's rights that was held in Seneca Falls in 1848. Around this historic occasion, Monfredo has fashioned an entertaining murder mystery with *Seneca Falls Inheritance* (St. Martin, 1992), which was an Agatha and Macavity nominee for Best First Novel. By the time of the second novel in the series, *North Star Conspiracy* (St. Martin, 1993), the time is 1854, and Monfredo wraps her tale around the story of the Underground Railroad. Though Glynis is determined to remain independent, the town constable Cullen Stuart has set his sights on making Glynis his wife, and their relationship adds emotional depth to an intriguing series. Readers looking for a satisfying blend of historical fiction and mystery novel will find Monfredo a welcome discovery.

Those acquainted with Glynis Tryon should try the work of Anne Perry and Amy Myers, who write about England of the nineteenth century. Also, readers might find Gillian Linscott's novels about Edwardian suffragette Nell Bray of interest because of the interest in women's rights. The other librarian detectives are all twentieth-century, in the Jacqueline Kirby novels of Elizabeth Peters, the work of Kate Morgan, Charlaine Harris, and L. R. Wright.

Moody, Susan. British writer Susan Moody has created a series of mysteries starring Penny Wanawake, a black amateur investigator. Penny is the daughter of an African ambassador and a titled Englishwoman; she is six feet tall, outspoken, and a talented photographer. She and her lover, Barnaby Midas, an antique dealer and jewelry thief, have set up a scam in which he steals jewels from the rich, and they give the proceeds to feed famine victims in Africa. Penny is beautiful and flippant, with an active sex life in these novels. In the first book in the series, *Penny Black* (Fawcett, 1984), Penny's school friend, Marfa Lund, is murdered in a bathroom at Los Angeles Airport. Penny's investigation of her death takes her to Washington, D.C. and California. In *Penny Pinching* (Fawcett, 1989), a murder victim who looks just like Penny is deposited on her doorstep in California. *Penny Dreadful* (Ballantine, 1986) is set in Canterbury, England, and revolves around the killing of an obnoxious thriller writer. The Penny Wanawake books are tongue-in-cheek and lively, with a distinctly wry wit.

Moody also has written a romantic suspense novel, *Mosaic* (Delacorte, 1991), and a thriller about the kidnapping of a baby, *Hush-a-bye* (London: Macdonald, 1991).

Readers who enjoy flippant heroines may want to try mysteries by Carole Berry, Liza Cody, Dorothy Dunnett, Marissa Piesman, and Natasha Cooper. Kerry Tucker writes a series of crime novels with a photographer character, Libby Kincaid.

Morgan, Kate. Morgan is a pseudonym for Ann Hamilton Whitman. Her cozy mysteries, published as paperback originals, feature Dewey James as an amateur sleuth. Dewey is an elderly librarian who is the widow of a police chief. She is known in her hometown of Hamilton as an eccentric who quotes endlessly from literary classics. The setting for most of the novels is a typical small town, and Dewey is an updated American version of Miss Marple, with a fund of sharp observations on local behavior. In the first book in the series, *A Slay at the Races* (Berkley, 1990), Dewey, in a neighbor's stable, finds a dead banker under the hooves of a racehorse. In *Days of Crime and Roses* (Berkley, 1992), she goes to New York City to visit an old friend. There she inevitably finds murder at an arts foundation, where her friend is on the board. Dewey's investigations often involve her old friend and suitor George Farnham, and the current Hamilton police captain Fielding Booker. Morgan gives her readers cozy mysteries, with time-honored elements like the traditional denouement where suspects are gathered together in one room to establish who's guilty.

Stefanie Matteson, Mary Bowen Hall, and Corinne Holt Sawyer write American cozies with elderly sleuths.

Morice, Anne. The late Felicity Shaw, who wrote crime novels as Ann Morice, was a playwright, and her skill with dialogue and dramatic pacing is evident in the long-running series about actress Theresa "Tessa" Crichton. In the first of the series, *Death in the Grand Manor* (London: Macmillan, 1970), Tessa is still in the early stages of her career when she encounters her first murder. Morice here introduces several of the characters who are regulars in the series: Tessa's eccentric cousin Toby Crichton, a well-known playwright; Toby's daughter, Ellen; and Robin Price, a detective inspector who has become Tessa's husband by the second book, *Murder in Married Life* (London: Macmillan, 1971). The novels are narrated in the first person by Tessa, and the dialogue, as well as Tessa's observations, can be sharp, witty, and insightful. Tessa's career generally offers the situations in which she encounters murders; an excellent example of this is *Death in the Round* (St. Martin, 1980), where murder occurs in a repertory company Tessa has briefly joined. Witty and elegant in style, Morice and her creation are enjoyable reading for those who like their murders mixed with the performing arts. Two of Morice's last three novels, *Design for Dying* (St. Martin, 1988) and *Planning for Murder* (St. Martin, 1990), do not feature Tessa.

Fans of Anne Morice might try the Charles Paris novels of Simon Brett and the series by American writer Jane Dentinger, as well as the theatrical mysteries of the late Dame Ngaio Marsh. P. M. Carlson has often made use of theatrical settings in her Maggie Ryan series.

Morison, B. J. Maine native Morison has created one of the more unusual series characters to grace the pages of an adult mystery novel. Elizabeth Lamb Worthington, the star of these books, is eight years old when the series begins with *Champagne and a Gardener* (Thorndike Press, 1982); the time is the early 1970s, for Nixon is still President. Elizabeth Lamb (as she is called by her family) and her mother have come to Mount Desert Island, off the coast of Maine, after living for a number of years in Europe, while her father, scion of an old Maine family, was off in South America trying to revive his fortunes. Her continental experiences, along with her own natural intelligence, have combined to give Elizabeth Lamb a perspicacity unnerving, even downright terrifying, to many of the adults around her. Through the course of the series, Elizabeth Lamb has aged to thirteen in the latest installment, *The Martini Effect* (North Country Press, 1992). Morison has penned a distinctive series, which is as much modern comedy of manners as murder mystery, for she delights in skewering the pretensions of the rich. The series is chock-full of information about the history and society of the inhabitants of Mount Desert Island and Bar Harbor.

Readers looking for more murder Down East should try the work of J. S. Borthwick and Susan Kenney. For more general New England settings, Sally Gunning, Charlotte MacLeod, and Phoebe Atwood Taylor all have series set in Massachusetts.

Moyes, Patricia. An accident while on a skiing holiday led Moyes to write her first mystery novel, and though Moyes may not have spent her holiday entirely as planned, this fortuitous accident witnessed the birth of a distinguished career in the mystery field. This first novel, titled, aptly enough, *Dead Men Don't Ski* (Rinehart, 1960), introduced Scotland Yard Inspector Henry Tibbett and his good-natured wife Emmy, who are on a skiing holiday in the Italian Alps. For more than three decades now Moyes has delighted fans of the traditional English mystery with her dazzling combination of razor-sharp wit, complex plots, and the knack for describing unusual settings vividly. Henry Tibbett is one of those who has a true nose for crime, and he has learned never to ignore his hunches, which have brought him success and recognition at Scotland Yard. Moyes also has a keen sense of humor and a talent for picking out the unusual, as evidenced by the engaging Manciple family, the centerpiece of two novels, *Murder Fantastical* (Holt, Rinehart, Winston, 1987) and *A Six-Letter Word for Death* (Holt, Rinehart, Winston, 1983). In *Johnny Under Ground* (Holt, Rinehart, Winston, 1965), Moyes tells a poignant tale of Emmy's reunion with some of her World War II Air Force buddies, and the easygoing Emmy proves as engaging a character as her husband. The Moyes books also offer a variety of settings, such as Switzerland, Holland, Washington, D.C., and the Caribbean, where Moyes now lives with her husband.

Those who enjoy the classic touch of Moyes might try the work of Marian Babson and Sarah Caudwell, both of whom infuse their works with their highly individual senses of humor. Readers looking for police detectives might try the work of Clare Curzon, Martha Grimes, June Thomson, Dorothy Simpson, or the early Dalgliesh novels of P. D. James.

Muller, Marcia. Her female private eye Sharon McCone debuted in *Edwin of the Iron Shoes* (McKay Washburn, 1977) five years before her best-selling peers, Sue Grafton and Sara Paretsky, published their first novels in their private eye series. According to the dust jackets of Muller's recent novels, Grafton has called Muller the "founding 'mother' of the contemporary female hard-boiled private eye." Based in San Francisco and working chiefly for a legal cooperative, All Souls, McCone is tough and independent, certainly an engaging epitome for the characters who have come after her. The early McCone novels have a softer-boiled feel to them, but with more recent works, such as the standouts *The Shape of Dread* (Mysterious, 1989) and *Wolf in the Shadows* (Mysterious, 1993), Muller displays a strong reflective and hard-edged voice, which makes her work equal the best of Grafton and Paretsky, for whom she opened the door. Muller has also written two other enjoyable but short-lived series. One featured Chicana museum curator Elena Oliverez, beginning with *The Tree of Death* (Walker, 1983), and the other starred art security expert Joanna Stark, who first appeared in *The Cavalier in White* (St. Martin, 1986).

Fans of Sharon McCone generally enjoy Sue Grafton's Kinsey Millhone novels, though McCone is a little older and more consciously political than Kinsey. Linda Grant, Maxine O'Callaghan, and Janet Dawson also have created enjoyable, California-based female private eyes.

Myers, Amy.   Myers mixes history with cooking to dish up an entertaining series that features maître chef Auguste Didier as detective par excellence in late Victorian England. Half-English and half-French, Didier was trained by the maître Escoffier himself, and the pages of Didier's adventures are peppered with the names of mouthwatering dishes (sadly, no recipes are given). In his first appearance, *Murder in Pug's Parlour* (Headline, 1986; Avon, 1992), Didier is chef at Stockbery Towers, rural seat of the Duke of Stockbery. He becomes the chief suspect when the duke's much-hated steward is murdered, and Didier turns sleuth to save himself. Scotland Yard soon appears, in the guise of Inspector Egbert Rose, and a new detective duo is born. In the second book, *Murder in the Limelight* (Headline, 1987; Avon, 1992), Didier is in London, chef of the café at the famed Galaxy Theatre. As always, Didier's nose for crime is equaled only by his skills as a chef. Myers has a light touch, endowing Didier with charm despite his healthy ego. The plots are neatly constructed, and the period detail adds an excellent flavor to the mélange.

Readers who enjoy the Victorian period might try the work of Anne Perry, Alanna Knight, L. B. Greenwood, Carole Nelson Douglas, the Amelia Peabody Emerson series of Elizabeth Peters, or Gillian Linscott's novels about Edwardian sleuth Nell Bray. Contemporary series with a culinary twist include the works of Janet Laurence, Diane Mott Davidson, and Katherine Hall Page.

Nabb, Magdalen. An Englishwoman long resident in Florence, Italy, Nabb as a neophyte mystery writer could hardly have
asked for higher praise than that which greeted her first novel,
Death of an Englishman (Scribner, 1982), and from no less a writer
than the late Georges Simenon. Writing about her adopted city,
Nabb has created a superb series of novels starring a humane
and very human character, Marshal Salvatore Guarnaccia. Sici-
lian by birth, the Marshal finds himself posted to Florence,
where he learns to cope with the often mysterious ways of northern Italy and its people. Florence itself is an important character
in these novels, but it is the Marshal, working slowly and steadily
in each case, persisting against the stultifying pace of Italian bureaucracy, persevering in the name of justice, who makes the
series so appealing. *Death of a Dutchman* (Scribner, 1983) and *The
Marshal and the Madwoman* (Scribner, 1988) are excellent examples of Nabb's skill with plotting and characterization.

Readers longing to visit other parts of contemporary Italy
might try Donna Leon's series set in Venice, and the works of
Edward Sklepowich and Michael Dibdin, who also write about
Venice. Those who enjoy the character of Guarnaccia might try

the work of M. R. D. Meek and the late Georges Simenon. For the lighter side, there is always wickedly funny Sarah Caudwell's *Thus Was Adonis Murdered* (Scribner, 1981).

Neel, Janet. British novelist Neel (aka Janet Cohen) has written a well-received series of books with protagonists Detective Inspector John McLeish of the London Metropolitan Police and Francesca Wilson, a civil servant in the Department of Trade and Industry. The books are an engrossing mixture of police procedural and the British psychological crime novel. John and Francesca meet in the first book, *Death's Bright Angel* (St. Martin, 1988), and they begin a stormy relationship against a backdrop of police work and financial malfeasance. Francesca has a fast-lane career, as well as four younger brothers whom she mothers and overprotects. Several of the brothers are brilliant singers, and Neel's creation of an eccentric family and their musical obsessions is well done. In her novels, Neel also has written an insider's description of the workings of the British civil service system. The suspense is potent and the writing strong in this worthy English series.

Death's Bright Angel won the John Creasey First Novel Award from the British Crime Writers' Association. *The Highest Bidder* (London: Michael Joseph, 1992), a financial thriller, has been published under the author's own name, Janet Cohen.

Other novelists that readers may enjoy include P. D. James, Emma Lathen, and Annette Meyers. Ruth Dudley Edwards and Natasha Cooper also write about the British civil service.

O'Brien, Meg. O'Brien's journalist/sleuth, Jessica James (inevitably nicknamed Jesse) fights a recurring attraction toward criminality and irresponsibility. But Jesse is also an award-winning journalist, a recovering alcoholic, and a wise-cracking, impetuous, and persistent investigator. She falls off the wagon, suffers bouts of self-recrimination, and possesses all the human failings needed to keep the reader fascinated. Jesse has an on-again, off-again relationship with a sexy, upscale Mafioso, Marcus Andrelli. Andrelli, his bodyguard Tark, and the teenaged Genesee Three help Jesse investigate crimes that involve her family and friends. The Rochester, New York setting is unusual and memorable, and Jesse's first-person narrative is smart, quick, and profane.

It helps to read the Jesse James mysteries sequentially; the first title in the series is *The Daphne Decisions* (Bantam, 1990). O'Brien has also written a riveting novel of suspense, *The Keeper* (Doubleday, 1992), about a mother's search for her kidnapped daughter.

Other writers with journalist sleuths include Sarah Shankman, Alison Gordon, Annette Roome, Mickey Friedman, and

Barbara D'Amato. Readers also might want to try Liza Cody, whose private eye Anna Lee is equally prone to personal failure. A classic predecessor of O'Brien's is the screwball comedy-mystery writer Craig Rice; Gabrielle Kraft is writing contemporary screwball mysteries.

O'Callaghan, Maxine. Private eye Delilah West is the heroine of O'Callaghan's mysteries, which are set in Orange County, California. Delilah and her husband, Jack West, jointly operated a detective agency, West & West. Jack is killed in the first book in the series, *Death Is Forever* (Worldwide, 1981), and of course Delilah must go after her husband's murderer. She won't give up and she keeps the agency going by herself. In *Hit & Run* (St. Martin, 1989), Delilah is reduced to doing small-time work, like serving subpoenas and delivering legal papers. Even with a second job, she has little money, so she uses a sleeping bag in her office and showers at friends' houses. She has little self-confidence, and she is still grieving for her dead husband. In *Set-Up* (St. Martin, 1991), Delilah is doing better financially, largely due to the help of a wealthy developer friend, Erik Lundgren. Delilah, however, loses some of her hard-won affluence by taking on the case of an antidevelopment activist accused of murder. In the tradition of California hard-boiled detectives, Delilah must fend off violent attacks during her investigations.

O'Callaghan also writes horror novels such as *Dark Time* (Diamond, 1992).

Other mystery novelists who set books in Orange County are Wendy Hornsby, Jean Femling, and A. E. Maxwell. Authors who write about Western private eyes include Sue Grafton, Karen Kijewski, Janet Dawson, Catherine Dain, Linda Grant, and Margaret Lucke.

O'Donnell, Lillian. O'Donnell has written several series of mysteries. She began her best-known series, the Norah Mulcahaney mysteries, with *The Phone Calls* (Putnam, 1972). In the story, young widows receive threatening anonymous phone calls and are driven to commit suicide. Norah is a young policewoman with good instincts, who gets a chance to prove herself on the case. Norah starts at the bottom of the New York City police force, and eventually she is promoted into homicide. She is a perceptive, honest cop, who is devoted to what she calls "The Job." Norah grows and changes in her personal life, as well as her career, over the years depicted in the books. She always works in homicide, except in *Leisure Dying* (Putnam, 1976), where she sets up a Senior Citizens Task Force within the police department. Norah is one of the first strong policewomen who care deeply about their careers to be depicted in mystery fiction. The Norah Mulcahaney books are well done, methodical, detailed police procedurals. O'Donnell often uses contemporary news items, like the stories of mugging victims who shoot their assailants, or a teacher who hires teenagers to kill her husband, to add verisimilitude to her books. She also creates realistic New York City settings for her crime novels.

O'Donnell also is writing a series featuring Mici Anhalt, a compassionate young caseworker for the Crime Victims Compensation Board. The first novel in this series is *Aftershock* (Putnam, 1977). Again, O'Donnell creates vibrant New York backgrounds to go with her detailed exposition of Anhalt's daily workload. O'Donnell's newest mystery series features New York private eye Gwenn Ramadge, who is somewhat reminiscent of P. D. James's character Cordelia Gray. The first book in the series is *A Wreath for the Bride* (Putnam, 1990).

Readers also may want to try Sue Dunlap's Jill Smith novels; Margaret Maron's Lt. Sigrid Harald novels; L. V. Sims's Dixie Struthers mysteries; and the police procedurals of Dorothy Uhnak and Katherine V. Forrest. For a view of a very different policewoman, try Julie Smith's Skip Langdon books.

Oliphant, B. J./Orde, A. J. Oliphant is a pseudonym for science fiction writer Sheri S. Tepper, who writes a second mystery

series under the pseudonym A. J. Orde. Oliphant's series character is crusty and intrepid Colorado rancher Shirley Mc-
Clintock, who debuted in *Dead in the Scrub* (Fawcett, 1990), which
was an Edgar nominee for Best Paperback Original. After spend-
ing a number of years in Washington, D.C., in an influential
position, the fifty-something, six-foot-two Shirley has returned to
the ranch her parents left her. Intolerant of fools, with a razor-
sharp mind, Shirley is a natural when it comes to ferreting out
the truth behind mysterious deaths. Shirley also has strong opinions on many subjects, and she gives these opinions free rein in
each book. Oliphant/Orde's other series character, Jason Lynx,
is much the same in this regard. Writing as Orde, the author has
created another complex and intriguing character. Mysteriously
orphaned, Lynx was taken in as an adolescent by a well-to-do
Jewish businessman, who has turned his interior design business
over to Jason when the series begins, with *A Little Neighborhood
Murder* (Doubleday, 1990). In the third book of the series, *Death
for Old Times' Sake* (Doubleday, 1992), Orde finally reveals the
secret of Lynx's past. Literate and thought-provoking, both these
series offer rewarding reading.

Those who've enjoyed the work of Oliphant/Orde might try
series written by M. K. Lorens, Mary Monica Pulver, and P. M.
Carlson. In addition to hiding behind initials, these authors also
specialize in complex and intense characters with strongly held
opinions. Readers looking for mysteries with Colorado settings
should try the work of Diane Mott Davidson and Yvonne Montgomery.

O'Marie, Sister Carol Anne. Perhaps the only nun actively
publishing crime fiction, Sister Carol Anne has created a popular
character in her nun detective, Sister Mary Helen. At seventy-
five, Sister Mary Helen is nominally retired, but in her first appearance, in *A Novena for Murder* (Scribner, 1984), the good
sister is anything but retired, as she pokes her nose into the
murder of a history professor at Mount St. Francis College for

Women in San Francisco. With the wisdom and the wit that has come from fifty years of service to her order, Sister Mary Helen and her cohorts, the other nuns and San Francisco homicide detectives Kate Murphy and Dennis Gallagher, solve the murder. Sister Mary Helen, who loves murder mysteries and disguises them with her prayer book cover, is a charming character. Like other older women sleuths, the good sister proves that age does not necessarily diminish one's capacities, and in this case, certainly, age has provided a thorough understanding of human nature and its many foibles and follies.

Ralph McInerny, creator of the Father Dowling series, uses the name Monica Quill to write a series of mysteries featuring Sister M. T. Dempsey. English writer Veronica Black is currently writing a series with a nun as the detective. Other clerical mysteries of interest are the series of D. M. Greenwood and Kate Charles. Readers looking for active, older women sleuths might try the works of Virginia Rich and Stefanie Matteson.

Orde, A. J. See **Oliphant, B. J.**

P

Page, Katherine Hall. Winner of the Agatha for Best First Novel for *The Body in the Belfry* (St. Martin, 1990), Page is quickly becoming a favorite with readers of the traditional mystery. Page's series character is Faith Sibley Fairchild, the daughter of a minister who is now married to a minister and living in the small Massachusetts town of Aleford. Before her marriage, Faith had an exclusive catering business in Manhattan called Have Faith. She's making an adjustment to life in a small town with her husband Tom and their small son Ben. Something of a food snob, Faith is nevertheless a charming character as she comments inwardly on the food habits of her fellow townspeople and other amusing information about small-town life. Page handles the conventions of the traditional mystery novel, with its enclosed setting and relatively small cast of characters, very well.

Another mystery series with culinary associations is the work of the late Virginia Rich. Janet Laurence and Diane Mott Davidson both write series whose main characters are caterers. For small-town New England or suburban Northeastern flavor, readers might try Sally Gunning, B. J. Morison, or Valerie Wolzien.

Papazoglou, Orania. See **Haddam, Jane.**

Paretsky, Sara. Along with Sue Grafton, Paretsky is one of the few American women mystery writers who consistently receives serious critical attention and acclaim for her novels. She has revolutionized the genre with her creation of the independent private eye V. I. Warshawski, and her bleak settings in corrupt and grimy industrial Chicago. One does not read Paretsky for an escape into a Christie-type intellectual puzzle; the reader instead is grabbed by the throat in the first chapter and dragged into Warshawski's world of injustice, pollution, and vicious urban politicking. V. I., like her male counterparts in hard-boiled novels, follows the tradition of packing a gun, drinking whiskey neat, and operating as a lone wolf to right wrongs. But she transcends the stereotypes by virtue of being a fully rounded character, with her own failings, idiosyncracies, and strengths. The crimes she solves are generally not simple individual antisocial acts; each book reflects a social problem about which Warshawski can exercise her legendary anger and frustration.

The first Warshawski book is *Indemnity Only* (Dial Press, 1982). Paretsky worked in the insurance industry for many years, and she began her series of mysteries by telling a strong story of insurance fraud. In later novels, Warshawski investigates arson, environmental, and medical crimes.

Blood Shot (Delacorte, 1988), published in Great Britain as *Toxic Shock* (London: Gollancz, 1988), won the British Crime Writers' Association Silver Dagger Award in 1988. Paretsky founded and was the first president of the Sisters in Crime organization, and she has edited the short story anthology *A Woman's Eye* (Delacorte, 1991).

Admirers of Paretsky should certainly try the works of Sue Grafton. Other writers of interest are Marcia Muller, the originator of the hard-boiled female private eye genre; Linda Barnes, whose protagonist Carlotta Carlyle is a remarkable creation;

Karen Kijewski; Catherine Dain; Gloria White; and Liza Cody and Gillian Slovo for a view of hard-boiled British PIs.

Paul, Barbara. Paul is a former English and drama teacher, who has directed plays as well. Many of her mysteries have theatrical backgrounds, including her series of three opera mysteries with Enrico Caruso and Geraldine Farrar as amateur sleuths. They are *A Cadenza for Caruso* (St. Martin, 1984), *Prima Donna at Large* (St. Martin, 1985), and *A Chorus of Detectives* (St. Martin, 1987). These mysteries share New York City historical backgrounds, memorable characterizations of celebrities, and an operatic backstage ambience. In *The Renewable Virgin* (Scribner, 1985), Paul writes about a series of crimes that entangle three very different women. The characters of Marian Larch, a police detective; Kelly Ingram, a television actress; and Fiona Benedict, a history professor, are drawn clearly through their first-person reflections on the crimes. Paul has written several more novels featuring New York policewoman Marian Larch. In her later books, Paul often creates plots that feature manipulative, Machiavellian characters. She is excellent at characterizing the sort of fiendishly self-obsessed people among whom murder seems liable to brew. *He Huffed and He Puffed* (Scribner, 1989) has no positive characters, just crafty connivers deceiving each other and outwitting each others' complex plans. A. J. Strode is attempting to buy shares from three people, so he can close down a business competitor. He tries to blackmail them when he discovers that each of the three has gotten away with murder. His victims get together and conceive a detailed plan to murder him. The novel is funny and wonderfully nasty, just like its characters. Paul has a distinct talent for creating vivid villains.

Other musical mysteries include the works of Janet Neel, Lucille Kallen, and Audrey Peterson. Marian Babson writes cozy mysteries with amusing, distinctive characters, and Sarah Caudwell's humorous mysteries are memorable.

Perry, Anne. The Victorian era offers a rich vein of subject matter for the writer, and Perry brings her novelist's imagination and sensitivity to two series of novels set in this fascinating and complex period of English history. The longer-running series, set during the mid- to late 1880s, features Inspector Thomas Pitt and his wife Charlotte, who has come down in the world by marrying a humble policeman. Having forsaken her comfortable upper-middle-class lifestyle after the first novel in the series, *The Cater Street Hangman* (St. Martin, 1979), the intelligent and socially conscious Charlotte aids her educated and sensitive husband in all his cases. Using her own family connections to gain entrance to the homes of the wealthy and powerful, Charlotte, often assisted by her sister Emily (who married as far up the social scale as Charlotte married down), pokes her nose into the secrets of the Victorian upper crust. In the second series, set in the mid-1850s after the end of the Crimean War, the main characters are Inspector William Monk and nurse Hester Latterly. In the brilliant debut of this series, the Agatha-nominated *The Face of a Stranger* (Fawcett Columbine, 1990), Monk wakes in hospital with no memory of who he is. Confronted by a brutal murder case and a superior who would enjoy his disgrace, Monk struggles to solve the mystery of his own identity along with the murder. In both series Perry takes a keen sense of social justice and unsparingly lays bare all the hypocrisy and injustice of Victorian England, when a minute percentage of the population literally held the power of life and death over the vast majority. Perry's later works, such as *Belgrave Square* (Fawcett Columbine, 1992) and *A Dangerous Mourning* (Fawcett Columbine, 1992), are particularly compelling. In Perry's hands the joining of social commentary, mystery plot, and historical novel means compelling reading.

Other novelists who use the Victorian era as a setting are Amy Myers and Carole Nelson Douglas. Taking a slightly different part of the realm for her series, Alanna Knight writes an unusual series set in Victorian Edinburgh. Gillian Linscott, in her series about suffragette Nell Bray, writes about Edwardian England.

Peters, Elizabeth/Michaels, Barbara. The legendary and prolific Barbara Mertz uses two pseudonyms for her books: Elizabeth Peters and Barbara Michaels. She also has written nonfiction books on Egyptology under her own name.

Under the Peters name, Mertz has created the series characters of Vicky Bliss, art historian; Jacqueline Kirby, librarian; and Amelia Peabody, Victorian archaeologist and adventurer. The Peters books are generally humorous and lively, with strong-willed and appealing heroines who find mysteries in exotic locations. Peters's first novel was *The Jackal's Head* (Meredith, 1968).

The first Jacqueline Kirby book is *The Seventh Sinner* (Dodd, Mead, 1972). Kirby is a middle-aged woman who thoroughly enjoys her forays into adventure and mystery. In *Die for Love* (Congdon & Weed, 1984), for example, she decides to make money by writing a swashbuckling romance novel and ends up at a romance convention by way of doing research. A hilarious satire on the excesses of the genre ensues, as do murder and a bit of romance for Jacqueline herself.

The first Vicky Bliss novel is *Borrower of the Night* (Dodd, Mead, 1973). Vicky is tall, voluptuous, and smart; she works in a museum in Germany and has occasional adventures with the mysterious Sir John Smythe, a charming rogue and art forger.

The first appearance of Amelia Peabody is in *Crocodile on the Sandbank* (Dodd, Mead, 1975). These novels are particularly noteworthy for the characterizations of the intelligent and adventurous Peabody, her irascible husband, Egyptologist Radcliffe Emerson, and their precocious son Ramses.

Under the Michaels name, Mertz writes suspense novels, often with a touch of the supernatural (more than a touch in the earlier novels). The first novel that appeared under this name was *The Master of Blacktower* (Appleton Century Crofts, 1966). The

Michaels novels are often set in Maryland or Virginia. Sometimes there is a tinge of the occult, and sometimes these are full-blooded ghost stories. Especially notable are *Ammie, Come Home* (Meredith, 1968) and *Shattered Silk* (Atheneum, 1986), which are set in the same historic house in Georgetown. In their setting, they are matched bookends, yet these quite different novels show Mertz's growth as a writer and are reflective of their times—the late 1960s and the mid-1980s. Books published under the Michaels name are known for their intriguing characters and vivid settings.

Naked Once More (Warner, 1989) won the Agatha Award for Best Novel in 1990.

Other writers who may appeal to the legions of Michaels/ Peters admirers include Dorothy Cannell, Sharyn McCrumb, Kathryn Lasky Knight, Margot Arnold, and Charlotte MacLeod.

Peters, Ellis. Novelist Edith Pargeter launched her mystery-writing career in the early 1950s with the novel *Fallen into the Pit* (Heinemann, 1951). But Pargeter fans, who were used to the author's historical novels and general fiction, were somewhat confused by the switch in genres, and thus the Peters pseudonym was born. For nearly thirty years Ellis Peters produced excellent novels of mystery and suspense with contemporary settings, many of them featuring the Felse family. The Felses, consisting of father George, a policeman, mother Bunty, a "retired" opera singer, and son Dominic, star in several outstanding novels, including the Edgar Award–winning *Death and the Joyful Woman* (Doubleday, 1962). In many of her contemporary novels Peters uses effectively her interest in music, such as in *Mourning Raga* (Morrow, 1970) or *The Horn of Roland* (Morrow, 1974). But in 1978, Peters wrote what was to be a single excursion into the historical mystery with *A Morbid Taste for Bones* (Morrow, 1978), which was based on the story of St. Winifred and the Abbey of St. Peter and St. Paul in Shrewsbury. Once the story was finished, however, the main character, the Welsh Benedictine monk Cadfael, refused to let go of his creator, and thus was born one of the most beloved of current mystery series. Weaving the actual historical events of the period, beginning in the late 1130s, through the plots of the mystery novels, Peters gives her readers a tantalizing glimpse of the medieval past. Peters does not, however, impose modern characters and modern psychology upon the period; her characters are distinctly medieval. Her long experience as a historical novelist has given Peters an unusual understanding of the complexities of medieval life, and her people are medieval to the core. The novels in the series often revolve, for example, around concepts that are peculiarly medieval, such as *The Sanctuary Sparrow* (Morrow, 1983), *The Pilgrim of Hate* (Morrow, 1984), or *The Potter's Field* (Mysterious, 1990). Peters's vivid prose, like that of Anne Perry and Lindsey Davis, conjures up the past and makes it almost tangible.

Both Kate Sedley and Margaret Frazer have recently begun series set in late fifteenth-century England, and Elizabeth Eyre has claimed Renaissance Italy with a new series. Sharan Newman has recently begun a series set in twelfth-century France. P. C. Doherty, who writes also as Michael Clynes, Paul Harding, and C. L. Grace, offers several series set in varying periods in medieval English history.

Peterson, Audrey. Peterson is a Californian who writes traditional cozy mysteries set in England, with American protagonists. In her first series, her sleuths are Jane Winfield and Andrew Quentin. Jane is an American scholar of music history, and Andrew is a professor and Jane's thesis advisor. In *Nocturne Murder* (Arbor House, 1987), Jane is in London working on a graduate fellowship in music history. She has an affair with a music critic who turns up dead in her room, and she is accused of his murder. In *Elegy in a Country Graveyard* (Pocket, 1990), Jane is writing a biography of an eminent pianist who died of AIDS. Her aunt dies suspiciously, and a long-lost cousin reappears to claim an inheritance. The settings are London and Yorkshire, and Peterson provides plenty of references to the Brontës. In her Winfield and Quentin series, Peterson has created entertaining, likable characters, including a gallery of eccentric musicians. Peterson has started a new mystery series with *Dartmoor Burial* (Pocket, 1992). The heroine is Claire Camden, an English literature professor at a California university. Claire has commuted between California and England for the many years of her marriage to an Englishman. She is now divorced, but still lives part of the year in London. In the first novel of the series, Claire is visiting her ex-mother-in-law in a small Dartmoor town where a body is found floating in a bog. Claire becomes friendly with the police inspector who is investigating the case. *Dartmoor Burial* is an atmospheric mystery, with strong parallels to the plot of a Victorian novel that Claire is researching.

Readers may want to try the musically oriented mysteries of Janet Neel, Lucille Kallen, and Barbara Paul. Elizabeth George, Marian Babson, and Martha Grimes are other American writers who set their mysteries in contemporary Great Britain.

Pickard, Nancy. Jenny Cain is the lively, thoughtful protagonist created by Pickard in her series of mysteries. Jenny's family once owned the biggest business in Port Frederick, Massachusetts (a town known locally as Poor Fred), until they closed it down in bankruptcy, throwing many out of work. Jenny is the director of a local philanthropic foundation, and many of the crimes she becomes involved with are linked to her work in evaluating and disbursing foundation grants. Her dysfunctional family haunts her, especially her mentally ill mother and her irresponsible father. Jenny marries a policeman, Geof Bushfield, and he tries with little success to protect her from the grim realities of life and crime. The mysteries are generally set in the fictional New England seaport of Port Frederick, although Jenny goes to Kansas on a case in *Bum Steer* (Pocket, 1990). *I.O.U.* (Pocket, 1991) is Pickard's most mature work to date. In this novel, Jenny tries to come to grips with the death of her mother and with the cause of her mother's long-term mental illness. It is a wise and caring book; it is also emotionally grueling but probably rewarding for readers who have experienced the death of a parent.

Pickard also has written *The 27-Ingredient Chili Con Carne Murders* (Delacorte, 1993), which is based on a manuscript left by Virginia Rich at the time of her death. It is a noteworthy blending of the writing styles of Pickard and Rich, with Rich's series protagonist, 'Genia Potter, finding murder on her Arizona ranch.

Pickard won an Agatha Award for Best Novel for *Bum Steer,* both Agatha and Anthony Awards for Best Novel for *I.O.U.,* and she won a Macavity Award for *Marriage Is Murder* (Scribner, 1987).

The first Jenny Cain novel is *Generous Death* (Avon, 1984).

American cozy mystery writers include Carolyn G. Hart, Gillian Roberts, Virginia Rich, Sharyn McCrumb, Jane Langton, and Charlotte MacLeod.

Piesman, Marissa. Piesman's lively amateur sleuth is Nina Fischman, who is ably assisted in her snooping by her elderly and equally spirited mother, Ida Fischman. Nina is an attorney for the New York Legal Services Project for Seniors. She is thirtyish, single, and increasingly dubious about her career and her single state. Nina maintains a constant flow of humor about New York City, men, clothing, religion, money, and the obsessions of her generation. Actually, Nina can obsess neurotically about almost anything. She was a red-diaper baby (a child of two leftwing social activists) and she continually tries to reconcile her upbringing with the practices of the greedy 1980s. The first book in the series, *Unorthodox Practices* (Pocket, 1989), deals with the cutthroat New York City real estate market in affordable Manhattan apartments. In *Personal Effects* (Pocket, 1991), Nina's best friend is murdered after answering a personal ad; naturally Nina needs to find out what happened to her and who could be such a murderous date. In *Heading Uptown* (Delacorte, 1993), Nina is named the executor of the estate of her mother's best friend.

The dead woman's son recently has been killed in a suspicious car crash, and Nina assumes his wife must have murdered him, since she turns up at her mother-in-law's funeral wearing a black leather miniskirt and high heels. Anyone that tacky certainly could be a murderer, Nina theorizes. Nina analyzes endlessly, and she's interested in everything around her. Nina's humor, kvetching, and self-deprecation are beautifully brought out by Piesman. A funny, observant sleuth and a strong sense of place make Piesman's books memorable.

Gabrielle Kraft, Joan Hess, and Barbara Paul write humorous mysteries. The heroines of both Lia Matera's and Linda Barnes's mysteries, like Nina, were red-diaper babies and now muse humorously on their radical backgrounds. Serita Stevens and Rayanne Moore are writing a mystery series featuring an elderly Jewish woman who is active and smart, like Ida Fischman.

Powell, Deborah. Houston, Texas, in the 1930s is the setting for this series of mysteries featuring lesbian crime reporter Hollis Carpenter, who writes for the Houston *Times*. When, in the winter of 1936, her bosses at the paper try to shunt Hollis off on a seemingly innocuous society-page story, Hollis quits the paper and noses around on her own into a story about guns stolen from a police department warehouse. Hollis has a sharp and funny tongue, and she uses it on practically everyone. She talks tough, but she lets her schnauzer Anice walk all over her. The supporting characters, including a crime boss who treats Hollis like a daughter, are lively and engaging. Readers familiar with contemporary Houston will find much amusement in reading of the city of over half a century ago. The first novel in the series is *Bayou City Secrets* (Naiad, 1991). Powell has an enjoyable light touch in this series, which is a throwback to the humorous hard-boiled detective novels of yesteryear.

Another writer with a reporter-detective of yesteryear is Diane K. Shah, whose tales feature post–World War II Hollywood and Los Angeles. Readers looking for other lesbian detectives might try the work of Vicki P. McConnell, Ellen Hart, and Barbara Wilson.

Pulver, Mary Monica. A member of the Society for Creative Anachronism, which is devoted to the study of the European Middle Ages and whose members spend time in activities like medieval tournaments and wars, Pulver has endowed her series characters with her own interests. In the first published novel of the series, *Murder at the War* (St. Martin, 1987), policeman Peter Brichter and his wife Kori are traveling with friends to a field in the Pennsylvania countryside where they and fellow SCA members will hold a battle, medieval-style. In the midst of the mock battle, however, one death turns out to be real, and Peter uses his detective skills to solve the crime. The second published novel, *The Unforgiving Minutes* (St. Martin, 1988), is actually chronologically the first in the series. In this novel, readers learn the true story of Katherine "Kori" Price and how she came to know Peter Brichter, and a riveting story it is. This novel demonstrates one of Pulver's strengths, the ability to create compelling and likable characters. Later novels in the series show the developing relationship between Kori and Peter. *Original Sin* (Walker, 1991) is an excellent variation on the snowbound country house mystery. Recently, Pulver and a friend, Gail Bacon, have collaborated on a medieval mystery, *The Novice's Tale* (Diamond, 1992) as Margaret Frazer. This series features fifteenth-century English nun Dame Frevisse as detective. The period detail is nicely handled, and Dame Frevisse has promise to be a worthy series character.

Readers who have enjoyed Pulver might try writers like P. M. Carlson, M. K. Lorens, Kate Wilhelm, B. J. Oliphant/A. J. Orde, or Kathryn Lasky Knight, all of whom write series with distinctive and interesting series characters who are quite unlike anyone else's. Those who have read Pulver as Frazer might try the work of Ellis Peters, Kate Sedley, and Sharan Newman.

Quest, Erica. After publishing three enjoyable novels of romantic suspense, beginning with *The Silver Castle* (Doubleday, 1978), this pseudonymous wife-and-husband writing team turned to a more traditional English mystery series. Quest's Detective Chief Inspector Kate Maddox is one of the few English women police detectives as chief series character in current mystery fiction. In her first case, *Death Walk* (Doubleday, 1988), Kate delves into the murder of the mistress of the local stately home. This series has the comforting feel of the traditional English police mystery, combined with the small town/village setting. But the selection of a woman detective has made this series different. Kate Maddox is intelligent, forceful, and committed to her work. She has a sharp eye for discrimination and a steely determination to succeed despite the chauvinistic odds piled against her. Kate makes an attractive and likable centerpiece for a deftly conceived and executed series.

The detective series of Jill McGown also features a woman police detective, Judy Hill, in a lead role. Jennie Melville (aka

Gwendoline Butler) has a long-running series about police-woman Charmian Daniels, while P. D. James and Sheila Radley both feature women police detectives in supporting roles to their respective male central characters.

Radley, Sheila. Her first novel, *Death in the Morning* (Scribner, 1979), marked Radley as a writer to watch develop. This novel, featuring English police detective Douglas Quantrill, set the tone for much of Radley's work to follow: a fairly traditional mystery in its framework, but with a blending of the psychological style in the vein of Rendell and James. Radley at some point worked for the postal service in a village, and her experience there has come through in her writing. Her keen eye for characters and their motivations never fail to make her novels interesting, and her ability with characterization has allowed her to experiment successfully with the traditional form of the English detective story. *A Talent for Destruction* (Scribner, 1982) is more a psychological study than a tale of detection, and the recent *This Way Out* (Scribner, 1990), though it again features Inspector Quantrill, offers an intriguing variation on Patricia Highsmith's *Strangers on a Train* (Harper, 1950). The blend of psychology and detection that is such a prominent feature of contemporary English mystery fiction at its best is a staple with Sheila Radley.

Those who like Radley and her village settings might also try the Wexford novels of Ruth Rendell, the work of June Thomson, who also handles the village setting with considerable skill, Caroline Graham, Jill McGown, or the novels of Lin Summerfield and Minette Walters. Both of these last writers offer intriguing variations on the English village mystery.

Redmann, J. M. This series about tough private eye Michele "Micky" Knight is set in New Orleans and its environs, and, as always, the Crescent City lends its distinctive flavor to the books. Micky, who is described as a hard-hitting, tough-talking dyke detective, conforms to this description, at least on the surface. In the course of her first appearance, *Death by the Riverside* (New Victoria, 1990), Micky must confront the demons of her own past in order to solve the case, and readers come to understand just what the tough talk serves to protect. Micky physically endures beatings that would convince many others to seek other employment, but her dedication to her work and her own pursuit of justice make her indomitable. Redmann spices the detective story with some explicit sex scenes, offbeat characters, and humor to create a mixture just right for readers looking for a Cajun surprise.

Other writers with New Orleans area settings are Julie Smith and Chris Wiltz. Readers interested in other lesbian detectives should try the work of Katherine V. Forrest, Claire McNab, and Sandra Scoppettone.

Rendell, Ruth/Vine, Barbara. She has been hailed by some critics as the best mystery writer in the English language anywhere in the world, and she is generally mentioned in the same breath as her peer and countrywoman, P. D. James, as one of the leading lights of the modern crime novel. Rendell's career began, modestly enough, in the mid-1960s, with two novels that were to set some of the patterns of her career. *From Doon with Death* (Doubleday, 1965) introduced Reginald Wexford, her popular policeman detective, and *To Fear a Painted Devil* (Doubleday, 1965) introduced readers to the psychological Rendell, one for whom the abnormal and unusual exerts a powerful fascination. Many books of both types, and many awards and laudatory reviews later, Rendell is one of the most celebrated of current crime writers. The Wexford novels in the early years followed the fairly traditional pattern of the English police detective mystery, but Rendell's skill in characterization and puzzle-making has lifted the Wexford books far above the ordinary. These same skills, plus her interest in the "why" of crime, have made her psychological novels, such as *A Judgment in Stone* (Doubleday, 1978), some of the most original in contemporary mystery fiction. These latter also make uncomfortable reading for some crime fiction fans, who don't wish to know so much about the abnormal psychology of the criminal mind. Lately Rendell has written several novels under the pseudonym of Barbara Vine. These works have also attracted their share of awards and critical praise, such as *A Dark-Adapted Eye* (Bantam, 1986) and *King Solomon's Carpet* (Harmony Books, 1992). Though darker and certainly more psychological than the Wexford books, the Vine novels are often more approachable for crime fiction fans than the psychological Rendell novels. Whatever the reader's choice, Rendell has much to offer crime fiction aficionados.

Fans of the Wexford novels generally also enjoy the Adam Dalgliesh series of P. D. James. American writer Elizabeth George has a powerful appeal for English mystery lovers with her novels of English policeman Thomas Lynley. Other recommendations are the series of Cynthia Harrod-Eagles, Gwendoline Butler, Jennie Melville, Sheila Radley, and Magdalen Nabb. Those who prefer the psychological approach may try the work of Margaret Millar, Frances Hegarty, Patricia Highsmith, Rosamond Smith, Minette Walters, or Margaret Yorke.

Rich, Virginia. The late Virginia Rich wrote only three novels, but she achieved a reputation for well-crafted classic mysteries, and her books have remained popular. Her sleuth, 'Genia Potter, is a widow and a good cook, who lives part of the time in Arizona and part of the time in New England. Rich's first novel, *The Cooking School Murders* (Dutton, 1982), is set in Mrs. Potter's old hometown in Iowa. 'Genia is charmingly unassuming and warm, with a large and eccentric group of friends and neighbors. Rich writes Christie-like puzzles; she introduces the suspects in the first chapter, then sets up a murder, then she gives further details on each suspect gradually as the plot unfolds. There are plenty of cooking details and dinner parties in each story, and the plots are worked out meticulously. Another popular writer of cozy mysteries, Nancy Pickard, was commissioned to write a new 'Genia Potter book, *The 27-Ingredient Chili Con Carne Murders* (Delacorte, 1993), based on a story and notes left by Virginia Rich at the time of her death.

Readers inclined toward culinary mysteries may want to sample the offerings of Diane Mott Davidson and Trella Crespi. Susan Dunlap has written a mystery set around a trendy restaurant in Berkeley, *A Dinner to Die For* (St. Martin, 1987). And then, of course, there's *A Diet to Die For* (St. Martin, 1989) by Joan Hess, and even *The Thin Woman* (St. Martin, 1984) by Dorothy Cannell.

Roberts, Gillian. Judith Greber has adopted the pen name of Gillian Roberts for her series of mysteries about thirtyish Philadelphia schoolteacher Amanda Pepper. The author is a former high school English teacher, and her mysteries are full of amusing stories about the horrors of teaching English to adolescents. In the series, Amanda teaches English at Philly Prep, a school for rich, underachieving kids. Amanda is a lively and funny character, with a group of meddlesome acquaintances and family. She has something going (she's never sure exactly what) with the reticent C. K. Mackenzie, a Philadelphia cop. A recurring joke in the books is the spate of phone calls from Amanda's mother in Florida, who keeps trying to contrive ways to get her daughter married off. The first book in the series is *Caught Dead in Philadelphia* (Scribner, 1987), which won an Anthony Award for Best First Novel in 1987. *I'd Rather Be in Philadelphia* (Ballantine, 1992) is about wife-beating and is the most serious and harrowing book so far in the series. Its structure is that of the average person who finds evidence that a crime will be committed, but doesn't know the identity of either the criminal or the victim, as in the classic *Warrant for X* (Doubleday, 1938) by Philip MacDonald.

Other distinctive character studies may be found in the works of Nancy Pickard, Janet LaPierre, Meg O'Brien, Jane Dentinger, and Marissa Piesman. Jane Haddam uses Philadelphia settings in many of her holiday mysteries.

Roome, Annette. Chris Martin, a forty-year-old English housewife, looks in the mirror one morning and feels only despair at what she sees. So begins *A Real Shot in the Arm* (Crown, 1989), a fine novel of detection and self-discovery. Chris gets a job as a rookie reporter on the local weekly newspaper (against her husband's wishes) and learns her trade. Chris finds that she is actually good at being a reporter, she gains self-confidence, and she learns that men still appreciate her. She also solves a perplexing local murder that everyone around her has discouraged her from investigating. In Roome's second book, *A Second Shot in the Dark* (Crown, 1990), Chris becomes involved again in a local murder investigation, and her level of assurance and skill at detection and journalism grow stronger. She finds information by interviewing people and paying attention to details the police have missed. Roome's writing is humorous, light, and acerbic, with a deft interweaving of character development and mystery plot.

A Real Shot in the Arm was a winner of the John Creasey Award for Best First Mystery, given by the British Crime Writers' Association.

Readers also might enjoy the Claire Malloy novels of Joan Hess, the Rain Morgan books of Lesley Grant-Adamson, and the Paris Chandler novels of Diane K. Shah. Dorothy Cannell's *The*

Thin Woman and Sarah Caudwell's books are recommended as well.

Rowe, Jennifer. Editor of *The Australian Women's Weekly*, Rowe has made murder Down Under increasingly popular with her series of clever mysteries set in Australia. The first novel in the series, *Grim Pickings* (Bantam, 1991), which has already been a miniseries in Australia, is cast in the traditional mold. There is a good-sized cast of characters in an enclosed setting—in this case, an apple farm. The Tender family, along with various friends, has gathered to help elderly Aunt Alice gather in her crop, and immediately the tensions begin to surface. On the scene is Verity Birdwood, known as Birdie, researcher for one of the television networks, and her nimble mind makes her a natural as an amateur detective. Birdie is a prickly, difficult character. She hides her feelings, even from her best friend, Kate Delaney, who also appears throughout the series, along with Kate's husband and daughter. The Australian setting makes a pleasing change from the usual venue of the traditional mystery, and Rowe's skill in devising intricate plots makes her work delightfully reminiscent of the best of the Golden Age detective story. *Murder by the Book* (Bantam, 1992) offers murder in a publishing house, and the recent *Death in Store* (Doubleday, 1993), a collection of short stories featuring Birdie, demonstrates that Rowe is very much at home with the short form as well.

Readers looking for Australian settings might try the work of Arthur W. Upfield and Jon Cleary. Otherwise, writers with qualities similar to Rowe's are Jill McGown, Carolyn G. Hart, Betty Rowlands, and Paula Gosling. They all write mysteries in the traditional vein, but with decidedly modern themes.

Rowlands, Betty. Rowlands writes traditional cozy English mysteries in her Melissa Craig series of novels. Melissa is a famous crime writer who has bought a cottage in the Cotswolds. Her next-door neighbor and friend is Iris Ash, an artist and textile designer. In the first book in the series, *A Little Gentle Sleuthing* (Walker, 1990), Melissa is learning to live independently in the countryside. Iris finds a body in the woods, and Melissa's curiosity impels her to investigate. *Over the Edge* (Walker, 1993) is set at an adult school in the south of France. A German visitor is found at the bottom of a cliff at the beginning of the novel. Was he pushed by a disturbed former member of the French Resistance who hates Germans, or by an unknown enemy with contemporary problems? Rowlands evokes the fascinating medieval and World War II history of the area as an essential element of her plot. Rowlands's mysteries are peopled with eccentric characters, and she strews her red herrings adroitly.

Readers who enjoy Rowlands should look for cozy mysteries by Carolyn G. Hart, Audrey Peterson, Hazel Holt, Kay Mitchell, Caroline Graham, and Pat Burden.

S

Sale, Medora. This Canadian author has a Ph.D. in medieval studies from the University of Toronto, but when she turned to a life of crime-writing, she chose as her setting contemporary Toronto. Her first novel, *Murder on the Run* (Paperjacks, 1986), won the Arthur Ellis Award for Best First Novel from the Crime Writers of Canada and introduced Inspector John Sanders of the Toronto police. In her second novel, *Murder in Focus* (Scribner, 1989), Sale introduced Sanders's companion in crime, architectural photographer Harriet Jeffries. The slowly developing relationship between Sanders and Jeffries, both of whom are definitely wary of emotional entanglements, is one of the chief appeals of this series. Sale handles the emotional topography of the relationship with restraint and insight. Above this, however, Sale also provides entertaining plots and an intriguing cast of secondary characters, some of whom sometimes take the lead role in the novels. An excellent example of this is *Sleep of the Innocent* (Scribner, 1991), in which Sergeant Rob Lucas investigates a murder involving an attractive young rock singer, while John and Harriet are on a disastrous vacation. This is a good, solid series that builds on the author's various strengths with each new book.

Writers looking for crime in Canada might try the work of Eric Wright, whose series of novels about Toronto cop Charlie Salter have won considerable critical acclaim, or the sports mysteries of Canadian sports writer Alison Gordon. Edgar-winner L. R. Wright sets her mysteries on the opposite side of the country. An excellent English series is that of Cynthia Harrod-Eagles.

Sandstrom, Eve K. A columnist and former award-winning reporter for the Lawton, Oklahoma, *Constitution,* Sandstrom uses her reporter's eye for detail to create soundly constructed puzzles as the basis for her Down Home series set in southwestern Oklahoma. Sandstrom's detectives are husband and wife Sam and Nicky Titus. Sam is an officer in the Army's Criminal Investigation Division, and Nicky is the daughter of a general. In their debut, *Death Down Home* (Scribner, 1990), the newlyweds are just moving into their new quarters in Frankfurt, Germany, when they get a call from Sam's brother, telling them that Sam's father, "Big" Sam, lies critically ill from a mysterious accident. Sam and Nicky immediately return to Holton, Oklahoma, to help out the family. As they make adjustments to the ranch and to small-town life, Sam and Nicky delve further into the mystery. Sam uses his skill as an army investigator, and Nicky uses hers as a photojournalist. Sandstrom writes convincingly about her people and her places, and the second novel, *The Devil Down Home* (Scribner, 1991) is an effective and entertaining tale of small-town murder and mayhem.

Another Oklahoma writer who uses the small-town setting to good advantage is Jean Hager, currently writing two series. Otherwise, readers might try the works of Carolyn G. Hart, Susan Rogers Cooper, and D. R. Meredith.

Sawyer, Corinne Holt. Little old lady detectives have been a staple of mystery fiction almost from the beginning, and Sawyer has taken a stock character and added an enjoyable spin. Her series, set in a posh retirement community in southern California, features not one, but two little old ladies who are nothing like the stereotypes. One of the main characters is the peppery and often irritating Angela Benbow, widow of an admiral. Though she might look like a small, delicate blossom, Angela is just about as tough as old boots. Her boon companion is Caledonia Wingate, also the widow of an admiral, but physically the opposite of Angela. Tall, imposing, and never afraid to throw her considerable weight around, Caledonia serves as an effective damper on Angela's sometimes ill-conceived plans. When murder strikes their exclusive retirement community in *The J. Alfred Prufrock Murders* (Donald I. Fine, 1988), Angela, Caledonia, and a small circle of their friends decide to investigate. Eventually the officer in charge of the case, suave and attractive—but young—Lieutenant Martinez, allows them to "help." Sawyer writes with clear eyes and no false sentimentality about the elderly. Her characters are engaging and believable, her plots solidly constructed, and her humor restrained but effectively employed. The first novel in the series was an Agatha nominee for Best First Malice Domestic Mystery Novel.

Like Sawyer, Margot Arnold, Mary Bowen Hall, E. X. Ferrars, Eleanor Boylan, and Gallagher Gray write about the elderly, proving that the skills for detecting crimes don't necessarily diminish with age. Readers who enjoy little old lady detectives might also try two of the classics, Agatha Christie's Miss Marple and Patricia Wentworth's Miss Silver.

Scoppettone, Sandra/Early, Jack. Under the pseudonym of Jack Early, Scoppettone has written three hard-boiled mysteries. The first was *A Creative Kind of Killer* (Franklin Watts, 1984). It features Fortune Fanelli, a private eye who lives in the SoHo area of New York City. A teenager from the New Jersey suburbs is killed across the street from his apartment, and the girl's uncle hires him to investigate. Fortune is a single father of two teenagers, and is a sympathetic, charming character. As in her later novels, the author creates vivid scenes of Italian-American family life in New York. *Donato & Daughter* (Dutton, 1988) is a darkly dramatic suspense novel about a series of killings of nuns. Police lieutenant Dina Donato heads up a crime team set up for these cases and her father, Sergeant Michael Donato, assists her.

Under her own name, Scoppettone now is writing a series of mysteries with lesbian private eye Lauren Laurano. The first Lauren Laurano novel is *Everything You Have Is Mine* (Little, Brown, 1991). Lauren is a bright and observant character, and she shares her life with her long-term lover Kip, a psychotherapist. These novels are fairly hard-boiled mysteries, with humorous observations by Lauren on the foibles of humanity. They are atmospheric, with settings primarily in Greenwich Village. Lauren likes to compare herself to fictional sleuths; she often asks herself, "What would Kinsey Millhone [or another fictional detective] do?" *I'll Be Leaving You Always* (Little, Brown, 1993) is a darker novel, with an exploration of the nature of friendship and the eternal possibility of betrayal. Scoppettone creates well-realized New York City backdrops for her stories.

Sue Grafton, J. M. Redmann, Linda Grant, Sara Paretsky, and Liza Cody are some other writers who have created feisty women who are private eyes. Lillian O'Donnell, Dorothy Uhnak, and Dorothy Salisbury Davis use vivid New York settings.

Sedley, Kate. Medieval England is becoming increasingly popular as a setting for mystery fiction, and Sedley's new series takes as its time frame a particularly turbulent era of English history, the Wars of the Roses. This period of political strife affords the author excellent opportunity to weave tales of murder into the fabric of history, as Ellis Peters does with her series set just over three centuries earlier. Sedley's detective is Roger the Chapman, a young man who had been sent as a novice to the Benedictine monastery at Glastonbury by his widowed mother. But Roger felt the call of the world outside the abbey, so he left the cloisters and eventually ended up as a chapman, or peddler. Following this trade, Roger can travel around England as he pleases. In the first of the series, *Death and the Chapman* (St. Martin, 1992), the year is 1471. While the York-Lancaster war rages on, Roger agrees to look for a wealthy young man who disappeared in London. Along the way, Roger becomes acquainted with Richard, Duke of Gloucester, the future Richard III, and does the duke a service. The duke calls upon Roger for help in the second book, *The Plymouth Cloak* (St. Martin, 1993), and thus Sedley establishes a strong link for her detective with the troubled figure of Richard III. Sedley handles the period detail with ease, and her sleuth, Roger, is an amiable and intelligent protagonist.

Fans of the medieval mystery are certainly acquainted with Brother Cadfael and his creator, Ellis Peters. Other writers of medieval mysteries are Elizabeth Eyre, Margaret Frazer, Sharan Newman, and P. C. Doherty, who writes under three additional names, Michael Clynes, C. L. Grace, and Paul Harding.

Shah, Diane K. Shah is a veteran journalist who also writes mysteries. Her first novel, *The Mackin Cover* (Dodd, Mead, 1977), featured journalist Lindsie Hollis, an associate editor of the fictional *Monday* magazine. Alexander Mackin, a star quarterback, disappears shortly after Lindsie interviews him, and she must find him again to finish her cover story. Using her knowledge of California and her journalism background, Shah then began a series of books starring Paris Chandler, a legman for the gossip writer on the Los Angeles *Examiner.* These newspaper mysteries are set in the L.A. of the late forties, and Shah does a superb job of fictionally recreating the postwar city, especially the Hollywood movie colony that is just about to be revolutionized by television. Chandler, who is the war widow of a son of the L.A. *Times* owners, is also a Hollywood insider. Her coworkers, servants, and friends are depicted as typically zany southern Californians, but it is the meticulous and loving detailing of an L.A.

that is gone forever that lifts Shah's books above run-of-the-mill mysteries. Paris Chandler's exploits in pursuit of a good story and a move up the ranks toward a real reporter's job are irresistible.

The first Paris Chandler novel is *As Crime Goes By* (Bantam, 1990). Shah has also coauthored LAPD chief Daryl Gates's autobiography, *Chief* (Bantam, 1992).

Readers also might appreciate Gabrielle Kraft's humorous view of contemporary Los Angeles, and the stories of rookie reporters written by Annette Roome and Lucille Kallen. Readers of *The Mackin Cover* also may enjoy Alison Gordon's baseball mysteries. Deborah Powell writes mysteries set in the city of Houston in the 1930s.

Shankman, Sarah. She began her life in crime as Alice Storey, to separate the criminous Storey from the mainstream fiction–writing Shankman, at an editor's insistence. Thus the first two novels in her Samantha Adams series, *First Kill All the Lawyers* (Pocket, 1988) and *Then Hang All the Liars* (Pocket, 1989), were published under the Storey name. Sam Adams is a journalist, born and bred in Atlanta. After the death of her policeman lover in San Francisco, the formerly hard-drinking Sam has returned to her native Atlanta, where she now works for the *Constitution*. The two Storey novels are thoroughly enjoyable stories with a nicely realized setting and interesting characters. But with the switch back to her real name with the third novel of the series, *Now Let's Talk of Graves* (Pocket, 1990), Shankman's full voice unleashed itself, and the result was a wickedly funny novel. Set in New Orleans during Mardi Gras, *Graves* is a veritable feast of eccentric characters, pitch-perfect Southern dialogue, and a rollicking plot that keeps the reader gasping with laughter and guessing until the end. The fourth novel, *She Walks in Beauty* (Pocket, 1991), peeks behind the scenes at the Miss America pageant, and Atlantic City will never be the same. Shankman gives the reader an unusual combination of unsparingly satiric humor and a keen eye for the often absurd contradictions of the contemporary South. Her work is evolving into her own unique style of crime novel.

Like Shankman, Joan Hess has a satiric eye and pen with her Maggody series. Those who enjoy the Atlanta setting should try the works of Celestine Sibley and Kathy Hogan Trocheck. Meg O'Brien writes a series about another hard-edged journalist. Readers who have enjoyed Shankman's view of the modern South might try the New Orleans series of Julie Smith and Chris Wiltz as well, though they are much harder-edged than Shankman.

Shannon, Dell. See **Linington, Elizabeth.**

Shepherd, Stella. Before turning to writing full time, Shepherd studied medicine and worked as a doctor specializing in radiotherapy. She brings her knowledge of medicine to her series of mysteries featuring Inspector Richard Montgomery of Nottingham CID. In the first book, *Black Justice* (Doubleday, 1989), the action is centered around the murder of a young doctor, which occurs during a weekend meeting of the Medieval Circle. This society is made up of mostly amateurs interested in the Middle Ages, and some of the amateurs are colleagues at a Nottingham hospital. The action in the second book, *Murderous Remedy* (Doubleday, 1990), takes place in a Nottingham teaching hospital, but in the third book, *Thinner Than Blood* (Doubleday, 1992), Shepherd has moved out of the hospital and into the village. Shepherd's medical knowledge plays a strong role in the methods of murder; various drugs are used in devious and effective ways, and Shepherd paints an interesting picture of medical life and culture in England. She reveals bits and pieces of the life of her main character and his subordinates as the series unfolds, in time-honored English police procedural fashion.

Readers looking for the combination of the medical world and the mystery should try P. D. James, whose own work in hospitals has given her extensive knowledge of the milieu, and the two series of American writer Mary Kittredge. Other good English traditional mystery writers in much the same vein as Shepherd are E. X. Ferrars, Anthea Fraser, and Ann Cleeves (with her series about Inspector Ramsay).

Sibley, Celestine. Sibley, a veteran Atlanta reporter, may well hold the record for the number of years between debut and second appearance of a mystery series character. Sibley's first murder mystery was *The Malignant Heart* (Doubleday, 1958), which featured as its detective a young reporter, Katherine "Katy" Kincaid. Someone has murdered a powerful woman columnist at Katy's paper, and Katy is a suspect. The policeman investigating the crime is Katy's childhood chum, Lieutenant Benjamin Mulcay, and muted sparks fly between them until the crime is solved. When Katy makes her second appearance, it is as the widowed Kate Mulcay in *Ah, Sweet Mystery* (HarperCollins, 1991). In the thirty-three years between her appearances, Kate has married and lost her beloved Benjy. She is still a reporter, writing a thrice-weekly column for an Atlanta newspaper and living in a log cabin in a tranquil and sparsely populated suburb of Atlanta. Then one of Kate's neighbors, a beloved elderly woman friend, confesses to the murder of her own obnoxious stepson, and Kate becomes involved in sorting out the mess. Kate is sensible, albeit stubborn, and altogether an attractive character. Sibley's depiction of the modern South is adroit, and fans of the regional crime story will find much to enjoy.

Other reporter-detectives whom readers might enjoy are Samantha Adams (created by Sarah Shankman), Kate Henry (created by sports journalist Alison Gordon), and Henrietta 0. Collins (the new series character created by Carolyn G. Hart). Readers looking for an Atlanta setting might try some of the works of Patricia H. Sprinkle, Kay Hooper, and Kathy Hogan Trocheck.

Simpson, Dorothy. Her first novel, *Harbingers of Fear* (London: Macdonald, 1977), was suspense; her second, *The Night She Died* (Scribner, 1981), was an English police procedural in the traditional vein. With this traditional series, starring policeman Luke Thanet, however, Simpson found a special place in contemporary mystery fiction. Her cop, Thanet, is an ordinary family man with a wife and two children. As the series begins, Thanet's wife Joan is at home with two young children, and as the series progresses, the reader watches the natural growth and evolution of the Thanet family. This core of ordinariness, with a series character grappling with the common problems of daily life, offers a center to Simpson's fiction which is, actually, rather unusual in contemporary mystery fiction. The Kent town of Sturrenden and its environs serve as the setting for the series. Simpson delineates her area with a loving eye and brings to her writing an excellent understanding of English urban life in the latter decades of the twentieth century. The excellent *Last Seen Alive* (Scribner, 1985) won the Silver Dagger from the British Crime Writers' Association.

Those who like their mysteries set in England's villages and smaller urban areas should try also the work of Marjorie Eccles, June Thomson, and Anthea Fraser. Pat Burden, Patricia Moyes, and Susan B. Kelly also write police procedural series in the traditional vein.

Sims, L. V. Sims writes hard-boiled police procedurals set in San Jose, California and the Silicon Valley. Her protagonist is Sergeant Dixie T. Struthers, one of the first women on the San Jose police force. In the first book, *Murder Is Only Skin Deep* (Charter, 1987), she is confronted with a sexist boss and colleagues who don't think that she can ever measure up to male police officers. However, Dixie is the daughter and granddaughter of Irish cops, and she is determined to prove herself their equal. Her partner, Herb Woodall, is quickly won over by her competence. She is accepted more slowly by her other colleagues, but their sexual harassment lessens as she proves herself to be a loyal partner and a good cop. In *To Sleep, Perchance to Kill* (Charter, 1988), Sims juxtaposes scenes of an American traitor in a Japanese prison camp in World War II with a recent murder in a high-tech computer laboratory. Sims's mysteries reflect the violence of urban police work and the odd twists possible in relationships between coworkers.

Readers looking for tales of policewomen's lives should try Susan Dunlap's Jill Smith books, Katherine V. Forrest, Lillian O'Donnell, and Dorothy Uhnak.

Singer, Shelley. A former journalist and editor, Singer uses the Bay Area, where she herself lives, as the setting for her two series of mysteries. The first series features Jake Samson, who debuted in *Samson's Deal* (St. Martin, 1983). Once a cop in his native Chicago, Jake found his enthusiasm for his job waning in the wake of the 1968 riots, and he left the Midwest for California. Eventually, after several moves and several career changes, Jake settled in Oakland, where he lives off the income from a trust fund and from some rental property he owns. In the first book Jake helps out the friend of a friend with a problem, which turns out to be solving the murder of the man's wife. Jake doesn't have a license for private investigation, but he does have a friend who's an editor for an investigative magazine who gives him press credentials so that he can nose around. Helping Jake in his investigations is his tenant, Rosie Vicente, a woman given to wearing cowboy boots and Gertrude Stein T-shirts. She also has a standard poodle named Alice B. Toklas. Jake himself is a cat lover. This series, like Jake, is pretty mellow, with the feel of somewhat other-worldly northern California. Recently, Singer created a new series, starring Barrett Lake, high school history teacher, who decides she'd rather become a private eye instead. Her debut is *Following Jane* (Signet, 1993). Singer uses the Bay Area settings effectively. Her characters are genial, and the plots are engaging puzzles.

Readers who have enjoyed Singer might try the work of other Bay Area writers, like Marilyn Wallace, Susan Dunlap, Linda Grant, or Marcia Muller.

Slovo, Gillian. Slovo is an expatriate South African novelist and journalist. Her mysteries are hard-boiled stories with sleuth Kate Baeier. Kate is a freelance journalist who moves gradually into private investigations as the series develops. She is Portuguese, plays the saxophone, and lives in a racially diverse area of London. Her politics are decidedly left-wing and her cases generally have political overtones. In the first book, *Morbid Symptoms* (Dembner, 1984), she is asked to look into the death of a fellow writer who has been doing research on South Africa. In a later mystery, *Death Comes Staccato* (Doubleday, 1988), she has set up her own investigative agency and has enough business to employ an assistant. In her novels, Slovo provides absorbing portraits of a London far different from that seen in most English crime novels; this London is full of left-wing students, squatters, poor immigrants, street markets, and high-minded communes of argumentative intellectuals. Slovo, whose father is a senior official of the African National Congress and whose mother, Ruth First, was an anti-apartheid activist killed by a letter bomb, also has written two novels about South Africa, *Ties of Blood* (Morrow, 1990) and *The Betrayal* (London: Michael Joseph, 1991). *Facade* (London: Michael Joseph, 1993) is a novel of psychological suspense in which Laura Weber, an actor, uncovers the shadowy past of her mother who committed suicide and her famous father who has died mysteriously.

Liza Cody and Sarah Dunant also write hard-boiled tales of women detectives in London, and Val McDermid's crime novels are set in locales such as Glasgow and Manchester.

Smith, Evelyn E. Smith has created, in Miss Susan Melville, perhaps the only gently bred assassin in contemporary mystery fiction. Miss Melville, descendant of a long line of Melvilles, whose family fortunes were begun by a Caribbean pirate, has fallen on hard times in the first book of the series, *Miss Melville Regrets* (Donald I. Fine, 1986). When the genteel New York school at which she teaches art must close, Miss Melville begins a downward spiral, at the nadir of which she decides to kill herself at a society function as something of a political protest. At the last moment, however, she decides to kill the speaker, an obnoxious and morally corrupt man who is the son of an old family friend. What Miss Melville didn't know was that her victim was already the target of a highly secret organization in the assassination business. Soon Miss Melville has a lucrative new career as a highly paid assassin in New York City, but she insists that her hits must be for persons who, for moral reasons, deserve to die. Through the eyes of Miss Melville, Smith offers mordant and humorous observations of life in contemporary New York City, with particular attention given to the foibles of the rich and pretentious. Miss Melville's life changes considerably during the course of the series, but Smith wisely focuses on the character of Miss Melville herself. This is an unusual series, but those looking for an uncommon heroine will enjoy it.

Like Evelyn E. Smith, Joyce Christmas also sets her novels among society in the Big Apple. Other entertaining series with New York settings are those by Gallagher Gray, Jane Dentinger, Annette Meyers, and Margaret Maron.

Smith, Janet L. Smith's series character, Annie MacPherson, is, like Smith, a lawyer in Seattle. In the first book, *Sea of Troubles* (Perseverance Press, 1990), Annie and her partner Joel Feinstein have their own firm. Annie travels to a resort hotel in the San Juan islands to look into its sale for a client. The buyer's girlfriend is kidnapped, and all negotiations are halted until the case is solved. Annie learns about kayaking and whale watching while investigating the kidnapping and multiple murders. At the beginning of *Practice to Deceive* (Fawcett, 1992), Annie is returning to work from an extended leave of absence. Her partnership is merging with a much larger and more prestigious law firm, and she goes to work for the powerful and sexist Gordon Barclay. He is planning to secede from the company and take his clients with him. Smith provides plenty of back-stabbing and office politics in her insider's view of law firms. Annie is a smart, interesting character, and the legal backgrounds are as well described as the northwestern scenery.

Readers also may enjoy Susan Wolfe's *The Last Billable Hour,* another novel of murder and mayhem in a West Coast legal firm. Lia Matera, Carolyn Wheat, Judith Van Gieson, and Julie Smith have female series characters who are lawyers. J. A. Jance, Barbara Wilson, and Mary Daheim use Seattle settings for their crime novels, and Dana Stabenow writes about a lawyer turned investigator in Alaska.

Smith, Joan. British novelist Smith has written a series of mysteries about Loretta Lawson, a professor of English at the University of London. Loretta is a thoughtful, analytic sleuth, as well as an active feminist theoretician. The first book, *A Masculine Ending* (Scribner, 1988), involves the murder of a deconstructionist English literature professor in Paris. Loretta, assisted by her Oxford friend Bridget Bennett, looks into this murder as a matter of self-defense, since she found the body and might be a suspect. *Why Aren't They Screaming?* (Scribner, 1989) is set in Oxfordshire, where Loretta has taken a country cottage in which to recuperate from an illness. Unfortunately, she finds that the owner has turned the back garden over to a women's peace camp. Loretta gets little peace and quiet, especially when her landlady is killed. In *Don't Leave Me This Way* (Scribner, 1990), a woman Loretta knew years ago shows up on Christmas Eve in need of a place to sleep. She disappears, however, on New Year's Eve. Loretta finds out later that she's been killed in a suspicious car crash on that same night. Loretta's curiosity impels her to look into this mystery, and she is subsequently threatened and injured while engaged in her search. Smith's novels are densely written academic mysteries, and her protagonist, Loretta, is a deliberative, mature scholar.

Readers in search of other academic mysteries might turn to Amanda Cross, Susan Kenney, Nora Kelly, and Edith Skom. Maggie Elliott, in the mysteries of Elizabeth Atwood Taylor, is another self-reflective, intense character.

Smith, Julie. The first Edgar Award for Best Novel given to an American woman since 1956 was awarded to Smith for *New Orleans Mourning* (St. Martin, 1990). Smith started her writing career as a journalist, then began to write mysteries with a series that featured San Francisco lawyer Rebecca Schwartz. The first book in this series is *Death Turns a Trick* (Walker, 1982). Rebecca, who identities herself as a Jewish feminist lawyer, matures in her personal approach to life and in her career throughout the series. The Schwartz novels are generally light, amusing fare, although *Dead in the Water* (Ivy, 1991) is more harrowing and violent than the earlier books. Smith's second series of mysteries set in the Bay Area stars Paul McDonald, freelance writer and former journalist. There are two Paul McDonald novels to date; these are humorous, hard-boiled private eye novels. The first is *True-Life Adventure* (Mysterious, 1985); the second is *Huckleberry Fiend* (Mysterious, 1987). Julie Smith's most recent crime series chronicles the adventures of Skip Langdon, a policewoman in New Orleans. Smith hit her stride as a mature writer with these novels. The first, *New Orleans Mourning*, gives the reader an insider's view of Mardi Gras and particularly its high society participants. Skip Langdon is a fully rounded, believable character; readers learn about her neuroses, weaknesses, and insecurities, as well as her talent as an investigator. She is confident and skilled in her job, but she feels awkward about almost everything else. The Garden District social background that Skip grew up in has been of assistance in her crime-solving, even though she felt out of place there and has abandoned that life to become a cop. The second Skip Langdon novel is *The Axeman's Jazz* (St.

Martin, 1991); it's another excellent examination of New Orleans murders. This time a serial killer is repeating the modus operandi of a legendary killer from earlier in the century. Smith brings a vivid, bawdy, drunken, and hedonistic New Orleans to life in her novels, but she also captures the inner lives and motives of the natives of this city as well as other Southerners.

San Francisco lawyers also appear in the works of Lia Matera and Chelsea Quinn Yarbro. Mysteries set in New Orleans include Sarah Shankman's *Now Let's Talk of Graves* (Pocket, 1990) and the novels of Chris Wiltz. Lillian O'Donnell's Norah Mulcahaney novels and Margaret Maron's Sigrid Harald novels portray the lives of policewomen, and Elizabeth George's mysteries give us psychological insights into the minds of investigators.

Smith, Rosamond. One of the premiere names in American belles lettres, Joyce Carol Oates, has adopted the Smith pseudonym to pen her masterful novels of psychological suspense. Like Ruth Rendell, Smith writes about disturbed personalities or about how a crime can affect the people concerned with it. In her first novel, *Lives of the Twins* (Simon & Schuster, 1987), Molly Marks finds herself intrigued with a puzzle from her lover's past. When she and her lover, a psychotherapist, move in together, he tells her that he has an identical twin brother with whom he has no contact any longer. Molly, for reasons she can't understand, seeks out her lover's twin and becomes enmeshed in a relationship with him as well. How will she get herself out of this increasingly difficult dilemma? Another Smith novel, *Nemesis* (Dutton, 1990), probes the aftermath of an accusation of rape brought by a male graduate student against a world-famous male composer at a select New England school of music. Eventually a murder complicates the situation, and Smith unravels the mystery with great skill. The complexities of human behavior are fertile ground for Rosamond Smith, whose work is very much in the tradition of writers like Margaret Millar and the aforementioned Ruth Rendell.

In addition to Millar and Rendell, those who have read Rosamond Smith might enjoy the suspense novels of Frances Hegarty, Patricia Highsmith, and Minette Walters.

Sprinkle, Patricia H. The star of this series, Sheila Travis, is recently widowed when the series begins with *Murder at Markham* (St. Martin, 1988). Sheila's husband, an abusive and controlling man, had been a diplomat in Japan, and Sheila's experience as a diplomatic wife wins her a job at the Markham Institute of International Studies in Chicago, which trains students for the diplomatic corps. Sheila's sleuthing skills quickly come to the fore, however, when an uneasy situation erupts into murder. Aided by her wealthy and charming elderly aunt Mary, Sheila sorts out the situation. Subsequent books find Sheila moving back to her native South. In *Murder in the Charleston Manner* (St. Martin, 1990), Sheila goes to South Carolina to aid an old school friend of Aunt Mary's. Recent books find Sheila, who grew up in Japan, living and working in Atlanta for a large Japanese corporation. Sprinkle writes about the Southern setting and her mostly Southern characters with warmth and understanding. The mood of the stories is definitely cozy, but Sprinkle has a keen eye for the often odd contrasts of life in the modern South, and she uses them to good effect.

Other Southern series of interest are the works of Mignon F. Ballard, Charlaine Harris, Taylor McCafferty, and Sharyn McCrumb. Those looking specifically for the Atlanta setting might try the work of Celestine Sibley, Kathy Hogan Trochek, and the first two books of Sarah Shankman (as Alice Storey).

Stabenow, Dana. Stabenow writes a highly atmospheric series of mysteries set in Alaska. The heroine is Kate Shugak, who is a former investigator for the District Attorney's office in Anchorage. Kate, an Aleut, has retreated to live in the bush after being seriously injured while trying to stop a father from sexually abusing his daughter. Her throat was cut, so she has trouble with her voice, but she is still curious and vital. The first two books in the series are set in a fictional national park that covers thousands of acres of mountains, glaciers, and forests. In the first book, *A Cold Day for Murder* (Berkley, 1992), Kate needs to find out what has happened to a missing park ranger and an investigator sent in after him. *A Fatal Thaw* (Berkley, 1993) begins on the first day of spring with multiple murders. The mass murderer confesses immediately, but forensic tests show that one victim was killed by a different gun. Kate is hired to find the hidden killer, and during her search she discovers many of the concealed activities that go on daily in the bush country, like growing marijuana and poaching protected animals. In *Dead in the Water* (Berkley, 1993), Kate goes undercover on a fishing boat to find the killers of two crewmen. Kate is assisted in her investigations by Mutt, her half-wolf, half-husky dog; her on-again, off-again lover Jack Morgan; and Bobby Clark, a raucous, intelligent, and wheelchair-bound black Vietnam vet. The novels are notable for their vivid descriptions of the Alaskan bush, Aleut towns, and the fiercely independent bush dwellers. The reader is held by the fascination of such an exotic setting for mysterious events.

A Cold Day for Murder won an Edgar Award for Best Paperback Original.

Readers who enjoy Stabenow's books should try *Murder on the Iditarod Trail* by Sue Henry and the legal mysteries, set in Seattle, of Janet L. Smith. Chelsea Quinn Yarbro and Jean Hager write mysteries with Native American sleuths.

Stacey, Susannah/Eyre, Elizabeth. Jill Staynes and Margaret Storey are former teachers and lifelong friends who are the joint authors of two series of crime novels. Under the Stacey pseudonym, they write a series of police procedurals with a continuing protagonist in Superintendent Robert Bone. He appears to be a typically quiet, omniscient English policeman. Tragedy has affected Bone deeply, however; his wife has been killed in a car accident and he is bringing up his teenage daughter, Charlotte, alone. Charlotte has a speech impediment and other injuries from the accident, and she is a strong and charming character in the novels. Bone works out of Tunbridge Wells, and the mysteries he solves occur in the villages and countryside of Kent. The people he encounters in the course of his investigations are idiosyncratic individuals whose psychology Stacey explores as an integral part of her plotting. For example, an intelligent and charismatic rock star, Ken Cryer, appears in several stories. The first Superintendent Bone mystery is *Goodbye Nanny Gray* (Summit, 1987). A nanny is murdered, and there are many suspects in this well-done English village mystery. *Grave Responsibility* (Summit, 1990) is a bleak and rather gory tale of multiple murders that occur within the very peculiar Clare family.

Under the pseudonym of Elizabeth Eyre, the writers have begun a new series of historical mysteries set in Renaissance Italy. Sigismondo, the Duke of Rocca's agent, is an enigmatic sleuth in the atmospheric *Death of the Duchess* (Harcourt Brace Jovanovich, 1992) and *Curtains for the Cardinal* (Harcourt Brace Jovanovich, 1993). The authors' plots reflect the conspiracies and the Machiavellian scheming of the times, along with detailed historical settings.

Fans of Stacey's mysteries should try the works of P. D. James, M. C. Beaton, and Ruth Rendell. Jean Hager writes about a policeman, Mitch Bushyhead, who is a devoted single father of a teenage girl. Kate Sedley, Margaret Frazer, and Sharan Newman write medieval mysteries.

Stewart, Mary. Stewart began her writing career in the 1950s and eventually she became the foremost practitioner of the romantic suspense novel. She is known especially for the use of exotic locations and for her masterly descriptions of landscapes. Several of her novels, such as *The Moon-Spinners* (Mill, 1963) and *This Rough Magic* (Morrow, 1964), are set in Greece, but her stories also take place in Scotland, France, Lebanon, Austria, and England. *My Brother Michael* (Mill & Morrow, 1960), one of her best, brings together brooding, austere Greek backgrounds with a twentieth-century revenge tragedy in the shape of a wartime murder and a postwar search for justice and vengeance. In many of her novels, Stewart uses the archetypal gothic plot device of a young woman caught in a dangerous situation, from which she uses her own agile wits to escape. But she brings to this classic form her own touch of magic, exemplified by her elegant and educated use of language and history. A superior example is *Nine Coaches Waiting* (Mill & Morrow, 1959), set in the French Alps, which tells of a young boy protected by his teacher from the ill-will of his evil relatives and a series of potentially fatal mishaps. Stewart's recent novel, *The Stormy Petrel* (Morrow, 1991), is an impressionistic story of mysterious events on a small island off the west coast of Scotland.

Stewart also has written an admirable set of historical novels that weave together the legends of Merlin, King Arthur, and Mordred, with her own splendid evocation of fifth-century Britain.

Stewart's first novel was *Madam, Will You Talk?* (Mill, 1956). Her first Arthurian novel was *The Crystal Cave* (Morrow, 1970).

Many later writers in the field have been influenced by Stewart's style and popularity, including Caroline Llewellyn, D. F. Mills, Phyllis Whitney, Victoria Holt, Elizabeth Peters, and Dorothy Cannell.

Storey, Alice. See **Shankman, Sarah.**

Sucher, Dorothy. With the intriguingly titled *Dead Men Don't Give Seminars* (St. Martin, 1988), Sucher introduced a detective duo in the grand tradition of Nero Wolfe and Archie Goodwin. Young private eye Vic Newman serves as legman to the brilliant Sabina Swift. Though Vic has a knack for the type of observations that Archie is famous for, Sabina Swift is not the recluse that Wolfe generally was. In their debut, Sabina and her physicist husband are attending a conference in Vermont, where a Nobel laureate is murdered. Sabina calls Vic in to help investigate. In *Dead Men Don't Marry* (St. Martin, 1989), Vic is disturbed by the odd death of a neighbor who had recently married a man Vic finds a little too mysterious. Literate, intelligent, and witty, Sucher combines the private eye novel with the traditional mystery in a very entertaining fashion. *Dead Men Don't Give Seminars* was an Agatha nominee for Best First Novel.

Those who have enjoyed the exploits of Swift and Newman might try the novels of Rex Stout, the Stout-influenced work of William Love, the series by Gallagher Gray, and the Gregor Demarkian novels of Jane Haddam.

Taylor, Elizabeth Atwood. Taylor writes a series of mysteries with heroine Maggie Elliott. The first novel, *The Cable Car Murder* (St. Martin, 1981), has a San Francisco background of wealthy couples with spoiled children and snobbish friends. Maggie is a young widow who has spent her recent years drunk, depressed, and increasingly impecunious. However, her half-sister is killed under a cable car, and the grisly death brings Maggie out of her inertia. Maggie teams up with Pat O'Reagan, a retired cop, to investigate her sister's murder. They do so well at their sleuthing that they decide to open a private eye agency. In *Murder at Vassar* (St. Martin, 1987), Maggie returns east for her Vassar College reunion, only to find more murder and her first solo assignment as a professional investigator. *The Northwest Murders* (St. Martin, 1992) is about the murder and scalping of a hiker on the Pacific Crest Trail near the California-Oregon border. Maggie is staying in a backwoods cabin borrowed from O'Reagan while she recovers from chronic fatigue syndrome. She is hired to find the killer after a local man is falsely accused of the murder. As a backdrop to the detection, Taylor paints a vivid portrait of the Pacific

Northwest woods and their Native American inhabitants. The historical prejudices against the local Karuk and Shasta Indians, and against immigrant Chinese workers in California, become an integral part of her mystery plot.

Other writers who set mysteries in San Francisco and northern California include Janet LaPierre, Chelsea Quinn Yarbro, Susan Dunlap, and Marcia Muller. Isabelle Holland and Joan Smith also write novels with heroines who, like Maggie, are intensely self-reflective.

Thomson, June. Thomson has the distinction of being perhaps the only current mystery writer whose series detective has a different name on either side of the Atlantic. Known to British readers as Inspector Finch, the character had his name changed to Rudd in the United States because Thomson's longtime American publisher, Doubleday, already had a detective named Finch on its list (the Inspector Finch of the novels by the late Margaret Erskine). Finch/Rudd first appeared in *Not One of Us* (Harper, 1971). From the beginning, Thomson demonstrated a keen insight into the psychology of her characters, many of whom live in the smaller towns and villages of England. Her writing style is succinct, with no excess verbiage to trim, particularly when compared to that of P. D. James, but, at her best, Thomson is no less compelling or less psychologically acute. Finch/Rudd is an intriguing and believable character, and Thomson gives him tantalizing puzzles to solve. Especially noteworthy are *The Long Revenge* (Doubleday, 1975) and *The Habit of Loving* (Doubleday, 1979).

Readers of Thomson generally also will enjoy the work of her peers Patricia Moyes and Dorothy Simpson. Other writers who make effective use of the small towns and villages of England for their crime-writing are Susan B. Kelly, Anthea Fraser, Marjorie Eccles, and Clare Curzon.

Travis, Elizabeth. *Deadlines* (St. Martin, 1987), Travis's first book, is a suspense novel about the drugging and eventual murder of an elderly woman. Travis then moved on to write a series of mysteries featuring Ben and Carrie Porter, who live in the suburban town of Riverdale, Connecticut and own a book publishing business. The Porters have arranged their lives so that they can be interchangeable at work and at home. Ben often stays at home, cooking gourmet food and painting, while Carrie takes care of the business. The first book in the series, *Under the Influence* (St. Martin, 1989), is a fairly traditional cozy mystery. A local artist and philanderer is killed in Ben's office with Ben's fishing knife. Ben must, of course, find the murderer in order to clear himself. *Finders Keepers* (St. Martin, 1990) is set on the French Riviera, where Carrie and Ben are in pursuit of the last work of a recently deceased literary giant. The manuscript has been divided among various heirs, with a proviso that one heir must gain possession of the whole book and have it published within one year. Inevitably, the heirs all scramble to steal from each other and the result is mayhem. Travis creates an interesting setting, with tantalizing descriptions of elaborate French meals.

Other writers who have created husband-and-wife detective teams include Carolyn G. Hart, Mollie Hardwick, and Charlotte MacLeod. Orania Papazoglou writes mysteries about the publishing industry, and Valerie Wolzien sets her crime novels in suburban Connecticut.

Trocheck, Kathy Hogan. Formerly a reporter for the *Atlanta Journal-Constitution,* Trocheck has turned a sharply observant eye on life in the modern South in a new series about former cop and not-quite-former private eye, Julia Callahan Garrity, Callahan to her friends. Burned out by the male-dominated worlds of the police and the private eye game, Callahan has gone into business with her mother Edna Mae Garrity. As owners of House Mouse, Callahan and her mother, along with a deliciously funny staff of "mice," clean houses in some of the best sections of Atlanta. In the first book of the series, *Every Crooked Nanny* (HarperCollins, 1992), Callahan takes on a cleaning job for an old sorority sister, Lilah Rose Beemish, who soon turns to Callahan for help with more than just overgrown dust bunnies. Her family's Mormon nanny has absconded with jewelry, furs, and files of a secret business deal which could land Lilah Rose's husband deeply in trouble. Callahan dusts off her private eye license and tries her best to help the obnoxious Beemish family. Callahan Garrity is smart, funny, and tenacious, whether she's tracking down a murder suspect or trying to get that noisome stain out of the living room carpet. With helpers like Neva Jean, one of her cheerfully white trash House Mouse employees, the elderly black sisters, Sister and Baby Easterbrook, and the irrepressible Edna Mae Garrity, Callahan has her hands full solving crimes in Atlanta. Trocheck's trenchant humor takes no prisoners when it comes to the idiosyncracies of modern American society or of Southern culture.

Readers acquainted with Trocheck's books might try Kay Hooper, Sarah Shankman, Celestine Sibley, and Patricia Houck Sprinkle, all of whom use Atlanta as settings for their books. For other Southern series with satirical overtones, readers should look for the work of Sharyn McCrumb and Charlaine Harris.

Truman, Margaret. Truman writes mysteries in the classic puzzle whodunit mode, all set in and around Washington, D.C. The novels have murders committed in Washington landmarks such as the White House, the Supreme Court, the Kennedy Center, and the National Cathedral. Often a dash of romance between male and female investigators accompanies the working out of the plot, and politics is always present in the story. Truman has an insider's knowledge of government and the political process, especially as practiced in the Washington corridors of power. She shows her acquaintance with the details and minutiae of White House life, for example, in *Murder in the White House* (Arbor, 1980). Oddly enough for a President's daughter, Truman doesn't even mind casting revered and august figures like the President or the Chief Justice of the Supreme Court (in fictional form, of course) as murder suspects. Another offspring of a President has written Washington mysteries: Elliott Roosevelt's series of mysteries depicts his mother Eleanor Roosevelt as the sleuth.

R. B. Dominic (aka Emma Lathen) writes a series with a congressman-sleuth that readers may enjoy.

Tucker, Kerry. Tucker's series heroine is Libby Kincaid, a photographer. In the first mystery, *Still Waters* (HarperCollins, 1991), she is taking photographs of celebrities for a glitzy New York magazine when her brother dies in southern Ohio. Libby goes out for his funeral and discovers that not everyone is convinced that he committed suicide and tried to shoot his beloved dog as well. As she cleans out his belongings and stays in his house, mysterious events begin to happen. Tucker's second book, *Cold Feet* (HarperCollins, 1992), is set in New York City, during a brutally hot summer. Libby is on leave from her magazine job and she is taking a series of photographs of a group of jazz tap dancers. Her life is consumed by her project, at least until murder occurs and her wandering father reenters her life in a dramatic fashion. As well as creating lively mystery plots, Tucker provides a detailed view of how Libby thinks about her art, and how she handles the technical aspects of her photography.

Susan Moody's heroine Penny Wanawake is also a photographer. Sandra Scoppettone's richly detailed New York City settings also might prove enjoyable for readers of Tucker's mysteries.

Uhnak, Dorothy. New Yorker Uhnak spent fourteen years with the city's Transit Police, won several medals, then quit because of sex discrimination and wrote *Policewoman: A Young Woman's Initiation into the Realities of Justice* (Simon & Schuster, 1964). She has since written a number of realistic police procedurals set in New York that feature female characters. Her first novel, *The Bait* (Simon & Schuster, 1968) won an Edgar Award for Best First Mystery, and introduced a series character, Christie Opara. Opara is an NYPD detective, who encounters sexism and violence routinely in her job. In *The Ledger* (Simon & Schuster, 1970), for example, Christie uncovers the story of a mobster's girlfriend, who became a prostitute after starting out in a convent. *The Ledger* won the Grande Prix de Litterature Policiere. *False Witness* (Simon & Schuster, 1981), one of Uhnak's most acclaimed works, involves Lynne Jacobi, a Bureau Chief in the New York District Attorney's office. Lynne, in the midst of an affair with a subordinate, is assigned to the case of a top-ranked black fashion model and part-time revolutionary talk show host who, in the novel's opening scene, is assaulted with particular savagery. *False Witness* is memorably successful in fooling the reader about the identity of the culprit. *Victims* (Simon & Schuster, 1985) is the story of a brutal killing of a young woman on a middle-class street in Queens, where no one helps her or even calls the police. Uhnak shows why each witness refused to help, and how people become brutalized through the difficulties and crime of contemporary urban life. *The Ryer Avenue Story* (St. Martin, 1993) is Uhnak's first book in almost a decade. It begins in the Bronx in 1935 with a brutal attack on a drunken man. Six neighborhood kids are involved, and one of their fathers is executed for the crime. Uhnak's story covers the children as they grow up and as social customs change. Uhnak's stories are often violent and portray the world of big-city politics and police work with a gritty frankness. She vividly portrays New York's ethnic groups and neighborhoods.

Readers also may want to try the realistic urban novels of Lillian O'Donnell, Soledad Santiago, Teri White, Dorothy Salisbury Davis, and Katherine V. Forrest.

Valentine, Deborah. "Intense" and "dark-hued" are two adjectives one might use to describe the work of Valentine. The emotional terrain of her novels can be tricky for the characters to navigate, but fascinating for the readers. In the first of the series, *Unorthodox Methods* (Gollancz, 1989; Avon, 1991), Valentine introduces her recurring characters, sculptress Katharine Craig and policeman Kevin Bryce. Someone in an affluent community near Lake Tahoe has been stealing valuable art, and Bryce is on the trail. Katharine Craig returns to the area to visit her cousin. When a man is murdered on a bizarre piece of sculpture, Katharine is implicated. Bryce finds himself intrigued by her, and their relationship develops through this book and continues in the subsequent novels. The second, *A Collector of Photographs* (Bantam, 1989), has Bryce, who has resigned from the force, investigating a strange situation for the husband of a friend of Katharine's. Readers who enjoy mysteries about the art world will find this one compelling reading, as Valentine demonstrates with telling force that "art has no ethics," as one character declares. Valentine's third novel, *Fine Distinctions* (Avon,

1991), received an Edgar nomination for Best Paperback Original.

Readers looking for suspense and mystery novels with a darker edge to them might try the work of Faye Kellerman, the non-Wexford novels of Ruth Rendell, and the work of Rosamond Smith.

Van Gieson, Judith. Hard-boiled, atmospheric mystery novels are the metier of Van Gieson. Her series with lawyer and investigator Neil Hamel is set in a vividly realized New Mexico landscape. Neil has a small, slow law practice with an ineffectual law partner, Brink, and an equally inept secretary. She chiefly handles divorces and real estate closings. This leaves her plenty of time to get caught up in causes, like reintroducing an endangered species of wolf to its former habitat in *The Wolf Path* (HarperCollins, 1992), or opposing urban redevelopment in *The Other Side of Death* (HarperCollins, 1991). Aside from her casework, Neil has a young Mexican lover known only as The Kid; he's her auto mechanic, but also the person who gets her through bad times and lonely nights. Essentially a loner, Neil tries not to rely on him or on the tequila she drinks so much of when she's feeling morose. Van Gieson's descriptive powers bring home to the reader the heat and the austere beauty of the desert Southwest, although most of *Raptor* (Harper & Row, 1990) is set in Montana. Throughout the series, Van Gieson's writing is spare, economical, and often cynical.

The first Neil Hamel novel is *North of the Border* (Walker, 1988).

Other novelists of interest include Lia Matera and Mercedes Lambert for their depictions of hard-boiled female lawyers, and Jane Langton, M. K. Wren, and Janet LaPierre for environmentally oriented mysteries.

Vine, Barbara. See **Rendell, Ruth.**

· **Wallace, Marilyn.** With her debut novel, *A Case of Loyalties* (St. Martin, 1986), Wallace won the Macavity Award for Best First Novel. This book also introduced her series characters, Jay Goldstein and Carlos Cruz, who work out of the Oakland, California, Police Department's homicide division. Goldstein, who likes to spend his spare time reading philosophy, comes from a prominent Bay Area family; his father is an influential lawyer. Cruz is a family man with two sons and a working wife. Both men, despite their widely differing backgrounds, are dedicated to their work and their ideals of justice, and they balance each other's weaknesses with their strengths to make an effective team. Wallace tells her stories through multiple viewpoints, allowing the reader to have a wider view of the story than just through the eyes of the detectives. This is particularly effective in *Primary Target* (Bantam, 1988), in which a mysterious group named the Brotherhood of Men attacks the presidential campaign of Congresswoman Jean Talbot. Most recently, Wallace penned a suspense novel, *So Shall You Reap* (Doubleday Perfect Crime, 1992), somewhat in the vein of Barbara Michaels. Wallace writes crisply, with intelligence, and her stories are suspenseful and absorbing. Wallace has also edited the *Sisters in Crime* anthologies (Berkley) and coedited the first *Deadly Allies* anthology (Doubleday).

Those who have enjoyed Wallace and her Bay Area settings might try the work of Shelley Singer, Marcia Muller, Susan Dunlap (the Jill Smith books), and Linda Grant.

Those who have read *So Shall You Reap* might try the work of Barbara Michaels, Phyllis A. Whitney, or Caroline Llewellyn.

Walters, Minette. With *The Ice House* (St. Martin, 1992), Walters won the John Creasey Award for Best First Novel, bestowed by the British Crime Writers' Association. Upon first look, *The Ice House* appears to be a fairly conventional English mystery. A body has been discovered in the abandoned ice house on an estate in Hampshire. Could it be the body of the estate owner's husband, who disappeared ten years ago? Or does it belong to someone else? From this starting point, Walters takes the conventions of the traditional English mystery and turns them topsy-turvy, sideways, and any which way she pleases, and the result is a compelling and engrossing story that never takes the tack the reader expects. With her second novel, *The Sculptress* (St. Martin, 1993), Walters explores our modern fascination with brutal murderers. Roz Leigh, a journalist whose life is in a shambles, reluctantly agrees to write a book about Olive Martin, a monstrous young woman who murdered her mother and sister, then calmly dismembered their bodies before calling the police to confess the crime. Fascinated by Olive, Roz delves further and further into the background of the crime to understand why it happened, and she finds herself drawn deeper into Olive's disturbing world. Walters conjures up a dark and brooding atmosphere in her novels in which nothing—and no one—are ever quite what they seem.

Like Minette Walters, Ruth Rendell, in her non-Wexford books and as Barbara Vine, writes novels that playfully stretch the conventions of crime fiction. Readers who enjoy such novels as these might try in addition the work of B. M. Gill, S. T. Haymon, Frances Hegarty, Margaret Millar, and Rosamond Smith.

Webb, Martha G. See **Wingate, Anne.**

Wheat, Carolyn. A former defense attorney with the Legal Aid Society in Brooklyn, New York, Wheat uses her extensive knowledge of the law and of the court system to lend a sometimes harrowing authenticity to her novels about Cass Jameson. When the series begins, with *Dead Man's Thoughts* (St. Martin, 1983), Cass, like her creator, is a lawyer with Legal Aid. One day Cass finds her lover and colleague, Nathan Wasserstein, murdered in his apartment in an apparent gay killing by a young Puerto Rican hustler. Cass refuses to believe what looks like a setup to her, and she turns detective to clear Nathan's name. By the second book, *Where Nobody Dies* (St. Martin, 1986), Cass has left Legal Aid and set up her own practice, but she finds herself visiting all the familiar places of the system from her days as a Legal Aid attorney. Cass is tough, principled, compassionate, and committed to seeing that justice is done to the best of her ability. The plots of the novels are neatly and tightly constructed, an excellent blend of the traditional mystery plot with contemporary, well-rounded characters. *Dead Man's Thoughts* was nominated for an Edgar for Best First Novel.

Readers acquainted with Carolyn Wheat might try the series of Janet L. Smith, Julie Smith (the Rebecca Schwartz books), Frances Fyfield, and Dana Stabenow, all of whom have women lawyers as main characters.

White, Teri. White writes hard-boiled, gritty suspense novels and police procedurals. Her books often concentrate on the psychological dynamic of male bonding, and they generally feature a team of men, either cops or criminals. White's first novel, *Triangle* (Ace Charter, 1982), won an Edgar award for best paperback original. The plot follows two Vietnam vets, Johnny and

Mac, who hire out as a team of hit men. They kill, as part of a mob rubout, an undercover cop. The cop's partner, Simon, abandons everything else in his life to seek his partner's killer. *Bleeding Hearts* (Mysterious, 1984) introduces Blue Maguire and Spaceman Kowalski, detective partners in the Los Angeles Police Department; *Tightrope* (Mysterious, 1986) continues their adventures. Maguire is rich, educated, and angst-ridden, while Kowalski is a tough, macho, streetwise cop. The evolution of two such different individuals into an effective team is set against a bleak backdrop of bloody, hideous L.A. crimes. *Tightrope* is a particularly unusual book; it's one of the very few caper novels written by a woman. *Max Trueblood and the Jersey Desperado* (Mysterious, 1987) is the story of two New York City police detectives (one veteran, one novice) and two mob hit men (again, an old-timer and his protégé). In this novel, White has written effective underworld scenes in New York and New Jersey, with authentic-sounding dialogue.

Readers also may want to try hard-edged urban mysteries by Wendy Hornsby, Dorothy Uhnak, and Faye Kellerman.

Whitehead, Barbara. After publishing several Regency romances, Whitehead has written what is described as the York cycle of mysteries. The cycle is notable for her vivid descriptions of the city of York and its magnificent cathedral, the York Minster. *Playing God* (St. Martin, 1988) is set at a summer theater festival of medieval mystery plays, performed in the ancient parts of the city. Poison Peters, a punk rock star, is brought in to play the part of Christ. A storm of protest, attempts on his life, and an eventual murder are played out against a religious and theatrical background. Whitehead turns to the secular world for the setting of a police procedural, *The Girl in Red Suspenders* (St. Martin, 1990), and an atmospheric mystery set in a family-run chocolate factory, *Sweet Death, Come Softly* (St. Martin, 1993). She returned to a religious setting for *The Dean It Was That Died* (St. Martin, 1991), which revolves around the mysterious death of the dean of a cathedral during a church service. Canons Grindal and Oglethorpe and Lucy Grindal, who appeared in *Playing God,* become key characters here as they discover a group of criminals that is attempting to use the church for evil purposes.

Isabelle Holland, Veronica Black, and Mollie Hardwick write other clerical mysteries.

Whitney, Phyllis A. Named Grand Master by the Mystery Writers of America in 1988 and given an Agatha Award for Lifetime Achievement by Malice Domestic in 1989, Whitney has been producing entertaining mystery fiction for adults and young adults for five decades. Her first novel was *Red Is for Murder* (Ziff Davis, 1943). Along with Mary Stewart and the late Victoria Holt, Whitney was a regular on the best-seller lists of the late 1960s and 1970s, the heyday of what is called romantic suspense. These mysteries with a romantic twist remain popular, as evidenced by the longevity of such practitioners as Whitney, Holt, Stewart, Barbara Michaels/Elizabeth Peters, Velda Johnston, and Mary Higgins Clark. One of the hallmarks of Whitney's fiction is its strong sense of place. Born to American missionaries in Japan, Whitney was a world traveler at an early age, and this taste for unusual and interesting places makes a distinctive contribution to her work. Her novels vary in setting from Turkey, South Africa, Greece, Japan, and various parts of the United States. Along with an expertly sketched setting, Whitney gives her readers entertaining stories with a masterful sense of pace and suspense. Whitney's heroines are generally young, sometimes a bit inexperienced, but always with a sense of self-responsibility and the courage to carry them through often life-threatening situations. Among Whitney's best mysteries are *Emerald* (Doubleday, 1983) and *The Glass Flame* (Doubleday, 1978).

Those who enjoy Whitney for her sense of place might also try the work of M. M. Kaye, whose novels of far-flung places are a nostalgic and evocative travelogue of a vanished world. The novels of Mary Stewart also make the most of exotic locales. A newer writer, Caroline Llewellyn, is a bright new voice in this same tradition. Another new writer, D. F. Mills, writes convincingly about young women caught up in mysterious events seemingly beyond their control.

Wilhelm, Kate. Winner of the two most prestigious prizes in science fiction, the Hugo and the Nebula awards, Wilhelm is perhaps better known as a science fiction writer. But her very first novel, *More Bitter Than Death* (Simon & Schuster, 1963), was a mystery. Conventional in plot and setting, this book exhibits the staple elements in Wilhelm's later mystery novels. There is a strong sense of place, underscored by the belief that environment plays a significant role in the shaping of character. Wilhelm pays much attention to the development of her characters, creating her people through disciplined, descriptive language. First introduced in a short story, the husband-and-wife team of Charlie Meiklejohn and Constance Leidl has been featured in several novels, beginning with *The Hamlet Trap* (St. Martin, 1987). Charlie, a former New York City arson investigator, now works as a private investigator, and Constance is a professional psychologist, a Ph.D. with impressive credentials. In combination these two make a very effective team, and their relationship provides a strong emotional core to the novels. Wilhelm is not afraid to experiment, as with *The Dark Door* (St. Martin, 1988), a Charlie and Constance novel that blends science fiction and mystery, or *Death Qualified* (St. Martin, 1991), a highly unusual legal mystery. Other books, such as the recent *Seven Kinds of Death* (St. Martin, 1992), are more traditional, though Wilhelm remains strongly individual, whatever she writes.

Those who have enjoyed Wilhelm's mysteries might try the series of P. M. Carlson, M. K. Lorens, B. J. Oliphant/A. J. Orde, and Mary Monica Pulver.

Wilson, Barbara. Seattle writer Wilson is cofounder of Seal Press, which happens to be the publisher of Wilson's two series of lesbian, feminist mysteries. *Murder in the Collective* (Seal Press, 1984) introduces Pam Nilsen, who with her twin sister Penny, has turned their family business, Best Printing, into a collective after the death of their parents. The collective receives an offer to merge with lesbian-owned B. Violet Typesetting, and the stage is set for murder. As she sorts warily through the tangles of politics and sexual relationships among the collective, Pam also seeks an answer to her own troubling questions about her sexuality. In subsequent books of the series, Pam adjusts to her new identity as a lesbian and finds her attention captured by murders that help her explore her beliefs as a feminist. Teenage prostitutes are the theme in *Sisters of the Road* (Seal Press, 1986) and pornography and lesbian sadomasochism in *The Dog Collar Murders* (Seal Press, 1989). With *Gaudi Afternoon* (Seal Press, 1990), Wilson introduced Cassandra Reilly, globe-trotting Spanish translator, who dashes through her paces in a delicious comic thriller set in Barcelona. This novel won an award from the British Crime Writers' Association for Best Crime Novel with a European Setting. Whether writing about Pam or Cassandra, Wilson has a crisp style.She mixes characters with differing political viewpoints with ease and makes them articulate and believable.

Readers who have enjoyed the work of Wilson might try writers such as Ellen Hart, Katherine V. Forrest, Claire McNab, and Sandra Scoppettone, all of whose characters are lesbian amateur or professional detectives. Readers looking for Seattle settings might try the work of Mary Daheim and Janet L. Smith.

Wiltz, Chris. Wiltz, a native of New Orleans, has set her series of hard-boiled private eye novels in the Crescent City and endowed them with that special flavor that can belong only to New Orleans. Wiltz's detective is Neal Rafferty, who grew up in the tough area on the wrong side of the tracks known as the Irish Channel. A cop like his father and his grandfather before him, Neal leaves the force after the murder of his lover, a prostitute Neal believes was killed by the powerful district attorney. Since striking out on his own as a private cop, Neal finds it difficult to get along with his father and his father's cronies on the police force. Neal Rafferty exhibits many of the characteristics common to the hard-boiled private eye. He drinks and smokes too much on occasion, he sometimes gets involved with the wrong woman, and he's stubborn about doing things his way. Wiltz makes New Orleans as much a character in the series as any person, and this gives her books a strong sense of place. First in the series is *The Killing Circle* (Macmillan, 1981). The most recent novel, *The Emerald Lizard* (Dutton, 1991), has as an underlying theme the seductiveness of violence, and this book displays Wiltz's skills with people and place at their best.

Readers looking for other series set in New Orleans and Louisiana might try the Skip Langdon novels of Julie Smith, the work of Tony Fennelly, and the series about lesbian private eye Micky Knight, written by J. M. Redmann.

Wingate, Anne. Wingate is actually the third literary incarnation for this prolific mystery writer who has a Ph.D. in English. She began her career as Martha G. Webb, penning three novels. About the same time as Webb appeared, Lee Martin published her first novel, then a few years later came Wingate, her real name. Several characteristics are common to all three, including Texas settings. The veteran of eight years of police work, mostly with the major crime scene unit, Wingate uses her experiences to lend an authentic feel of police procedure to her novels. The Lee Martin books feature Fort Worth homicide detective Deb Ralston, who first appeared in *Too Sane a Murder* (St. Martin, 1984). Deb is called to a horrifying crime scene in which a young man, previously diagnosed as a schizophrenic, has allegedly murdered five members of his family. As Wingate, the author introduced Mark Shigata in *Death by Deception* (Walker, 1988) as an FBI agent based in Bayport (on the Gulf Coast near Galveston). In the second book, *The Eye of Anna* (Walker, 1989), Shigata copes with his duties as the new chief of police in Bayport as a hurricane rages. Whether writing as Webb, Martin, or Wingate, this author packs her novels full of authentic police procedure and rapidly paced action. An underlying theme of antiracism lends a strong message to the books. For example, Shigata is Nisei, and Deb Ralston and her husband have three adopted children of different ethnic backgrounds. In addition, Wingate has recently published *Scene of the Crime: A Writer's Guide to Crime-Scene Investigations* (Writer's Digest Books, 1992).

Those who have enjoyed any of the works of this author might try the various series of Elizabeth Linington, Dell Shannon, and Lesley Egan, the novels of J. A. Jance, the Skip Langdon series of Julie Smith, Dorothy Uhnak, Medora Sale, and Lillian O'Donnell.

Wings, Mary. Wings has written a series of mysteries with lesbian sleuth Emma Victor. The first Emma Victor novel is *She Came Too Late* (Crossing Press, 1987). Emma is a former publicist and activist, now suffering burnout and working at the women's hot line in Boston. A woman who calls for help is murdered, and her death leads Emma into a shadowy world of biological engineering and drugs. In *She Came in a Flash* (New American Library, 1988), Emma has moved to California and is doing publicity for an old friend. Her friend asks her to look into the death of a religious cult member as a favor, and Emma becomes involved with the activities of a self-absorbed rock star, Nebraska Storm. The claustrophobic atmosphere of the cult is conveyed forcefully, and Emma is a strong female investigator in the classic hard-boiled mode. *Divine Victim* (Dutton, 1992) has the unnamed narrator traveling with her new lover, Marya, to clean out an old house in Montana that Marya has recently inherited from her aunt. The novel is full of religious intensity as the narrator slowly uncovers the story behind the aunt's obsession with images of the Virgin Mary and female saints, and reveals her own dangerous activities.

Other lesbian sleuths have been created by Ellen Hart, Sarah Dreher, and Lauren Wright Douglas.

Wolzien, Valerie. Susan Henshaw, the housewife who serves as Wolzien's series detective, inhabits a world in suburban Connecticut that many readers well may envy. The wife of a highly successful advertising executive, Susan has a beautiful home, two children, and a loving and generally attentive husband. This is a world where husbands might give wives expensive vintage automobiles for Christmas, or where families might spend as much on Christmas decorations as many people make in one year. Beginning with *Murder at the PTA Luncheon* (St. Martin, 1988), Susan becomes involved with the fatal goings-on in her suburban corner of the world, and she proves that the ability to run a successful household evinces some skills at solving domestic murders. The woman who becomes Susan's best friend, Kathleen Gordon, luckily has experience as a police detective and private security consultant, and Kathleen's professional knowledge, linked with Susan's in-depth knowledge of the inner workings of suburbia, make an effective combination.

Other writers who set their series in suburbia include Jill Churchill, Caroline Crane, and Susan Isaacs. Readers might also try the series of Elizabeth Travis and Katherine Hall Page. Best-selling suspense novelist Mary Higgins Clark has also effectively mined the suburban setting for several of her successful novels.

Woods, Sara. The late Sara Woods wrote some forty-eight novels featuring barrister Antony Maitland, his wife Jenny, and Antony's uncle, Sir Nicholas Harding. Using her own experience of having worked in a solicitor's office, Woods made the English legal mystery particularly her own, and Antony Maitland is perhaps the character in English mystery fiction closest to Erle Stanley Gardner's Perry Mason. Maitland has a definite nose for crime, for he has hunches that nearly infallibly tell him when something is odd about a seemingly straightforward case. Courtroom scenes are often a part of the action in these novels, and Wood handles them with considerable aplomb, building tension in a manner worthy of Gardner himself. Through the course of the series, readers find out tidbits of the lives of the Maitlands; one book, *They Love Not Poison* (Holt, Rinehart, & Winston, 1972), takes the reader back to a period before Antony has qualified as a barrister and is thus a prequel to the rest of the series. Wood's literate style, attention to detail, and generally complex puzzles will appeal to readers who like their mysteries English and traditional. *Bloody Instructions* (Harper & Row, 1962) is the first in the series. Woods also wrote as Anne Burton, Mary Challis, and Margaret Leek.

Readers interested in English legal mysteries might try the work of Frances Fyfield, Ann C. Fallon, E. X. Giroux, the late Anthony Gilbert, and M. R. D. Meek.

Woods, Sherryl. Woods writes romantic mysteries as well as romance novels. The heroine of her first mystery series, Amanda Roberts, is a former New York hotshot journalist, who followed her husband to a job in rural Georgia. The husband rapidly decamped and Amanda now yearns for a more exciting career than working on a country weekly. The initial novel, *Reckless* (Warner, 1989), begins with a famous chef, Maurice, keeling over dead into the chocolate soufflé at a cooking demonstration. Amanda hopes that if she can solve the crime and write a prize-winning story she can get out of her dead-end job. However, Joe Donelli, a former Brooklyn cop, is unofficially helping his friend the sheriff with the investigation. Inevitably, he tries to thwart Amanda's sleuthing at every turn. Subsequent books chart a relationship that develops between Roberts and Donelli.

Woods's second romantic mystery series is set in south Florida. *Hot Property* (Dell, 1992) introduces Molly DeWitt, a single mother who finds a man dead one morning in her condominium card room. Homicide detective Michael O'Hara is the drop-dead-handsome Cuban cop assigned to the case. In *Hot Secret*

(Dell, 1993), Molly is working as a publicist in the Miami/Dade film office, and a famous film director is found dead on a location shoot that Molly has arranged. O'Hara turns up again to argue with Molly and to listen to her discoveries.

Readers who enjoy Woods might want to try Mignon F. Ballard, Caroline Llewellyn, and Kay Hooper.

Wren, M. K. Wren is the pseudonym of Martha Kay Renfroe, a West Coast writer and artist. Her mysteries star Conan Flagg, a bookstore owner in Holliday Beach, Oregon. Conan has a private investigator's license, the existence of which he usually tries to keep quiet, and he is a former intelligence agent. The independently wealthy heir to a ranching fortune, Conan is also half Nez Percé Indian, a collector of art, and the possessor of a classic Jaguar XKE and a luxurious beach house. As a sideline to his bookstore business, he helps out people in trouble who come to him. In *Nothing's Certain but Death* (Doubleday, 1978), for example, Conan helps a friend who is suspected of murdering an IRS agent. *Seasons of Death* (Doubleday, 1981) is set in a ghost town in Idaho, where Conan investigates a forty-year-old murder. Conan sets out to ensure justice when a friend is killed in *Wake Up, Darlin' Corey* (Doubleday, 1984). Wren uses the Oregon environmental movement as a backdrop to her story of greed and vengeance. In all of her mysteries, Wren is particularly adept at creating atmospheric settings, especially in the Oregon beach areas and the desert.

The first Conan Flagg novel is *Curiosity Didn't Kill the Cat* (Doubleday, 1973). Wren has also written a science fiction trilogy, *The Phoenix Legacy* (Berkley, 1981), and *A Gift Upon the Shore* (Ballantine, 1990), a science fiction novel.

Carolyn G. Hart, Joan Hess, and Sheila Simonson write about booksellers turned sleuths. Jane Haddam (aka Orania Papazoglou) features Gregor Demarkian, a former government agent turned private detective, in her cozy mysteries. Janet LaPierre creates mysteries noted for their vivid North Coast settings and environmental concerns.

Wright, L. R. Laurali Wright, who is a Canadian journalist and novelist, struck gold the first time out with a crime novel; her first, *The Suspect* (Viking, 1985), won the Edgar for Best Novel. Two elderly men are having a conversation, and suddenly one of them strikes the other dead, then toddles off home. Called in to investigate is Staff Sergeant Karl Alberg of the Royal Canadian Mounted Police, stationed in the town of Sechelt on Canada's Sunshine Coast. In his late forties, divorced but delving into the dating game again, Alberg is a shrewd, laconic detective. He works slowly through the evidence to identify the killer and the motive in this absorbing and inverted murder study. Subsequent novels in the series demonstrate Wright's interest in the reasons ordinary people commit crimes. Each novel is in some way a character study, either of a victim or a perpetrator, and of the people involved in the situation. As the series progresses, Alberg develops a romantic relationship with Cassandra Mitchell, the town's librarian. Thoughtful, compassionate, Wright looks into the nastiness in the human heart and creates fascinating novels of suspense. The Sunshine Coast is a vital part of her tapestry of crime, and her evocative descriptions of the area lend a strong sense of place to her work. In addition to her crime novels, Wright has written several novels of straight fiction.

Those who have enjoyed Wright's crime novels might try the work of English writers Ruth Rendell, P. D. James, Frances Fyfield, and Margaret Yorke, or the Toronto-based series of Medora Sale.

Yarbro, Chelsea Quinn. Yarbro is a prolific author of science fiction and children's books, as well as mysteries. She has created a series that features Charles Spotted Moon, a San Francisco attorney and Ojibwa tribal shaman. Charlie is a strictly ethical lawyer who takes seriously his obligation to get each client the best possible defense. In each novel, courtroom scenes and legal details alternate with Charlie's independent investigations. In order to establish a client's innocence, he sometimes goes on Ojibwa spirit walks to hear how a murder happened by listening to the voices of the dead. The difficult and sometimes gory realities of contemporary urban life often contrast with Charlie's clear awareness of his positive spiritual life. Charlie's prickly associate, Morgan Studevant, also plays a prominent part in the novels and in Charlie's life as well.

The first book in the series is *Ogilvie, Tallant & Moon* (Putnam, 1976), also published as *Bad Medicine* (Jove, 1990). Yarbro also has written eight volumes of a historical horror series featuring the Comte de Saint-Germaine, a vampire.

Readers who enjoy legal maneuvering also might try Sara

Woods's series with British barrister Antony Maitland. Susan Wolfe and Lia Matera have written crime novels about San Francisco attorneys. Jean Hager writes mysteries about Cherokee traditions, and Dana Stabenow about Aleuts.

Yorke, Margaret. Yorke began her mystery-writing with a series of conventional detective novels featuring Oxford don Patrick Grant, whose first appearance was in *Dead in the Morning* (Geoffrey Bles, 1970). Handsome, learned, and incurably nosy, Grant is much in the mold of the gifted amateur detective, and in his five appearances he serves as an entertaining, if not compelling, sleuth. After her fourth novel about Grant, Yorke wrote a novel that was to signal the direction of her career in crime. *No Medals for the Major* (Geoffrey Bles, 1974) is set in a much more contemporary version of the traditional English village. In this setting Yorke has full range for her considerable talent in observing the ordinary routines of life and how these routines, and the people who effect them, can be altered by crime. Yorke's world is no St. Mary Mead, and she mines this ground time after time with quiet effect. She focuses on ordinary people, not the psychopaths so beloved of her peer Ruth Rendell, and she demonstrates to the reader just how easily crime can upset the delicate balance of an ordinary person. Other excellent examples of Yorke's craft are *A Small Deceit* (Viking, 1991) and *Criminal Damage* (Mysterious, 1992).

Readers who have enjoyed the crime novels of Yorke might try the novels of Anna Clarke, Sheila Radley, Rosamond Smith, Celia Fremlin, Margaret Millar, June Thomson, and Ruth Rendell.

Anthologies

This list includes important short story anthologies of women mystery writers.

Deadly Allies, edited by Marilyn Wallace and Robert Randisi. New York: Doubleday, 1992.

The Fourth Womansleuth Anthology, edited by Irene Zahava. Freedom, CA: Crossing Press, 1991.

Lady on the Case, edited by Marcia Muller, Bill Pronzini, and Martin Greenberg. New York: Bonanza Books, 1988.

Malice Domestic 1, presented by Elizabeth Peters. New York: Pocket, 1992.

Malice Domestic 2, presented by Mary Higgins Clark. New York: Pocket, 1993.

More Ms. Murder, edited by Marie Smith. Secaucus, NJ: Carol, 1991.

Ms. Murder, edited by Marie Smith. Secaucus, NJ: Citadel, 1989.

Ms. Mysteries, edited by Arthur Liebman. New York: Washington Square, 1976.

Reader, I Murdered Him, edited by Jen Green. New York: St. Martin, 1989.

The Second Womansleuth Anthology, edited by Irene Zahava. Freedom, CA: Crossing Press, 1989.

Sisters in Crime, edited by Marilyn Wallace. New York: Berkley, 1989.

Sisters in Crime 2, edited by Marilyn Wallace. New York: Berkley, 1990.

Sisters in Crime 3, edited by Marilyn Wallace. New York: Berkley, 1990.

Sisters in Crime 4, edited by Marilyn Wallace. New York: Berkley, 1991.

Sisters in Crime 5, edited by Marilyn Wallace. New York: Berkley, 1992.

A Suit of Diamonds: A Commemorative Volume of Specially Commissioned Short Stories Published to Celebrate The Crime Club's Diamond Jubilee. New York: Dell, 1991.

The Third Womansleuth Anthology, edited by Irene Zahava. Freedom, CA: Crossing Press, 1990.

The Web She Weaves, edited by Marcia Muller and Bill Pronzini. New York: Morrow, 1983.

A Woman's Eye, edited by Sara Paretsky. New York: Delacorte, 1991.

The Womansleuth Anthology, edited by Irene Zahava. Freedom, CA: Crossing Press, 1988.

Women of Mystery, edited by Cynthia Manson. New York: Carroll & Graf, 1992.

Index by Series Character

Geographic Index

243

AUSTRALIA

REST OF WORLD

Gilman, Dorothy
Hadley, Joan
Langton, Jane
Livingston, Nancy
Leon, Donna
Llewellyn, Caroline
Moyes, Patricia
Nabb, Magdalen
Peters, Elizabeth
Stewart, Mary
Whitney, Phyllis A.
Wilson, Barbara

HISTORICAL SETTINGS

Beck, K. K.
Davis, Lindsey
Douglas, Carole Nelson
Eyre, Elizabeth

Frazer, Margaret
Greenwood, L. B.
Jackson, Marian J. A.
Johnston, Velda
Kellerman, Faye
Knight, Alanna
Linscott, Gillian
Meyers, Maan
Michaels, Barbara
Monfredo, Miriam Grace
Myers, Amy
Paul, Barbara
Perry, Anne
Peters, Elizabeth
Peters, Ellis
Sedley, Kate
Shah, Diane K.
Whitney, Phyllis A.

Index by Type of Detective

ACTORS/THEATRICAL

Babson, Marian
Carlson, P. M.
Dentinger, Jane
Hart, Ellen
Matteson, Stefanie
Morice, Anne

AMATEUR DETECTIVES

Adams, Deborah
Babson, Marian
Ballard, Mignon
Beck, K. K.
Boylan, Eleanor
Brown, Rita Mae
Cannell, Dorothy
Charles, Kate
Churchill, Jill
Clark, Mary Higgins
Craig, Alisa
Crane, Hamilton
Daheim, Mary
Dank, Gloria
Davis, Dorothy Salisbury
Dunlap, Susan
Ferrars, E. X.
Granger, Ann
Gray, Gallagher
Hadley, Joan
Hager, Jean
Harris, Charlaine
Hart, Ellen
Johnston, Velda
Kelman, Judith
Linscott, Gillian
Livingston, Nancy
Llewellyn, Caroline
MacLeod, Charlotte
Michaels, Barbara
Moffat, Gwen
Morison, B. J.

Muller, Marcia
Oliphant, B. J.
Orde, A. J.
Peters, Elizabeth
Peters, Ellis
Peterson, Audrey
Pickard, Nancy
Rowe, Jennifer
Sale, Medora
Sawyer, Corinne H.
Sedley, Kate
Singer, Shelley
Sprinkle, Patricia H.
Stewart, Mary
Truman, Margaret
Whitney, Phyllis A.
Wilson, Barbara
Wolzien, Valerie

ARCHAEOLOGISTS/ ANTHROPOLOGISTS

Arnold, Margot
Mann, Jessica
McCrumb, Sharyn
Peters, Elizabeth

ARTISTS

Charles, Kate
Dunnett, Dorothy
Knight, Kathryn L.
Moody, Susan
Peters, Elizabeth
Sale, Medora
Smith, Evelyn
Tucker, Kerry
Valentine, Deborah

BOOKSTORE OWNERS

Hart, Carolyn G.
Hess, Joan
Wren, M. K.

BUSINESSPEOPLE/OTHER PROFESSIONS

Babson, Marian
Berry, Carole
Carlson, P. M.
Crespi, Trella
Douglas, Carole N.
Dreher, Sarah
Femling, Jean
Girdner, Jaqueline
Gray, Gallagher
Hall, Mary Bowen
Hardwick, Mollie
Hart, Ellen
Lathen, Emma
Law, Janice
Maxwell, A. E.
Meyers, Annette
Travis, Elizabeth
Wilson, Barbara

CLERGY

Black, Veronica
Davis, Dorothy Salisbury
Frazer, Margaret
Greenwood, D. M.
Holland, Isabelle
O'Marie, Sister Carol Anne

Peters, Ellis
Whitehead, Barbara

COOKS

Davidson, Diane Mott
Laurence, Janet
Myers, Amy
Page, Katherine Hall
Pickard, Nancy
Rich, Virginia

ETHNIC DETECTIVES

Adamson, M. J.
Femling, Jean
Hager, Jean
Hornsby, Wendy
LaPierre, Janet
Moody, Susan
Muller, Marcia
Shannon, Dell
Singer, Shelley
Stabenow, Dana
Wallace, Marilyn
Wingate, Anne
Woods, Sherryl
Wren, M. K.
Yarbro, Chelsea Quinn

GOVERNMENT AGENTS/ WORKERS

Cooper, Natasha
Dominic, R. B.
Edwards, Ruth Dudley

Gilman, Dorothy
Mann, Jessica
Neel, Janet
Truman, Margaret

HEALTH PROFESSIONALS

Cornwell, Patricia D.
Dunlap, Susan
Kittredge, Mary
Millar, Margaret
Shepherd, Stella

JOURNALISTS

Braun, Lilian Jackson
D'Amato, Barbara
Fraser, Antonia
Friedman, Mickey
Gordon, Alison
Grant-Adamson, Lesley
Hart, Carolyn G.
Kallen, Lucille
O'Brien, Meg
Roome, Annette
Shah, Diane K.
Shankman, Sarah
Sibley, Celestine
Slovo, Gillian
Woods, Sherryl

LAWYERS

Caudwell, Sarah
Charles, Kate
Fallon, Ann C.
Fyfield, Frances

PRIVATE EYES

TEACHERS AND PROFESSORS

WRITERS